THE GOOD WEDDING GUIDE

THE GOOD WEDDING GUIDE

For Planning, Reference and Inspiration

Sue Carpenter

Illustrated by Angela McAllister

EQUATION

First published 1987

Every effort has been made to obtain
permission for use of the photographs in
this book but we apologize to those we
have been unable to trace

British Library
Cataloguing in Publication Data

Carpenter, Sue
The good wedding guide: for planning,
reference and inspiration
1. Weddings
I. Title
395'.22   HQ745

ISBN 1-85336-014-7

Equation is an imprint of the Thorsons
Publishing Group, Denington Estate,
Wellingborough, Northamptonshire
NN8 2RQ, England

Printed in Great Britain by
Butler & Tanner Ltd, Frome, Somerset

1 3 5 7 9 10 8 6 4 2

CONTENTS

Acknowledgements   6
Introduction   7

Section I
  Proposal and Engagement   9

Section II
  Arrangements Schedule   19
  The Church and Register Office   23
  Church Music   29
  Invitations and Other Stationery   33
  Wedding Presents   40
  Photographs   45
  Videos   56
  Transport   60

Section III
  Clothes   64
  Beauty   110
  Flowers   114

Section IV
  Catering   130
  Party Planning Services   147
  Venues   150
  Marquees   155
  Decor and Lighting   159
  Party Music   162

Section V
  Stag and Hen Nights   165
  The Day   168
  The Honeymoon   179

Colour Photograph Credits   187
Bibliography   188
Index   189

Colour Plates
  1-4   64
  5-12   96

ACKNOWLEDGEMENTS

I would especially like to thank Angela McAllister, who has provided invaluable help and support throughout the preparation of this book. Special thanks too to chief researcher Clare Faull. I am indebted to photographer Mark Houldsworth, and to all those who made the colour fashion photographs possible—notably models Eve, Lauren, Denise and Cressida, child models Max Austin and Cosima Hibbert and their parents, make-up artist Lucie Llewellyn, hair stylists Pascal from Neville Daniel and Mats, florist Jane Packer, Carol Adams of the Savoy Group, Claridge's and all those who lent clothes and accessories. Many thanks too to Lady Elizabeth Anson, Rose Coutts-Smith, Christopher Bowler of Abbey Studios, to the many brides and grooms who lent photographs and shared experiences and finally to all the people listed within the book, all of whom have been extremely helpful in its compilation.

INTRODUCTION

The stage is set, the spotlight's on and_ *you* are the star. Months of toil and preparation have paved the way for this moment: your wedding day. But, help, wait! Where and how on earth do you begin?

Begin with this book—a comprehensive guide for bride and mother, with hints for the groom, best man and guests, to help you sail through the whole daunting business of arranging the wedding, from the proposal right through to the honeymoon.

There are other how-to guides and etiquette books for the bride and groom, but I have found most of them to be long-winded, dated, unadventurous and too general. This book, while essentially practical and covering all aspects of a traditional wedding, is firmly Eighties in approach. The guide is packed with ideas and inspiration—both written and visual, advice from experts, information about wedding services, case histories, anecdotes and wedding lore. I intend prospective brides to be filled with enthusiasm, not dismay.

Some 346,000 couples tie the knot each year in England and Wales alone. Undoubtedly your wedding will be compared with those of friends: 'Oh, we didn't have such a long queue at *our* reception', or 'Jane and John had that hymn too', but you can follow tradition without following the crowd. Making your wedding original takes thought,

planning and imagination rather than a Swiss bank account. *The Good Wedding Guide* is not just for those who have cases of vintage champagne waiting in the cellar and the family tiara sitting in the bank vaults, it's more for those who want a wedding with bags of style and individuality, but may not have the means or know-how to create it.

To provide that know-how, I interviewed dozens of brides, grooms and parents who have recently been through the trials, traumas and triumphs of organizing a wedding, as well as an army of people who work in the wedding industry—the experts— from florists and dressmakers to photographers and cake-bakers. Their experience and inside knowledge have helped me make this book authoritative. Talking to specialists such as the Duchess of York's wedding-dressmaker, Lindka Cierach, and her florist, Jane Packer, has enabled me to pinpoint current fashions but without being faddish. Listed within are the names, addresses and details of such people and establishments, all of whom provide a wedding service. Gathered together for the first time, these sources—mostly recommended by word of mouth—form an invaluable directory.

This book, I hope, will take the headache out of planning your wedding and provide leads for making The Day extra-special for you.

SECTION I
PROPOSAL AND ENGAGEMENT

The formal betrothal, like other worth-while institutions so sneered at over the past two decades, has seen a solid revival in the Eighties. It involves the proposal of marriage, the acceptance, the announcement (verbally to family and friends, in print to *le monde*), and the giving of a ring.

One third of all men propose within six months of meeting, according to magazine statistics. It's a case of when the real thing comes along, it's patently obvious, so why hang around? However, speedy engagements can be dangerous, simply because you can't know each other well enough to consign your lives to each other. One couple met at a wedding and he proposed that weekend. She asked for some time to think it over, and rang him a few days later to accept. However, the romanticism ends there: they parted within a year.

Extreme youth is the other major factor against you. The chances of separation are high if you marry in your teens, and decrease as you get older. The more formed your characters, the less likely you are to grow apart. The getting of 'experience' may be an old chestnut, but it is invaluable where relationships are concerned. However, the likelihood of your marrying at all is reduced as you catapult beyond your mid-twenties, but at least these late unions have the best

chance of survival. The majority of couples get it right: the average bride is 22–23, the groom 24–25.

Proposal

Traditionally, the man asks the girl, 'Will you marry me?' and, on her acceptance, goes to see Father (or Mother if Father is unavailable) to request his daughter's hand in marriage. Father then consents to give his daughter away. Most men stick to this tradition, although they will probably have discussed marriage with their girlfriends before the actual proposal, and fathers are presented with a *fait accompli* rather than an option.

The proposal is by its very nature romantic and intimate. It doesn't actually require the trimmings of a candlelit *diner à deux* to make it special. One girl was puffing away on a forbidden cigarette at the bottom of the garden on Christmas Eve when her boyfriend came out to find her. While she braced herself for a chiding, he popped the question. However, the dinner remains the most popular setting, while about one third of men propose at his or her home and many others on holiday. And it all takes place, statistically speaking, between 10 pm and 11 pm.

One of the most public proposals occurred when Victor and Marilyn Lownes (who met at Victor's Playboy Club) appeared in a television documentary about couples. He was asked when they would marry. 'June', said he, and that was it. She turned pink and looked abashed, but the wedding went ahead.

Prince Andrew went down on both knees to propose to Sarah Ferguson at Floors Castle in the Scottish borders, seat of the Duke of Roxburghe. Prince Charles and Lady Diana Spencer also courted there, away from the heavy-breathing press.

Oldest bridegrooms

The oldest recorded groom was Harry Stevens, 103, who married Thelma Lucas, 84, in 1984 in Wisconsin. The British record for the oldest groom was set in London by Sir Robert Mayer, who married Jacqueline Noble, 51, in 1980 when he was 101.

When two women of the Choroti and Chaco tribes of Paraguay want to marry the same man, they don tapir-skin boxing gloves and fight it out between them.

Girls from the Trobriand Islands off Papua begin courting by going up to the man of their dreams and biting him.

A girl betrothed to a chieftain or dignitary in the Solomon Islands used to be kept imprisoned in a cage — sometimes for years — under the watchful eye of her father, until her wedding day.

One girl had been angling for the proposal for years, during which time her boyfriend had occasionally asked her out for a 'special dinner'. Each time she thought, 'This is it', and each time she was disappointed. Eventually, he took her to a French château for her birthday weekend. At midnight, he led her into the garden where he went down on bended knee, proposed, and presented her with a ring. When they went in, the waiter — primed in advance—cracked a bottle of bubbly at their table.

Another girl flew out to join her boyfriend in South Africa. He proposed at the top of Victoria Falls and presented her with a dazzling local diamond ring; she burst into tears — of happiness.

It certainly carries more impact and romance if the man presents the engagement ring (inherited or bought) to his bride-to-be when he proposes, though not many men would consider it if they were not sure of: (a) a positive reply, and (b) their good taste. Most couples choose the ring together. Occasionally, the man may be dispatched by his newly betrothed to buy her a 'surprise' ring. One such man, bemused, had to enlist his sister to guide his wallet towards a suitable ring.

Some men never actually propose — it just becomes an inevitability, a mutual under-standing. Some girls have to engineer the situation. Others go ahead and propose to the man. Each 29 February, there is a flood of female proposals, most of them successful.

Engagement

According to magazine statistics, 99.6 per cent of all couples have a formal engagement (0.4 per cent sneak off and marry in secret). You decide when you are officially engaged by announcing it — not necessarily in the newspapers, but at least to family and friends. The man gives the woman a ring at this time as a symbol of their love and commitment.

When the couple has the wherewithal to marry as soon as the wedding is organized, the engagement usually lasts for about six months (Andrew and Sarah's lasted four) — as long as it takes to organize the wedding comfortably. Where funds are flagging, engagements may stretch for years. One survey shows that most engagements last 20 months, since many men and women are still living with their parents when they get engaged and need that time to save up for their wedding (nearly all couples plan the full works), honeymoon and future home.

The intention is that the affianced are engaged *to be married*. Or is it? Some young couples treat the engagement as a stage reached in their relationship — a sort of pit stop after sticking it out for a couple of years — rather than a lead-up to marriage. That hurdle conquered, many months may lapse before the two even contemplate the greater hurdle of getting married.

Longest engagement and marriages

The longest engagement on record was between Octavio Guillen and Adriana Martinez. They finally took the plunge after 67 years, both aged 82, in 1969 in Mexico. The longest recorded marriages are both 86 years: one between Sir Temulji Bhicaji Nariman and Lady Nariman of Bombay, resulting from a cousin marriage when both were aged five; the other between Lazurus Rowe (1725-1829) and Molly Webber who were married in 1743.

Announcement

The traditional newspapers are *The Times* and/or the *Daily Telegraph*. *Guardian* readers can only announce marriages *after* the event, *The Independent*'s Court and Social column is as yet in its infancy and the tabloids don't have one.

DAILY TELEGRAPH
135 Fleet Street, London EC4

Announcements required in writing, at least two days in advance. State when you want the announcement to appear, where you want the invoice sent, a daytime telephone number and include a signature of the bride, groom or one of the parents. The announcement is presented in the paper's house style; £8.50 plus VAT a line.

THE TIMES
Court and Social Advertising, Times Newspapers Ltd, 1 Pennington Street, London E1

The same form as above; £6 plus VAT a line (about four to five words a line). The heading, consisting of the title (if any), initials and full surnames of the bride and groom, is free. Neither paper can guarantee inclusion on any particular day.

Correct wording
In the list of forthcoming marriages in newspapers, titled personages come first and commoners follow. The format is:

The engagement is announced between Joseph, son (younger son/only son/ second son) of Mr and Mrs B.D. Bloggs, of Oxford, and Mary, daughter of Vice-Admiral Sir John and Lady Miller, of Newbury.

If parents are divorced: . . . son of Mr B.D. Bloggs, of Oxford, and Mrs Joan Bloggs of Bournemouth . . .; *if mother has remarried:* . . . son of Mr B.D. Bloggs, of Oxford, and Mrs S.L. Green, of Bournemouth . . .; *if one parent is dead:* . . . son of the late Mr B.D. Bloggs, and Mrs Bloggs, of Bournemouth . . .; *if both parents are dead:* . . . son of the late Mr and Mrs B.D. Bloggs . . . .

It is not wise to give your exact address, which gives rise to the worst sort of bridal shower — that of bumf from photographers, caterers and the like (in the old days, it was contraceptives and double beds). However, you will still receive some unsolicited mail from companies that keep nationwide telephone directories. If they've gone to the trouble of seeking you out, it is worth considering the services offered before committing them to the file marked 'Bin'.

Being affianced

The first priority, if it has not already occurred, is for the parents to meet. There is often a celebration party for the immediate family on both sides. Each side may have a party to introduce the newcomer to their own family and friends. Parents usually give the couple a token present. There will be dozens of congratulations cards and letters (to which a thank-you note is appreciated), masses of celebratory bottles popped, and an *awful* lot to do.

From now on (just when you've decided you want to be together — alone), your time is not your own. You will be yanked from meeting one aged aunt to another, and from cakemaker to florist. Both sets of parents will be on the hot-line constantly to see how arrangements are going. It's a tense and emotional business, and most brides report a trickle of tears and rows during the lead-up to The Day. Just try and remain cool and unfazed by the inevitable annoyances and lap up the good bits (benevolent wishes, presents, and the fact that this is all for you . . .).

Photographs

You could have engagement portraits taken, like the royals do. It doesn't have to be his-hand-on-your-shoulder-and-your-hand-over-his-showing-off-the-ring. Neither, when standing, do you have to come up to his shoulder (no more, no less) to qualify. A good studio

11

will take happy, relaxed portraits which are a lovely informal keepsake for you and the family. You may also want a portrait of you alone à la *Country Life*. (For portrait photographer, see page 51.)

The ring

The engagement ring, originally the contractual seal on a betrothal, is a token of love between the couple, and a sign to the outside world that this woman is spoken for. There is always a ring, be it bought from a high street chain, a smart jeweller's, an antique shop or at auction; or be it designed specially, inherited, or made in metal class at school. In the year up to April 1986, £55 million was blown on 277,000 engagement rings costing around £200 each.

Fergie's ring must have bumped up the average. Estimated at £25,000, it was dreamed up by Prince Andrew in conjunction with a Garrard's designer. The oval ruby is surrounded by a cluster of ten diamonds in a band of 18-carat yellow and white gold.

Unofficial grins, chins and surprised eyes (above left) *at the Buckingham Palace photocall.* (Anwar Hussein)

The engagement of HRH Prince Andrew and Miss Sarah Ferguson (left): *official smiles gleam alongside £25,000 worth of ruby and diamond cluster.* (Anwar Hussein)

An informal engagement portrait of Lucinda Prior-Palmer Green (top right) *which appeared in* Country Life. (John & Annette Elliot)

Stones

Choosing the stone is largely a matter of colour preference and fashion. Nearly three-quarters of all girls go for an all-diamond engagement ring, a solitaire shining out above the rest. The diamond is classic and classy, ultra-wearable and ultra-durable (on a multi-stoned ring, you will see its sharp facets glinting long after the other jewels have worn smooth). Diamonds really are forever, the word deriving from the Greek 'adamas' — impenetrably hard.

Diana's sapphire and diamond cluster spawned a thousand clones (Fergie's loud red ruby failed to set a trend). The sapphire is now at its zenith, an easy-to-wear blue and a toughie — along with rubies, garnets and other less-usual gems. The expensive emerald, however, is easily fractured. Avoid

Choosing a ring

Go to a reputable jeweller. There is no such thing as a bargain. You get no more than you pay for (but if you buy from a non-professional, you may get *less*). Decide on an upper price limit, and ask the jeweller for the very best quality he has in your range. If you are looking around the £200 mark, simply choose a ring whose design and type of stone(s) pleases you. Small stones cost proportionately less than larger ones of the same quality — thus you get more for your money with a cluster than a solitaire.

If you want a ring with investment value, you will have to make an outlay of at least £500. The value of a modern ring from a high street chain will drop the moment you leave the shop, whereas an antique ring — unique and beautifully made — will hold its value. Similarly, a ring designed by a contemporary craftsman has lasting value as a one-off work of art. However precious in financial terms, don't forget to insure your ring as soon as possible.

Birthstones

An engagement ring containing your birthstone traditionally brings luck.

January: garnet — constancy, truth
February: amethyst — sincerity
March: aquamarine — courage
April: diamond — innocence, light
May: emerald — happiness, success
  in love
June: pearl — beauty
July: ruby — love, preserves chastity
August: peridot — joy
September: sapphire — wisdom
October: opal — hope
November: topaz — fidelity
December: turquoise — success,
  prevents matrimonial arguments

Sardonyx ensures married happiness, bloodstone courage. Pearls can symbolize tears, and the opal — inconstant and always changing its colours — represents these characteristics in the one who wears it; avoid it unless you are October-born.

pearls, turquoise, coral, opals and other porous stones which will not stand up to a soaking (pearls can also drop out as they are glued rather than set in a clasp).

Old stones have an iridescence and subtlety of colour that many cheap modern ones cannot match — sapphires are translucent cobalt blue and rubies a rosy pink, as against some of the dark, dull blues and reds we see on the high street.

Metal

All gold is alloyed with other metals to make it harder. The carat refers to the amount of pure gold out of 24 parts of metal. Thus 22-carat gold is almost pure and therefore the most expensive, but it is of less value in a ring, as it will wear down sooner than the hardy 18-carat. White gold is 18-carat gold — bleached. Platinum is the most practical metal — it can be made slender yet as strong as gold, and maintains its whiteness and polish. If your engagement ring is of the same carat as the wedding ring, it may stave off the wearing-down process a little, but it is inevit-able that a solid band will wear down the fine underside of an engagement ring. David Callaghan of Hancocks (see page 17) recommends that you wear the engagement ring on another finger.

High-street jewellers

Mass-market modern rings tend to be predictable — a diamond solitaire or a coloured stone plus diamonds, either set three in a row or in a cluster. Settings can be clumsy and unattractive. Some jewellery chains have a higher standard than others. The best are **Zales** (who manufacture their own rings) and **H. Samuel**. Both have branches all over the country.

> *To lose or damage an engagement ring bodes ill, lest the bond it represents should suffer; if another girl tries on the ring, the owner's future happiness could be jeopardized.*

A selection of antique rings from Trevor Allen.

Antique and second-hand rings

An old ring gives better value for money. What you pay for is the quality and size of stone (not labour). What you get is character, style, individuality, superior craftsmanship, a finer cut, a more intricate setting. The metalwork is an intrinsic part of the design and can be as pretty as the stones. Consider a second-hand modern ring, too — anything original and hand-crafted. If you are not buying through a jeweller, just make sure the stones are secure and the claws in good condition, as repairs can be expensive.

Most *antique* rings — that is, over 100 years old — are not serviceable in this day and age. They were not made to withstand constant wear, or to be plunged into washing-up detergent and suchlike. If you must have one, wear it sparingly and with care. From the Edwardian era onwards, rings became more practical, and most twentieth-century rings are suitable.

Styles

Elizabethans wore a gimmal ring which broke into three parts — one for the woman, one for the man, one for a witness — to be reunited later as the wedding ring. Gold or silver rings, perhaps twisted into a lovers' knot, where also favoured. It was not until the nineteenth century, when South African diamonds became more widely available, that these and other gemstones became fashionable.

Victorian betrothal rings included the forget-me-not in turquoise and diamonds, the pansy ring in the shape of the flower, symbolizing 'think of me' (from the French *penser*), a ring with a lock of hair in the centre, or an enamel, or an ivory miniature under glass. None of these is entirely practical as an engagement ring today. Look instead for rings containing precious stones whose initial letters spell such words as DEAREST (diamond, emerald, amethyst, ruby, epidote, sapphire, turquoise), LOVE ME (lapis lazuli, opal, verd antique, emerald, moonstone, epidote) or REGARD (ruby, emerald, garnet, amethyst, ruby, diamond). Or the carved half-

hoop in gold, its sides carved with scrolls, and a row of stones set on top. Or the gypsy-set ring, like a wide, tapered wedding ring with stones set into the band. There are also puzzle rings that should never be removed for fear that the wearer cannot complete the ring again — proof then of her infidelity.

Edwardian rings are highly favoured today. Elegant, traditional and well-constructed, most tend to have flattish settings that don't catch on clothes; you might find a small, flower-like diamond cluster, three sapphires encircled by tiny diamonds, or a square-shaped ring with a stone in the centre and square-cut stones at the corners. Decorative art nouveau and geometric art deco rings are all the rage, and their rarity makes them a good investment.

The wedding ring dates back to the ancient Egyptians. The ring is placed on the third finger of the bride's hand because it was thought that this finger carried a vein leading directly to the heart. Made from enduring, ever-valuable gold, it is supposed to bestow upon its wearer a similarly long-lasting and treasured marriage; a broken wedding ring, or the removal of the wedding ring, is a bad omen.

Thus, wearing someone else's discarded wedding ring seems ill-advised. For this reason, almost every couple likes a new wedding ring, or perhaps an inherited one. Wedding rings sell mainly for bullion at auction, unless they have a particular point of interest such as an inscription or date from the eighteenth century or earlier. Rings inscribed with poems or love ditties are occasionally available. A plain band of eighteen-carat gold is the most popular. Some men are wearing wedding rings too — in most cases a slim gold band worn on their little finger with a signet ring.

Fit and clean

The ring should be a perfect fit. If you can twist it on your finger, it is too big, and the motion will wear the gold down. It is easy enough to have the ring adjusted. Clean it regularly to avoid the condition deteriorating. Dip the ring into hand-hot water with crystal soda and brush with a toothbrush.

Wedding and engagement rings

Contemporary designers

An engagement (and/or wedding) ring designed to order is particularly special, since it's the only item created for your marriage that you will (may) wear, day in, day out, for the rest of your life. There are a number of talented young individuals who work mainly on commission, blending imaginative ideas with fine craftsmanship. They need not be too expensive and are best found through word of mouth.

London

VALERIE BLACK
The Garden House, 25 Beauchamp Place, London SW3 (01) 589 2706

If you are stumped for an idea, Valerie has dozens. She can make up a ring from an existing piece of jewellery or from stones you may have bought abroad. She will follow your design (provided she approves it). Sapphires are her most requested stone.

ESTHER EYRE
376 St John Street, London EC1
(01) 833 4403

Esther did a degree course in jewellery design and worked at Mappin & Webb before setting up her own business. She works mainly in precious metals and stones, and designs to your specifications or will suggest her own ideas. She can convert old jewellery. If not too busy, she can make a wedding ring in three days and an engagement ring in a week — but allow longer. She often makes the engagement ring, wedding ring and bridesmaids' presents too. Wedding rings from £70 and engagement rings from £500.

THEO FENNELL
177 Fulham Road, London SW3
(01) 352 7314

Understated, sophisticated designs for engagement and wedding rings, using mainly gold and diamonds. These can be made to order and altered slightly to suit you. Wedding rings are designed to fit around the engagement ring. Theo and assistant Justine Carmody can convert an undesirable hunk of jewellery into several more wearable items — a brooch into a ring and earrings, say. Engagement rings from around £1,000. Also cufflinks, silver frames, hip flasks and

Marina Reese (née Killery) designed her baroque pearl collar around a diamond and pearl brooch, a family heirloom of her husband's. Theo Fennell crafted the necklace, a diamond engagement ring with the couple's initials, A and M, intertwined in gold on the underside, and two slim gold wedding bands.
(Michael Howells)

16

bibelots that would make a good wedding present for your husband-to-be.

ELIZABETH GAGE
20 Albemarle Street, London W1
(01) 499 2879

Acclaimed modern designer. Rings made to your own specifications or one of her popular designs: the Templar, a wide gold band set with stones (from £1,000 to £2,500 depending on the stones); a rich, Egyptian-looking Zodiac ring (from £800); or the opulent Agincourt (from £1,000 to £7,000).

Country and Scotland
NICHOLA FLETCHER
Reediehill Farm, Auchtermuchty, Fife
(0337) 28369

Engagement rings designed to order — often with unusually cut stones, such as triangular or fan-shaped. From £200 for a simple design. Also square-shaped wedding rings ('very comfortable!' says Nicky) for about £80.

GOLD AND SILVER STUDIO
11a Queen Street, Bath, Avon
(0225) 62300

Friendly team who design and make simple, attractive jewellery. They undertake commissions, remodelling and repairs, and have a wide stock on display in their gallery.

JULES HENRI
22 East Street, Brighton, East Sussex
(0273) 25233

Individual work on commission plus stock designs in the shop. Wedding and engagement rings to match. Prices vary according to the quality of the stones and so on.

Antique and second-hand rings
TREVOR ALLEN
Antiquarius, Stands 1/2, 139 King's Road, London SW3
(01) 352 7061

Antique jewellery, silver and *objets d'art*. A wonderful collection of rings, mainly Edwardian and Victorian plus a few art deco ones. All are exquisitely pretty and original. Betro-

thal rings with clasped hands or hearts entwined from the Victorian days when love, courtship and marriage were at their zenith. Prices around £300 to £500.

ANTIQUE CLAUDE
Stand El, Chenil Galleries, 183 King's Road, London SW3 (01) 352 5964

Claude Lautreville has a fabulous collection of art nouveau and art deco rings with mainly square settings and beautiful angular stones. Some more unusual settings, too. From around £300 to £800. Also some Georgian rings and many silver objects for the attendants' or groom's presents.

HANCOCKS
1 Burlington Gardens, London W1
(01) 493 8904

David Callaghan is a fount of information, and has a good selection of top-quality jewellery dating from about 1840 to the present day. Rings from £350 upwards. They can renovate and convert old pieces, and have a team of outworkers who can craft contemporary designs.

RICHARD OGDEN
28 & 29 Burlington Arcade, Piccadilly, London W1
(01) 493 9136

The widest range of wedding rings in England in 18-carat or 9-carat gold, white gold (currently booming), platinum, or a mixture. The plainest 18-carat costs from £100. With a month's notice, Richard Ogden can make a ring to your specifications. Men's rings, too — a simple 9-carat gold band starts at £60. Diamond-set wedding rings for those whose engagement ring lacks sparkle. Antique engagement rings, new rings second-hand, and copies of old designs.

Established jewellers
GARRARD & CO.
112 Regent Street, London W1
(01) 734 3944

Garrard's have the distinction of being the sole jewellers responsible for the upkeep of the Crown Jewels in the Tower of London. Established since 1843, they have a loyal clientele — including the Royal Family — that spans generations. Garrard's have their workshops on the premises plus their own team of resident designers. Commissions take less time to materialize than at many other establishments — the Duchess of York's engagement ring took only 24 hours. For commoners, a made-to-order engagement ring takes more like two or three weeks — or longer if the stones need to be specially cut. Around £400 and *rising*. They report that classic styles — clusters and solitaires — are most in demand.

MAPPIN & WEBB

170 Regent Street, London W1
(01) 439 8297;
65 Brompton Road, London SW3
(01) 584 9361
and branches

Established in 1774, they were appointed the royal silversmiths by Queen Victoria. An extensive range of engagement rings, starting around £500 — and the sky's their limit. They can do special commissions, but prefer not to. Their main branch is in Regent Street; Brompton Road is more upmarket, but does fewer engagement rings.

COLLINGWOOD

46 Conduit Street, London W1
(01) 734 2565

They made Lady Diana Spencer's sapphire and diamond cluster engagement ring that has been so much copied (in fact Collingwood themselves can make you a replica of all the royal rings they've designed). Wide selection of sapphire, emerald and clustered diamond rings. Gold wedding bands from £100.

Auctions

Don't be intimidated by the idea of buying at auction. There is ample time to view, and, at the established houses, unbiased experts are on hand for advice. All these auction houses have offices spread throughout the country.

CHRISTIE'S

8 King Street, St James's, London SW1
(01) 839 9060; 85 Old Brompton Road,
London SW7 (01) 581 2231

Antique jewellery is auctioned on Tuesdays at 2 pm at the Old Brompton Road branch. A mine of rings, most of them set with precious stones, that go for anything from £50 to £4,000. Less-frequent auctions at St James's cover the top end of the market.

PHILLIPS

7 Blenheim Street, London W1
(01) 629 6602

Three auctions a month on Tuesdays, with viewing on Friday, Monday and the morning of the auction. The rings are categorized into antique and modern (ranging from £100 to £3,000) and fine (£400 to £25,000). There is a special art nouveau and art deco section.

SOTHEBY'S

34 New Bond Street, London W1
(01) 493 8080

A wide selection of rings is auctioned once or twice a month. Their middle range goes for up to £2,000 and their fine jewels up to £25,000.

> In bygone days, when the betrothal was a contract, sealed with the ring, it was customary to return the ring if breaking an engagement. Most women think it immoral to do anything else. But Shirley MacLaine has a chain set with ten diamonds — one for each of the engagement rings she's been given.

SECTION II
ARRANGEMENTS SCHEDULE

Here is a complete chronological checklist of all that has to be done when organizing a wedding. By each point there is an indication of who is responsible for arranging it (B = Bride and/or bride's mother; G = Groom) and a page reference to the relevant chapter for detailed information.

For May to July weddings, follow the six-month schedule as shown. Christmas weddings need careful planning, as all party services and equipment are booked up way in advance. Out-of-season weddings require less notice. Allow plenty of time when organizing a wedding in London, particularly during the party and events seasons (late October to early January; late April to early August).

Schedule

Before planning the wedding you must come to a decision over style of wedding and reception, location, date and time (with alternatives in case the church or reception venues are already booked).

Six months

Speak to your minister, priest, rabbi or registrar and agree a date and time for the wedding. Book church/Register Office, etc. (BG). See pages 23-32.

Put arrangements for any special licence in motion (BG). See page 24.

Book the hotel/hall/marquee, caterer/party planner. If the wedding is at home, plan a subsequent site meeting for marquee/lighting/decor (B). See pages 130-164.

Choose your attendants — bridesmaids, pages (B), best man and ushers (though ushers can be chosen at a later date) (G).

Decide on the number of guests; make list over next three months (BG).

Book your honeymoon and the hotel for your honeymoon night. Arrange travel insurance at the same time (G). See pages 179-186.

Five months

Order cars/horse and carriage, etc. for going to the church (B and G make separate arrangements) and between the church and reception. Book going-away transport. Or make firm arrangements to borrow cars from friends or family (B/G). See pages 60-63.

Book photographer and video (B/G). See pages 45-59.

Plan your wedding-present list (BG). See pages 40-44.

Four months

Order wedding invitations and envelopes, service sheets and cake boxes (B). See pages 33-39.

Book florist. Discuss flowers for church, reception, bouquets, head-dresses and button-holes. Arrange subsequent site meeting if necessary (B). See pages 114-129.

Order cake (B). See pages 138-141 and 147 (DIY see 138-140).

Start planning your wedding dress and accessories, and the attendants' clothes. Book dressmaker. Book shoemaker if applicable (B). See pages 64-106.

Book dressmaker and milliner, if required, for going-away outfit (B). See pages 70-75 and 97-100.

Choose and buy wedding ring(s) (BG). See pages 13-18.

Three months

Plan music for the ceremony. Talk to the organist and choir. Book any extra musicians /choir that are not attached to the church (BG). See pages 29-32.

Have second meeting with minister and arrange rehearsal near the day. Arrange pre-marriage course if it's a Catholic wedding (BG). See page 25.

Confirm in writing choice of food and drink with the caterer or hotel (B). See page 130.

DIY cake: commence rich fruit cake (B). See pages 138-140 for full schedule.

Confirm in writing flowers with florist (B).

Check passports are in order if going abroad for honeymoon (BG). Complete post office forms if you want a new passport carrying your married name for your honeymoon (B).

Start shopping for going-away and honey-moon outfits and for any special lingerie, shoes, etc. (B). See pages 77-85, 91-94 and 95-96.

If marrying in a Register Office or in a church other than the Church of England, give notice of marriage to superintendent registrar (B/G). See pages 25 and 27.

Two months to six weeks

DIY catering: make thorough plan, start cooking for freezer (B). See pages 135-140.

Plan DIY floristry: see pages 124-125 for full schedule (B).

Buy presents for the best man and attendants (G).

Send out invitations (BG). See page 36.

Make a list of guest acceptances and refusals as they arrive (B).

Send thank-you letters for wedding presents as they arrive (BG).

Arrange stag and hen parties (B/G with chief bridesmaid and best man). See pages 165-167.

One month

Book hairdresser/manicurist. Test hairstyle with head-dress and veil and hat for the day. Buy any new make-up and practise. Go to beauty classes/health spas now (B). See pages 110-113.

Inform caterer of the final number of guests (B).

Prepare table plan and place cards if required (B).

Check that the groom has organized the ring, his outfits and the honeymoon (BG).

Buy each other's special wedding present (BG).

Write to inform any official bodies of your new surname — driving licence, car registra-tion, AA, insurance policies, building society, bank for cheque book, cheque card, credit cards, etc. (B).

Make a plan of action for the day. Decide where you are dressing if not at home, trans-port logistics, etc. (BG).

One week

Have stag and hen parties (BG).

Prepare DIY flowers (B). See page 124-125.

Check all your wedding clothes and try on the whole outfit with shoes and underwear (B).

Groom to prepare his speech (G). See pages 172-173.

Have a full rehearsal at the church with all attendants. Practise not getting each other's names wrong. Give head usher seating plan for close relations (BG). See page 26.

Check timing of travel to the place of marriage and allow plenty of time on the day (BG).

Make a final check on arrangements for caterers, cake, transport, flowers, photography, video, etc. for exact timing and so on (B).

Check that you have everything for your honeymoon (BG). See pages 179-186.

Go to any last-minute hair/beauty appointments (B). See page 110.

The day

Individual checklists for each member of the wedding party are charted in the chapter on The Day (pages 168, 169, 170, 171, 172 and 173).

DIY flowers: final assembly (Bride's mother and team). See pages 125 and 168.

DIY cake: final assembly (Bride's mother and team).

Arrange display of wedding presents (Bride's mother).

Who pays for what
Bride's side

Printing of invitations and sending to guests; cake; everything for the reception — venue/marquee, caterer, food, decoration, lighting, etc. (except in practice, the groom's side often pays for drink or helps pay for another part of the reception); bride's and attendants' outfits (but in practice the attendants' parents often help out); all hire cars that involve the bride, though the groom may pay for the going-away transport as part of the honeymoon;

photographer; video; floral decorations in church and at reception; wedding present for the groom.

Most expensive weddings

The marriage of Mohammed, son of Shaik Zayid ibn Sai'id al-Makhtum to Princess Salama in Abu Dhabi in May 1981 lasted 7 days and cost an estimated £22 million, which included a purpose-built stadium for 20,000 people. This had nothing on Ferdinand and Imelda Marcos' $40 million blowout on their daughter Irene's Philippine wedding. A silver coach rolled in from Austria, seven white horses were flown over from Morocco, and Marcos' old home town of Sarrat was rebuilt to accommodate its starry—if fleeting—visitors.

Groom's side

Engagement and wedding rings; newspaper announcement; his outfit; church (including music) fees; certificates and licences; his car to church and possibly the going-away transport; bouquets, head-dresses and buttonholes (in practice the bride normally pays one bill for all the flowers, but the groom may reimburse her); presents for the best man and attendants; wedding present for the bride; (optional) help with reception costs, often the drink; the honeymoon.

Most married people

The greatest number of marriages in the monogamous world is 26 by the former Baptist minister Glynn 'Scotty' Wolfe (b. 1908) of Blythe, California. He first married in 1927 and has a total of 41 children. Mrs Beverly Nina Avery, a barmaid from Los Angeles, was married 16 times. She alleged that five of her 14 different spouses had broken her nose. The record for bigamous marriages is 104 by Giovanni Vigliotto who used some 50 aliases between 1949 and 1981. In 1983 he was sentenced to 28 years imprisonment for fraud and six for bigamy.

All this puts the likes of Zsa Zsa Gabor (married eight times) and Elizabeth Taylor (also married eight times but twice to Richard Burton) in the shade.

Some advice to the bride's mother from Country Cook Diana McKenzie: keep the wedding in perspective. Diana recalls countless brides' mothers who have confessed to her in dismay: 'I don't know what I'm going to do with myself now because I've spent every moment of the last three months organizing the wedding.'

Choosing attendants

The bride chooses her chief bridesmaid — often a friend of a similar age — and is instrumental in deciding on her other attendants, although pages and bridesmaids will normally be drawn from both sides. It is completely up to you whether you have just one grown-up bridesmaid; a herd of tiny attendants, more pages than bridesmaids or vice versa; on the one hand, budget rears its ugly head, as they all have to be clothed, and on the other, protocol has to be observed if there are many young brothers/sisters/nephews/neices/cousins on both sides. Write to each attendant individually, on a fun card if asking little ones.

The groom chooses his best man. The ushers — one head usher and several more — are chosen from both sides, but the groom's side is often more heavily represented as this is a diplomatic way of giving his almost-best-friends a role. It is nice if the groom writes to his best man, but there is no need to invite ushers formally.

Choosing guests

Discuss guests with your parents, your fiancé and his parents. To determine numbers, each side should make out a rough list, taking into account the number you can fit into the church and into the proposed reception venue, and, most importantly, your budget. Guests will include relations on both sides, bride's parents' friends, groom's parents' friends, bride's friends, groom's friends and joint friends of the couple. The allocation will normally be divided equally between bride's and groom's sides, but there are obvious exceptions according to the size and location of each side's family.

It is up to you and your parents to decide on the proportion of young and old guests. There is always a dispute when parents want to invite a far-flung aunt or a business associate whom you have never met. It is a valid argument that you should know all your guests but, on the other hand, if parents are forking out, they see it largely in terms of *their* party. The situation to avoid is that of the wedding becoming a vehicle for paying off or impressing acquaintances. Some couples are keen to make the wedding a young event, and try to cut down on obligatory oldies, asking instead more of their own friends. This is up to you to decide with your parents. Of course, if you are paying — which occurs increasingly — it is your prerogative to choose your guests.

Both sides should compile a final guest list and the groom's list should be sent to the bride's mother. Either the groom's side or the bride's side send out the groom's invitations, but all replies go to the bride's mother.

When to marry lore

Monday for health,
Tuesday for wealth,
Wednesday the best of all,
Thursday for losses,
Friday for crosses,
Saturday, no luck at all.

Perhaps this accounts for the high divorce rates, since most people marry on a Saturday. Both Charles and Diana and Andrew and Sarah married, prudently, on a Wednesday.

THE CHURCH AND REGISTER OFFICE

This aspect of your wedding requires serious thought and organization. Booking the church or Register Office is top on your list of priorities: the more notice you can give, the better. Make an appointment with your minister or registrar. Agree upon a date and time with him and book it. The time you choose depends greatly on your reception — whether you plan a lunch, canapés, tea or dinner. The royals marry in the morning followed by a wedding breakfast (more of a brunch); country weddings commence more often than not between 2 pm and 3 pm; London weddings are held increasingly at 5 pm midweek. You may have a Sunday wedding, although some ministers are not keen on this. Church weddings must take place between 8 am and 6 pm.

In the case of religious ceremonies, during the time between the first meeting and the wedding, you will be expected to meet at least once again to discuss Christianity, the religious aspect of marriage, children, the meaning of the vows, and the more immediate concerns of music and the order of service. You should also discuss fees which, on top of the marriage service (£33 plus £2 for a marriage certificate) could include the banns or licence, organist, choir, bell ringers, heating, flowers, photographers, video, clearing up confetti, etc. There will probably be a rehearsal in the week before the wedding.

There are several different sets of regulations, both for marrying in church and in a Register Office. It is possible to overcome

Folklore decrees, in its macabre fashion, that no bride should hear her banns being called lest her children be born deaf and dumb. It is bad luck for the banns to be called partly in one year and partly in the next, or even 'straddling the quarters'. The most favourable time for them to be called is between a new and full moon.

such rules as being a regular worshipper at the church for six months, or having the banns read. And if you marry by registrar's certificate and licence, the process can be cut down to a minimum of two days.

Church of England

Banns

The most traditional way to marry is in the parish in which either you or the groom, or either parents, reside. Customarily, it is the parish of the parental home of the bride. Provided the church is not booked up, and your minister is in agreement, this takes a minimum of about a month.

The banns announce your intended marriage. If the groom and bride have different parish churches, the banns must be called in both and a certificate of proof is required from the church where the wedding will not take place. On three Sundays prior to marriage, the names of each partner are read out (you don't *have* to disclose *all* your Christian names) and the public are given the opportunity to declare any just cause or impediment to the union — a chance for some unknown spouse to rear his head. The fee for publishing banns in one parish is £4 (£8 for two), a banns certificate £2.

Most married couple

Jack and Edna Moran of Seattle, Washington, have married each other 40 times since their first ceremony in 1937.

Common licence

The only requirement to marry by this method is that one of the couple should be resident in the parish for 15 days before applying for the licence via their minister. In practice, it is a way of speeding up the process and avoiding the banns. Some couples have used it as a way of marrying outside their parishes by leaving a pair of shoes in a suitcase at an address in the parish — but the church does not look kindly on such fraudulent behaviour. The licence costs £26.

Special licence

This is a discretionary licence granted by the Archbishop of Canterbury. Since it makes allowances as to the time and place of the wedding, it is normally applied for by couples who wish to marry outside their own parishes — perhaps their parish church is not suitable, or there is a church with sentimental or professional connections, such as a school, college or military chapel. As a courtesy, you should discuss your intentions with your own parish minister as well as with the minister of the chosen church. You will be required to fill in forms and supply letters of reference, etc. This licence costs £40.

It is also possible, though uncommon, to marry in the Church of England after obtaining a superintendent registrar's certificate (see page 27). NB: this is not a certificate of marriage — that would mean you were marrying twice.

You may wish to be married by a minister from outside your parish — an old family friend who has moved away, for example. Without offending anyone, discuss this with him and your own parish minister. They will need to get permission from their parishes, but it should not be a problem.

For more information, contact the Enquiry Centre, Church House, Dean's Yard, London SW1P 3NZ (01) 222 9011.

Which service?

Both the original marriage service of 1662 and the revised version of 1928 appear in the 1928 Book of Common Prayer. The authorized Book of Common Prayer of 1966, based on the 1928 version, is the most commonly used but omits the bride's vow of obedience. 'To love, cherish and to obey', was a vow the Duchess of York took, but the Princess of Wales forsook. The 1980 Alternative Service Book uses more blunt, less poetic language: 'I give you this ring as a sign of our marriage', rather than, 'With this ring I thee wed'; you promise either, 'to love and to cherish', or, 'to love, cherish and worship', but 'obedience' is optional. In America they say, 'I do', but in all versions of the marriage service in Britain, the response is, 'I will', which is why newspapers that splash headlines like, 'When Di says "I do"', and, 'Paula says "I do" again!' are incorrect.

See also page 36 for more about the Order of Service.

Largest joint wedding

The largest mass wedding ceremony was the famous Moonie event of 1982 when 5,837 couples from 83 countries tied the knot in Seoul, South Korea, officiated over by Sun Myung Moon.

Roman Catholic

The standard procedure is similar to the Church of England although, in practice, the banns are not often called. You will probably be required to give notice to your local Register Office (see page 27); unlike Church of England ministers, few Catholic priests are authorized to register marriages. If there are any special circumstances such as marrying outside your parish, it is best to speak to your parish priest who will know exactly what to do in your case, fill in any necessary forms and gain any dispensations or letters of freedom needed.

Your priest will want to talk at some length about the commitment of marriage, about children, and so on. Decide whether you want a Nuptial Mass or a simpler ceremony. It is usual to have special readings and prayers in addition to the basic service.

For more information, contact The Catholic Marriage Advisory Council, 15 Lansdown Road, London W11 (01) 727 0141.

Catholic and non-Catholic

Catholics need dispensation from the Catholic church to marry non-Catholics. This will be given by the parish priest on the assurance that the Catholic will preserve his or her faith and bring up any children in the Catholic faith. The non-Catholic is not required to make any promises or convert to Catholicism, but will be expected to go to several sessions to discuss the meaning of marriage to Catholics. Various forms have to be filled in by the priest. The marriage normally takes place in the Catholic church.

Church of Scotland

In Scotland, you don't need parental consent to marry between the ages of 16 and 18. Young lovers still flock to Gretna Green — first stop over the border — to tie the knot. The marriage service is similar to that of the Church of England, but you need to fill in a form obtained from the registrar in order to receive a marriage schedule — you need to have one of these to give to your minister. In this enlightened land there are many women ministers.

Seating in church

If it's a small church, decide exactly how many guests you can fit in, and make sure there is enough room on each pew. Don't try and squash eight onto a pew that is designed for six. Work out a seating plan for the immediate family in the first two or three pews on each side, and make sure the ushers stick to it rigorously on the day. If ushers are going to be at the rehearsal, take the seating plan along then.

Service of blessing

A church service of blessing is sometimes held after a wedding in a Register Office or abroad. It can be held directly after the marriage or on another day. The service includes hymns, prayers, readings, etc., but there are no vows. Discuss it with your minister and book a date in the usual way.

Lady Elizabeth Anson on . . . the church

' 'I'm a great believer in smelling salts and sweets — smelling salts for the bride's mother and sweets for the bridesmaids and pages. If you have small children as bridesmaids you should take a sheet to pin on the bride's dress at the rehearsal so the children get used to it. Send the children home once they have rehearsed their bit, otherwise they tend to get nerved up. The other thing that is terribly important is to find out beforehand where the loo is in church — if there is one. If you're going to have a complicated seating plan you must give the ushers a very good briefing at the rehearsal.

I think it's a great mistake to bring babies and small children into the church. I think it's fair, particularly if they've got a nanny, to ask for them to stay at the back.

One bride's mother asked me to send four bottles of champagne into the vestry for the signing of the register and I remember feeling rather shocked, that popping corks in the vestry was not quite right. *That* was an amenable vicar. The vicar can be very powerful. He may say he won't marry you after 5 pm; or that he doesn't want your florist, he wants his wife to do the flowers . . . '

Register Office

Just over half the marriages in Britain take place in a Register Office. This does, of course, include second marriages, since divorced persons where the ex-spouse is still living may not marry in church. Favourite Register Offices, particularly in showbiz circles, are Marylebone and Chelsea.

Giving notice

To marry in a register office, one party must have resided in that registration district for at least seven days. This entitles you to marry without a licence. You must then see the superintendent registrar to give notice of marriage, specifying the building in which marriage is to take place, giving other details and signing the official declaration. If the other party resides in another district, he or she must give separate notice to the local registrar. The registrar posts up the notice for 21 days and then produces a certificate giving his authority to marry. The marriage must then take place between the 22nd day and three months hence. This costs from £18 to £34, depending on whether both of you live in the same district and where you marry.

Licence

To marry by licence, one party must have resided in the registration district for 15 days prior to giving notice. Only one party need give notice, regardless of where the other lives. Only one clear day (not Sunday, Good Friday or Christmas Day) is needed between giving notice and being issued a certificate and licence, after which you may marry. This costs £44 to £52.

The superintendent registrar will be able to advise you about the service, how many guests may be invited (at least two to witness the signing of the register, up to 20 or 30), about flowers, and photographs (see page 48).

For more information, contact the General Register Office, St Catherine's House, 10 Kingsway, London WC2 (01) 242 0262, or your local superintendent registrar.

The good church guide

Church of England
Chapel Royal or Queen's Chapel, St James's Palace, London SW1 (for those with royal connections, including staff)
King Henry VII Chapel, Westminster Abbey, London SW1 (for members of the Order of the Bath and their families)
The Queen's Chapel of Savoy, Savoy Street, London WC2 (for members of the Royal Victorian Order and their families)
St Margaret's, Westminster or the House of Commons Crypt, London SW1 (for those with parliamentary connections)
St Paul's Cathedral Chapel, London EC4 (for members of the Order of the British Empire and the Order of St Michael and St George)
Temple Church, Inner Temple, London EC4 (for those connected with the Inns of Court)
Holy Trinity, Brompton Road, London SW7
St Bartholomew the Great, West Smithfield, London EC1
St George's, Hanover Square, London W1
St James's, Piccadilly, London W1
St Mary, The Boltons, London SW10
St Michael's, Chester Square, London SW1
St Paul's, Knightsbridge, London SW1

Roman Catholic
The Oratory, Brompton Road, London SW3
Church of the Immaculate Conception, Farm Street, London W1
Our Most Holy Redeemer, Cheyne Row, London SW3
St James's, Spanish Place, London W1
St Mary's, Cadogan Street, London SW3

Church of Scotland
St Columba's, Pont Street, London SW1

Inter-denominational
Guards' Chapel, Birdcage Walk, London SW1 (for guardsmen and their daughters)

Marrying abroad

WEDDINGS IN PARADISE
Wings Faraway Holidays, Travel
House, Broxbourne, Hertfordshire
(0992 87211)

They can arrange the whole works in St
Lucia, Antigua, Jamaica, Barbados, the
Bahamas or the Seychelles. They provide
a best man if necessary, wedding cake,
Champagne toast and photographer. The
hotels involved offer a free week's accommodation for your first anniversary. You
provide passport, birth certificate, a decree
absolute or death certificate if divorced or
widowed, registration/licence fees. They
sort out ways round residency and other
formalities. Ask for their Faraway Holiday
brochure as well as 'Weddings in Paradise'
details, as you have to be on a standard
holiday to marry their way.

Miranda Nicolle and Paul Berrow (below) *cut the
cake at their wedding in the South of France,
amid sprays of olive branches, orchids, birds of
paradise, lilies and roses, arranged by Tomasz
Starzewski, who also made Miranda's simple
fitted voile dress.*
(Richard Taylor)

*Romina Marshall, niece of the Marquis Scicluna
of Malta, had a traditional wedding at the family
home, the Palazzo Parisio. She wore a copy of
an 18th-century family dress, embroidered by
nuns of the Good Shepherd of Balzan. She and
husband Alan Short walked beneath an 18th-
century brocade canopy. That evening the sound
of buglers, a brass band, a string quartet and
fireworks rocked the town.*
(Jennifer Beeston)

CHURCH MUSIC

The church music is an intrinsic and important part of the marriage ceremony. As the Archdeacon of Westminster Abbey said at the time of the Duke and Duchess of York's wedding, 'Good music makes an impact that it would not on a lesser occasion, and many who don't usually worship can be brought to a deeper understanding, a deeper faith in God, through the medium of music.' It sets and echoes the mood of the service, from the subdued, anticipatory music while the congregation awaits the bride, breaking into a rousing tune at the entrance of the bride, continuing with hymns, psalms and anthems, until the jubilant, climactic chords strike out at the departure of the couple.

This is a chance for the bride and groom to stamp their own personality on their marriage service. Traditionally, it is the bride's prerogative to choose the music, but in practice — apart from the bride's entrance music — the couple choose together, often assisted by their church organist. The Duke and Duchess of York certainly handed over much of the decision-making to Simon Preston, organist and Master of the Choristers at Westminster Abbey. Perhaps they should have taken a keener interest, though, since some of the music was felt to be rather gloomy, particularly Elgar's *Imperial March* which played as the bride and her father made their way up the aisle. The wedding of the Prince and Princess of Wales, in contrast, was a musical feast. St Paul's Cathedral was chosen partly for its excellent acoustics. Three hundred musicians performed, including three orchestras — of which Prince Charles is patron — and the star soloist, Kiri Te Kanawa, who sang Handel's 'Let the bright Seraphim' from *Samson*.

Back at the average parish church, your first step is to find out, discreetly, the virtuosity of the regular organist and — if there is one — the choir. Most couples are happy with the resident team. However, if it doesn't match up to your musical aspirations (has any decrepit country organist ever tackled Widor's *Toccata* and won?), you may wish to draft your own musicians. Paula Yates enrolled her father, Jess Yates, as organist. Your team may encompass singers and/or instrumentalists drawn from family, friends, a local society or school choir. An outside choir may wish to provide their own organist. Meanwhile, you must check whether there are choir stalls and how many people can be accommodated. All this will have to be put, tactfully, to your minister and organist. You will, in any case, have to discuss your music with them, and they will undoubtedly have their own views and suggestions.

Once you have enlisted your musicians, you are free to choose what they play — within bounds. Bear in mind aptness of tempo, mood and words. Anything quirky is dreaded by most church organists. There are standard pieces, hackneyed pieces and frankly unsuitable pieces. Bach, Handel and Purcell top the church chart hits. Wagner's and Mendelssohn's Wedding Marches are the most clichéd entrance and departure tunes; Wagner's is rarely played (not surprisingly, since it's 'Here comes the bride . . .'), but Mendelssohn's gets an occasional airing. Unsuitable for the most part, though oft-requested, are pop songs (*Sailing, A Whiter Shade of Pale*), soundtracks from films and stage musicals (though the *Brideshead Revisited* theme sounded rather good, reports one trumpeter), and all things dirge-like and funereal.

Pre-service and processional music

The music leading up to the service should set the tone for the ceremony. The music played before the Queen arrived at Westminster Abbey for her wedding in 1947 was representative: Widor's *Andante Cantabile*, Bach's *Jesu, Joy of Man's Desiring*, selections from Handel's *Water Music* and Parry's *Bridal March and Finale*. The Duke of York had a selection of music by Handel, Purcell and Bach. Both Lady Diana Spencer and Sarah Ferguson were greeted by a fanfare of trumpets.

The processional music is dignified and stirring. It declares to the congregation: 'The time has come, the bride is here.' A trumpet's resonant tones herald her entrance beautifully. Several royal brides have walked up the aisle to a hymn. The Queen chose *Praise, my soul, the King of Heaven*, the Queen Mother, *Lead us, Heavenly Father, lead us*, and Princess Margaret, *Christ is made the sure Foundation*. Choose something with a steady pace that can be broken at a suitable moment when you reach the chancel steps.

Notes to enter on
Trumpet Voluntary — Clarke
Trumpet Tune and Air — Purcell
Grand March of *Aida* — Verdi
Fugue in G Minor — Bach
Water Music — Handel
Arrival of the Queen of Sheba — Handel
Wedding March from *The Marriage of Figaro* — Mozart
Wedding March from *Lohengrin* — Wagner

Hymns and psalms

The standard order of service goes hymn, psalm, hymn, but many couples prefer to

Top hymns
Praise, my soul, the King of heaven
Praise to the Lord, the Almighty
Guide, me O thou great Redeemer
The Lord is my Shepherd (Psalm 23)
  — to the tune of Crimond
Dear Lord and Father of Mankind
Immortal, invisible
I vow to thee, my country
Jerusalem
Lead us, Heavenly Father, lead us
Love divine, all loves excelling
Come down, O love divine
The King of love, my shepherd is
Glorious things of Thee are spoken
Lord of all hopefulness

Favourite psalms
23: The Lord is my Shepherd (various choral arrangements if not sung as a hymn)
121: I will lift up mine eyes unto the hills
128: Blessed is everyone that feareth the Lord
48: Great is the Lord

have three hymns — from the *English Hymnal, Hymns Ancient and Modern, (Standard* and *Revised* editions) and the *Book of Common Prayer*. It is best to choose hymns that the majority of your guests will recognize, although if yours is the fifteenth *Praise, my soul* or *Praise to the Lord* that season, it could be reduced to a meaningless chant. A choir to lead hymns and sing descants makes a world of difference. Go through the hymns with the organist beforehand to make sure he will play the right version, at the right tempo, in an acceptable key. It is worth checking verses for unsuitable words (the popular *Dear Lord and Father of Mankind* continues 'forgive our foolish ways' . . .). You can always cut an offending verse, but ask your minister for his advice if you are in doubt.

The Queen chose *The Lord is my Shepherd*; Princess Anne, *Immortal, invisible* and *Glorious things of Thee are spoken*; Princess Alexandra, *Holy, Holy, Holy* and *Love divine*, *all loves excelling*; Lady Diana, *Christ is made the sure foundation* and *I vow to thee, my country*; and Sarah *Praise to the Lord, the Almighty*, the appropriate *Lead us, Heavenly Father, lead us* (... o'er the world's tempestuous sea) and *Come down, O love divine*.

Notes to go out on
Toccata — Widor
Trumpet Voluntary — Clarke
Wedding March from *A Midsummer Night's Dream* — Mendelssohn
Ave Maria — Bach/Gounod
Music for the Royal Fireworks — Handel
Toccata in C — Pachelbel

During the signing of the register

The ten-minute gap while you are breathing sighs of relief in the vestry is the ideal time for instrumentalists to play or for the choir to sing an anthem. It is perhaps not so appropriate to have a soloist who may be nervous, and could divert attention from the couple who should be in the spotlight. This was partly the feeling at the Prince and Princess of Wales' wedding. And when Paula Yates and Bob Geldof married in the village of Davington, Kent, lark-alike Aled Jones's rendition of *Ave Maria* reduced the congregation — including Simon Le Bon and Jasper Conran — to tears. But it would be difficult to upstage the Waleses or the Geldofs for long. The musicians and soloists at the Duke and Duchess of York's wedding, however, remained out of view in the organ loft. Felicity Lott sang Mozart's *Laudate Dominum*, chosen by the Duchess of York, and Arleen Auger sang Mozart's *Exultate Jubilate*. You may prefer to have organ music. *Jesu, Joy of Man's Desiring* is a favourite.

Recessional music

The triumphant procession down the aisle should be carried off with true pomp and circumstance. The Duke and Duchess of Kent and then Princess Alexandra were in part responsible for ruining many an organist's credibility when they chose Widor's *Toccata*, now one of the most demanded pieces to stride out to.

Bell appeal

One of the most glorious sounds is that of church bells announcing your wedding day to the neighbourhood, and a further explosion ringing the changes as you emerge from church. Arranging bell-ringers should be no problem — your minister will know who to call upon if there are no regulars at your church. At the Duke and Duchess of York's wedding, ten muscle-bound bell-ringers had to pull the ropes for a marathon 3½ hours to complete the full peal. There were over 5,000 different changes, only ever attempted on days of national celebration.

Musicians and choirs

London

CHOIRS FOR WEDDINGS
Flat 5, 46 Harcourt Terrace, London SW10 (01) 370 7347

Charles Hattrell can provide choirs of four to twenty voices, organists, trumpet players, brass, percussion and string trios and string quartets (more popular at receptions). Part-professional, part-amateur, the choirs include some ex-choral scholars from Oxford and Cambridge; their aim is to continue the tradition of Oxbridge chapel music. Always happy to give advice, they are usually requested to play traditional English church music from the last hundred years or from the Golden Age, the sixteenth century. They tend to work in the south-east but will travel anywhere if expenses are paid. The basic rate for a choir of four is £330; eight, £400; twelve, £500 and so on. The organist and instrumentalists are extra.

THE REGAL BRASS CONSORT
22 Oxford Avenue, Raynes Park, London SW20 (01) 540 4724; (01) 207 0007.

Chris Guy and his colleagues form a brass quintet — two trumpets, a French horn, a trombone and a tuba, but this arrangement can shrink or expand as required. At weddings, they play Renaissance music, wedding marches, interlude music and hymn accompaniments. They will travel, but prefer to stay in the London area. Minimum fee is about £35 a player.

TRUMPET VOLUNTARY
13 Dell Way, Ealing, London W13 (01) 998 3096.

Raymond Gay can provide any scale of musical arrangement required, right up to a symphony orchestra. However, as expenses can mount, he — or a colleague — is often asked to play the trumpet solo. He has played at weddings in Trinity Chapel, Dublin, Westminster Cathedral and small village churches. Common requests are Clarke's *Trumpet Voluntary* and Purcell's *Trumpet Tune*, but he can play a variety of suites for trumpet and organ in three or four movements while the register is being signed, and can accompany the hymns, the last verse either in unison or descant. It encourages people to sing, he reports. He can provide organists and soloists — all professional BBC singers. He is happy to hunt for favourite music if given enough time and will travel anywhere in the British Isles as long as expenses are covered. He will send a cassette of sample trumpet music. Minimum fee £75 for one player. Book as early as possible.

INVITATIONS AND OTHER STATIONERY

A wedding is a formal social function where the traditional style for invitations is laid down to the last copperplate full stop. This style is accepted as 'correct' in as much as anything is correct in the social language — it's like wearing a grey morning suit to Ascot. Of course, you don't *have* to adhere to social conventions, and if your wedding is at a register office or is to be particularly small or casual, you may feel formal invitations inappropriate.

Stationery and printing also includes Order of Service sheets, maps, menus, cake boxes and cards, although none of these is obligatory.

Traditional invitations

A 'proper' invitation should be hand-engraved in copperplate script (this means for each set of invitations, a skilled craftsman engraves an individual copper plate in mirror-writing). It has a quivery fineness that cannot be achieved by machine typesetting. The print is customarily black on single-fold double-sheet card, 7 × 5½ in (178 × 140 mm) (Duke) although, nowadays, the majority of invitations are 8 × 6 in (203 × 152 mm) (Albert). The cheaper alternative printing processes are thermography — shiny, embossed and unarguably tacky, since it attempts, toadily, to emulate engraving; and lithography — plain, flat, unpretentious, and the cheapest of all.

Up-market printer John Service observes: 'Some people will be mean about invitations, yet they'll have vintage champagne, because in their minds the printing is not important. Yet we get others who are not at all grand who want proper engraved invitations.'

The quality and colour of paper is also a

Colonel Sir Henry and Lady Tremayne
request the pleasure of
your company at the marriage
of their daughter
Annabelle
to
Captain James Paul Parker-Allen
at St Luke's, Stamfordham
on Wednesday, 8th September, 1982
at 3 o'clock
and afterwards at
Wootton Old Hall.

R.S.V.P.
Wootton Old Hall,
Stamfordham,
Northumberland.

Sample of an engraved invitation by Lonsdale Engraving.

point of consideration. One printer describes how an aristocratic client was so keen to achieve a particular blue for his invitations that he brought in a pair of silk knickers in the desired shade.

Confounding all etiquette, the Prince and Princess of Wales' wedding invitations were on unfolded card of landscape rectangular shape with the royal coat of arms embossed at the top, and in plain lithographic printing. The Duke and Duchess of York, however, did the right thing and went engraved.

Wording

This is the only social invitation where the host and hostess invite you rather than just the hostess. The names of the guests should be handwritten in pen (not biro) in the top left-hand corner, yet the envelope should be addressed to Mrs Guest only. To add further confusion, Mrs Guest addresses her reply and the envelope to Mrs Hostess only.

Whether you request the *pleasure* or the *honour* of your guests' company, and whether your daughter's marriage will be *to* or *with* her fiancé is up to you. Beyond that the actual wording of the invitation is quite straightforward:

> Mr (*title*) and (*not* &) Mrs (*title*)
>   Ernest (*one name*) Bond
> request the pleasure (*or* honour) of
> your company at the marriage
> of their daughter
> Brooke (*one Christian name*)
> to (*or* with)
> Mr (*title*) Vernon John (*all Christian names*) Littlewoods-Pooles
> at St Mark's, Little Premium
>   (*church and location*)
> on Saturday, 31st May, 1986 (*day, date, month, year in that order*)
> at 2 o'clock (*correctly it's always o'clock as in 2.30 o'clock; common usage, 2.30 pm/noon*)

and afterwards at
White City Stadium (*name only*).

R.S.V.P.
29, Bond Street,
Littlehampton,
Sussex

Complications arise when there is a variant over the host(s): a widowed mother (Mrs John Host), a divorced mother (Mrs Mary Host), a mother and stepfather (Mr and Mrs John Host request . . . at the marriage of *her* daughter), remarried divorcees (Mr John Host and Mrs Mary Smith, on two lines), and so on — the possibilities are endless. *Debrett's Correct*

> *If your wedding is on any day other than a Saturday, you may like to make it doubly clear. One couple chose a Bank Holiday Monday for their wedding, and invited friends for the whole weekend; to their consternation, they found that some guests had assumed the wedding was on the Saturday, and had made other arrangements for the Monday.*

Form should enlighten you over titles and ranks; do note any variance between address on the invitation and on the envelope. If you are in doubt over wording some peculiar permutation such as proxy parents and a double wedding, do ask one of the professionals listed.

You should never state the form of dress. In certain circumstances where there is security, you may need to add 'Please bring this invitation with you'; for example, for a reception at the House of Lords or a gentlemen's club. (Receptions at St James's Palace, incidentally, require car stickers and admission cards.)

People are so lax about replying promptly — it is good manners to reply immediately in order to help the hostess — that more and more invitations include an RSVP by a certain

Fashion stylist Clare Gardner-Medwin and photographer Michael Woolley's informal invitation (below) *reflects the style of their wedding. Designed by Michael's sister Vanessa Woolley, the card opens at the centre to reveal wording on three facets* (right)

date; the American custom of enclosing a stamped addressed reply card is also catching on in Britain.

Preserving the die

The hand-engraved copper die is, to use advertising speak, a unique souvenir of your wedding. Your printer will present it to you with the invitations. If you would like to make more of a feature of the die, some printers can craft it into a dish or ashtray. Lonsdale Engraving can do this with a second plate that is right reading (the original will be in mirror-writing). The Walton Street Stationery Company can incorporate the copper die in a mahogony box.

The wedding invitation itself is a small memento of the day and could be kept and framed, either by you or as a present from one of the guests.

DIY and informal invitations

If you are on a tight budget or want something original, you could design your own invitations or work with the stationer to dream up an individual design. One couple made cards that incorporated a transparent envelope full of confetti, another printed the invitation on

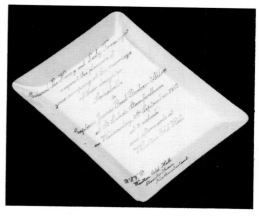

Copperplate ashtray from Lonsdale Engraving.

a balloon. You could design something modern and minimal, employ a calligrapher, or simply write it by hand yourself. Monograms or small hand-engravings of your house — used perhaps just on the envelope — can look very stylish. Unusual colour (and texture) of paper and print, unorthodox lettering, borders, ribbons, differently shaped cards, etc., all contribute a personal stamp — but avoid gilding the lily. It is much better to stick to tradition or to go for something jolly than to treat your guests to an overdose of schmaltz from the scalloped-silver-edged-cards-with-flowery-lettering-and-silver-bells school. Only the likes of Bob Geldof and Paula Yates — for whom kitsch is kool — could carry that off, as their invitations, all silver-lettered and horseshoed, proved.

The Marlow Suite,
Court Gardens,
Pound lane,
MARLOW

Mr. and Mrs. Alec Gardner-Medwin
Request the pleasure of
your Company at the Marriage
of their daughter
Clare
to
Michael Woolley
at
Holy Trinity Church, Cookham Village
Saturday 13th December 1986, at 2.00pm

Rose Cottage,
School lane,
Cookham Village,
BERKSHIRE
SL6 9QT

morning dress not Required

Reception only and evening party

An invitation to the reception only can be similar in layout to the wedding invitation or take the form of an 'At home' card. If there is a party in the evening as well as the wedding reception, it is best to have a separate 'At home' invitation to be sent with the wedding invitation.

Sending invitations

Invitations should be ordered at least three months before the day, to leave a comfortable margin, and sent out about six weeks in advance. John Service (see page 38) advises they are sent eight weeks ahead in the height of the season, for your wedding to gain precedence over the many others jostling to be attended.

It is usual to send a single invitation to a married couple and to include children below the age of majority (you can take either 18 or 21) on the same invitation. Children over 18 (or 21) should get their own invitation. The minister should be sent an invitation as a matter of courtesy. It is also courteous to send invitations to any friends and relations you know will not be able to attend the wedding. Everyone gets an invitation except the groom.

Order of Service sheets

The service sheet should not be engraved — it is not a formal or social item but a functional item simply to inform and assist guests. It gives the order of service, the titles of the passages of music and the words of the hymns. It is normally used in conjunction with prayer books and so there is no need to print out the marriage service itself or the prayers, except where there is a response from the congregation. It is normally a folded sheet of fine card (fine so that it can be folded again and put in a tailcoat pocket or handbag). On the cover it states the name and location of the church, the date, and the initials or Christian name of the bride (on the bottom left) and groom (bottom right). Inside, the format is:

Order of Service

(Introductory music)
At the entrance of the bride
(Entrance music)
HYMN (*all verses printed out*)
THE MARRIAGE
PSALM or HYMN (*all verses printed out*)
THE PRAYERS (*those with responses may be printed out*)
THE ADDRESS (*optional*)
HYMN (*all verses printed out*)
THE BLESSING
During the signing of the register
(Recessional music)
(Departure music)

To this basic order may be added a Reading, the Lesson, etc. Of course, you can print out the whole service — one grand wedding at Christ Church, Oxford ran to eight pages — but the typesetting bill will increase accordingly.

Most couples choose music and hymns and then go through the order of service with their minister to finalize readings/lessons/the address, and so on. When giving the order to the printer, you will need to state the hymn or psalm number, the first line, the number of verses required and which version (see pages 30-31). The sheets needn't be ordered at the same time as the invitations — a few weeks before the wedding should be ample.

Maps

For weddings in lesser known parts of the country it is worth enclosing a map and include the estimated driving time. Consider probable delays — a big event such as a rugby international at Twickenham can put timing vitally out. At one Sussex wedding, there were still 30 people missing when the bride

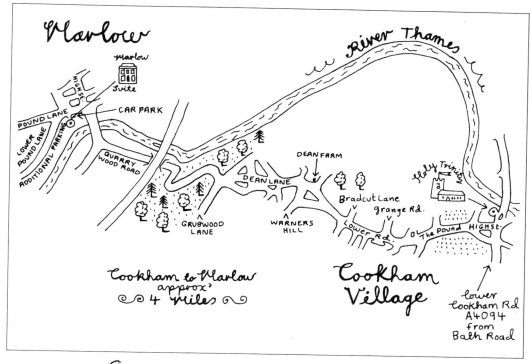

This map, designed by Vanessa Woolley, matches Michael and Clare Woolley's wedding invitation.

arrived; it turned out that they had been stuck on the A3 amid queues for the Farnborough Air Show. So consider putting an alternative route on your map.

Your printer can arrange to have a professional map drawn or can print from your own drawing or artwork (an existing line drawing in good order). One couple's invitation was printed inside with the same map that the hosting parents had used for their wedding in 1952. To save costs, you can always enclose a photocopied map.

Another consideration for weddings in Scotland, Ireland or abroad is to enclose a printed timetable of intercity train services and/or flights.

Menus

If you are having a special lunch or dinner, you may want to give the guests menus to keep. The cover of the menu could be mono-grammed, engraved with a picture of the bride's house, or could contain a hand-coloured drawing. The lettering could be engraved or handwritten, and the card tied with a ribbon or tassle. One girl had her menu printed inside a greetings card she particularly liked. The Walton Street Stationery Company have printed an elaborate seating plan for a reception for 600 guests.

Printers and stationers

There are very few old-fashioned engravers around, but you don't need a local printer — it can all be done by post. Ask stationers to show or send samples of their work — most have packs of sample invitations and service sheets plus an order form with suggested wording. Non-specialists such as Harrods are best avoided since they don't have their own engravers, take longer and cannot offer the same personal service.

All the stationers below can print in Hebrew and foreign languages if given due notice. They will be delighted to discuss ideas for personalized wedding stationery.

London

AQUILA PRESS
37 Bury Street, St James's, London SW1
(01) 839 4910; (01) 930 5969

One of the few old-established engravers, offering a bespoke service at competitive prices. The complete range of stationery, from invitations to direction slips. They can print onto handmade paper, with handmade envelopes to match. All invitations are hand-engraved ('When Gucci make plastic handbags we'll do thermography', shudders Andrew Ross). Work is completed in a fortnight, or

longer if a proof is required (at a small surcharge). Service sheets take a little longer. 7 × 5½ in (178 × 140 mm) invitations: £133 for 100, £165 for 200; 8 × 6 in (203 × 152 mm): £145 for 100, £178 for 200.

LONSDALE ENGRAVING
28 New King's Road, London SW6
(01) 736 9520

Although John Service founded this firm only a few years ago, he now leads the market in traditional wedding stationery ('It's our flagship'). They do a thorough daily mailing to all those newly betrotheds announced in *The Times* and *Daily Telegraph*, which yields almost all their wedding business — about 250 a year, divided evenly between London, and the rest of the UK (where goods can be despatched by British Rail's Red Star service). All work is hand-engraved on one of three qualities of card. Invitations take a month, including a proof stage: 7 × 5½ in (178 × 140 mm): from £125 for 100, £167 for 200; 8 × 6 in (203 × 152 mm): from £130 for 100, £175 for 200. Service sheets: £91 for 100, £107 for 200. The shop also sells hand-marbled albums, visitors' books, cards, etc. that would make beautiful wedding presents.

LOUDOUN PAPERS
1 Courtnell Street, London W2
(01) 229 1172

A fun shop for different invitations. Designer Rory McLaren has books of past designs for clients to see, but particularly enjoys creating something original and special. One past invitation displayed an engraving of the hosts' house on thick parchment, another used paper that had a watermark image of the couple, taken from a photograph. His ultimate job was a folder of no less than seven invitations per guest, edged in 22-carat gold and printed in gold, for an Indian client. A large variety of papers and cards. Also cake boxes, card matches, napkins, direction cards, etc. Prices on request.

An engraving of the bride's family home, (right) appears on the front cover of this invitation, printed by Loudoun Papers. It opens to conventional wording (below right) and on the back is another engraving (below).

I N V I T A T I O N

Mr and Mrs Cornelius Van Hage
REQUEST THE PLEASURE OF YOUR COMPANY
AT THE WEDDING OF THEIR DAUGHTER

MARY AN
WITH

ANTHONY CHARNLEY
AT ST. AUGUSTINE'S R.C. CHURCH, HODDESDON
ON SATURDAY, 18TH AUGUST AT 2.15 P.M.
AND AFTERWARDS AT AMWELL GROVE

AMWELL GROVE
CAUTHERLY LANE
GREAT AMWELL
Nr. WARE, HERTS

R.S.V.P.

SMYTHSON
54 New Bond Street, London W1
(01) 629 8558

The Queen's stationers. Invitations can be engraved in a variety of letterings as well as copperplate script. They have many styles of monogram which could be incorporated on your stationery. Also lavish photograph albums and other smart wedding presents. Prices — fit for a Queen — on request.

THE WALTON STREET STATIONERY COMPANY
97 Walton Street, London SW3
(01) 589 0777.

Claire Farnsworth offers a comprehensive range of wedding stationery, from engagement announcement cards and invitations to reply cards and thank-you notelets. They have done monogrammed invitations with silk ribbon ties (once in the racing colours of the bride's family); gilt-edged invitations; stationery that has been silk-screen printed with the bride's handwriting; Arabic, Hebrew and French invitations. A wide range of paper tints and textures such as parch-mark paper which has a soft marbled appearance; many styles of engraved lettering. Claire has catalogues to show past styles and formats and a store of ideas for commemorative work made from your copper plate. Prices on request.

WEDDING PRESENTS

The wedding list

If you are to avoid the ten-toast-racks syndrome, it is worth having a wedding list. Some couples feel it is mercenary and unspontaneous to state in precise detail what they want, but special friends who have their own ideas can always deviate from the list, while others who haven't got a clue what to give will find it invaluable. It also helps guests who live abroad or far away, who can just telephone through their order, and it cuts down on unwanted monstrosities as well as duplications.

Many major department stores offer a wedding list service. The system is this: eight to ten weeks before the wedding, you and your fiancé tramp round each floor making a note of all you want (some stores have suggestion lists for you to tick off); the shop then types out your personal list and takes care of all purchases and deliveries, striking out each item as it is bought. Arrange your list at one or two shops. A good combination is a serious, sensibly priced household store such as John Lewis plus a more decorative present-type shop like Liberty or the General Trading Company.

Alternatively, you could make out your own list — stating which model and colour of each item — and photocopy it for family and friends.

Put Mother in charge of keeping the list up-to-date, and ask everyone to check with her before they buy and inform her of any purchases.

Keep a note of all presents and their donors as they arrive. The first flurry of deliveries will occur soon after people receive their invitations and you should write thank-you letters as the parcels arrive. Most large stores will deliver within a certain catchment area and they will have a regular day for your area. Some firms are notorious for hashing up deliveries — if there's no one in they leave it on the doorstep, or with a neighbour, without checking first if you agree, and so on. Make sure there will be someone to accept and sign for deliveries when you are at work and when you are away on honeymoon. Otherwise, give an alternative address and also the address of a neighbour in case there is no one in at the first address. It may be easier for you to collect. Whatever the case, make your instructions crystal clear.

What presents?

Presents will range from purely practical to purely decorative. Remember that these are joint presents and, although you will both get

One of Alice Roosevelt's wedding presents in 1906 was a $1,500 Boston Terrier with a complete wardrobe of suits, shoes, furs and petticoats.

Bob Geldof was given a baseball bat at Marriage Mark II to Paula Yates. It was put to instant use: Simon Le Bon brought a further four bats with him to the reception, two teams were made up of about 100 friends and relations still clad in glad rags and morning suits, and they all played while Paula went up to change.

use from a soufflé dish, your husband-to-be may find it disheartening if there isn't something that fires his enthusiasm. Some of the ideas in the general section might generate a spark. You don't have to ask for conventional items, although one point about wedding presents is that they should last your married life.

Household: vacuum cleaner, washing machine, tumble dryer, heaters, iron, ironing board, wastepaper bins.
Kitchen: saucepans, pressure cooker, baking tins, oven-to-table ware such as Le Creuset casserole dishes, wok, coffee grinder, coffee maker, scales, colander, scissors, knives, sharpener, chopping board, pastry board, rolling pin, wooden spoons, cutlery, food processor (Magimix still the ultimate), electric whisk/mixer, kettle, toaster, slow cooker, toasted sandwich maker, ice-cream maker, yoghurt maker, electric hotplate, microwave, etc.
Dining room: dinner service, vegetable dishes, soufflé dishes, flan dish, bowls, tureens, ramekins, jugs, tea service, delicate coffee cups and jug, big breakfast cups; glassware — goblets, hock glasses, tumblers, cocktail glasses, liqueur glasses, carafes, decanters, fruit bowl; silverware — cutlery from place settings to sugar tongs and cake knives, candlesticks, salt, pepper and mustard set, toast rack; drinks accessories — cocktail shaker, corkscrew, ice bucket, wine cooler, wine rack; linen — tablecloths, napkins.

Bedroom: sheets, duvet covers, duvets, pillows, pillow cases, blankets, bedspreads.
Bathroom: scales, bath set, towels, mirror, cabinet, linen basket.
Sitting room: lighting, cushions, clock, hi-fi equipment, rugs.
General: photograph frames, antique objets, baskets, picnic hamper, sewing machine, luggage, vases, mirrors, pictures, radio, garden equipment and furniture, tools, photograph album, address book, desk set — blotter, letter rack, handle pencil sharpener, embossed address stamp, headed writing paper, records or tapes, magazine subscriptions, membership to a gallery, health club, etc. atlas, maps, dictionary, other reference or coffee-table books.

Royal lists

When the Queen married in the post-war years, even some of her wedding presents were drab and utilitarian. Princess Margaret's gift to her sister was 'a practical, well-designed picnic basket containing cutlery and equipment for four people'; the town of Leamington Spa sent an electric washing machine; and one precious pair of nylons was donated. Mahatma Gandhi crocheted a piece of lace, and one little American girl, used to sending 'bundles for Britain', sent a live turkey with her savings.

The Prince and Princess of Wales placed their wedding list at the General Trading Company, an example followed by the Duke and Duchess of York, who compiled a list of 500 presents. The gifts on the Duchess' list ranged from a Dartington glass vase at £3.95 to a Georgian mahogany dining table and eight repro chairs together worth £5,496. They also requested three dinner services, leather photo albums, china vases, a cache-pot, a brass fender, a nineteenth-century coal scuttle and a set of white plastic garden chairs with grey and white cushions.

Present lore

Sharp or pointed objects used to be taboo lest they sever the romance. Dutch brides would receive wafer irons with the groom's coat of arms, initials and the wedding date; English brides, brass warming-pans inscribed 'Love and live in peace'; Austrian girls, painted wooden tubs saying 'Be happy and industrious'. Finnish brides used to collect their own wedding presents from friends living in the neighbourhood, armed with a pillow case and escorted by an older married man with top hat and umbrella to symbolize his sheltering role. It amused each household to give the old chap a drink to help him on his way, and by evening his image would be shattered. Not to go bridal-collecting was considered snobbish.

Wedding present shops

Nearly every major department store in towns across the country offers a wedding list service. Some of the best are: Jenners of Edinburgh, Lewis of Manchester, Schofields of Leeds and all shops under the House of Fraser and John Lewis umbrellas. See also the shops listed on pages 16-18.

London

NINA CAMPBELL
9 Walton Street, London SW3
(01) 225 1011

You go round to list your presents. This list is mounted in a frame upstairs for friends to make their selection. Everything is gift-wrapped and the bride is kept informed so that she may collect what has been bought (presents can be posted but they prefer you to pick up). Mainly pretty, decorative presents — china, lamps, trays, vases, soft furnishing goods, tables, tooth mugs and soap dishes, carriage lamps, waste-paper baskets, magazine racks, breakfast sets (trays with tray cloths and napkins to match) and — their most popular wedding present — Tea for Two, a boxed teaset in a Nina Campbell design. Prices from £5.

THE CONRAN SHOP
77 Fulham Road, London SW3
(01) 589 7401

The trendy, designer branch of Sir Terence Conran's empire. A casual set-up, as it's a compact shop — you fill in a form and then go round alone, but can always ask advice. They gift-wrap and deliver free of charge even outside London. Beautiful modern-meets-ethnic bedlinen, cushions, towels, baskets, mirrors and rugs, glass, china, cutlery, special saucepans, lighting, and slick stationery, desk sets with more macho appeal.

EXIMIOUS
10 West Halkin Street, London SW1
(01) 627 2888

A small shop that has recently gained the approval of the Prince of Wales. Personalized presents include table mats with a print of your house, engraved glasses and decanters, photograph albums embossed with your name, visitors' books blocked with the name of your house, name tooth mugs, luggage, coat-hangers, towels, bathrobes and stationery. Also photo frames and a growing collection of goods for house and garden. A wedding-list service and also mail order by catalogue.

THE GENERAL TRADING COMPANY
144 Sloane Street, London SW1
(01) 730 0411

Suppliers of 'fancy goods' to the Queen Mother, the Queen, the Duke of Edinburgh and the younger Royals. The GTC has proved suitably discreet for royal lists (and royalists): prospective buyers had to flash their wedding invitation before being ushered into the private sitting room to peruse the Duke and Duchess of York's list. Lottie Quarry and two colleagues give you a folder with the company policy and conditions, a checklist and catalogue. They suggest you wander round noting things you like and then make an appointment with one of the team who will accompany you and list stock numbers, prices, etc. The list is ready in two days. They deliver free of charge in London or will hold items for collection. A beautifully selected range of goods — kitchen ware such as traditional iron and brass scales, bone dinner services to jolly picknicky items, glassware, linen, ornamental china, photo frames, prints, stationery, furniture, oriental gifts, cushions, garden furniture, baskets and vases that you could fill with their superior dried or silk flowers.

HARRODS
Knightsbridge, London SW1 (01) 730 1234

Anything and everything you care to imagine is stocked, but now that their Gift and Bridal Registry is fully computerized, there is no chance of a truly personal service. While the computer runs smoothly, the system is ultra-efficient. They provide you with a suggested list to fill in with your particular requirements,

then feed it through the computer and out comes a list complete with ranges, prices, sizes and colours. You are sent a copy for reference. When customers visit or telephone the Registry, a print-out of presents in their price-range can be produced. No charge for delivery within their normal zone; usual charges outside that area. There is a small charge for gift wrapping. Export and shipping facilities are available. After the wedding, you will receive a complete list of gifts purchased from your list including the names and addresses of the purchaser.

PETER JONES
Sloane Square, London SW1 (01) 730 3434; also **JOHN LEWIS**, Oxford Street, London W1 (01) 629 7711

The Bride's Book department on a Saturday is rather like a bank on a Friday afternoon. Simply *every* bride has a list at PJ's, since their stock is sound, comprehensive and 'never knowingly undersold'. The system is more regimented than at smaller shops. You must go round noting exactly what items you want, with stock number and current price. They check and type out the list within about a week and send you a copy. Not until then can your guests go buying, so it's best to organize the list well before you send out invitations. They stock a vast range of furniture, linens, china, glass, silverware, tableware, lighting, kitchen and electrical equipment. Do note that if any china, glass or silverware is out of stock, it may take several months for the new order to arrive.

Gift cards are supplied, but wrapping is

purely functional. Goods are delivered free of charge within a 30-mile radius of the store. There's a regular delivery schedule to each area, so find out when it's your day and make sure someone will be in to sign. PJ's van drivers are not always the most diligent. If you live outside the delivery zone, parcels are sent by post at a cost of £1.80 per purchase to the donor. Arrangements can be made for delivery of bulky items such as furniture.

LIBERTY
Regent Street, London W1 (01) 734 1234

Based in the main China and Glass department downstairs, Anna Cramphorn will go round with you to help you make your list, and offers advice to your friends and relations. She knows all her clients. Liberty informs you weekly, by letter, of all the gifts purchased, which enables the bread-and-butter process to be speeded up. They gift-wrap and supply a card for your message. Excellent for the dinner service — they can supply china by Royal Worcester, Rosenthal, Ginori, Wedgwood, etc., plus fine glassware. Bed and table linen by Descamps, Martex and Castellini, thick-pile towels and bathrobes. British crafts from the One-Off department, stationery, delectable kitchen equipment and a treasure-house of presents in the Oriental department, from Japanese lacquerware to wooden ducks.

PHOTOGRAPHS

(Tom Hustler)

Wedding photographs have an importance all of their own. BV (Before Video), they were the only lasting, tangible reminder of the day. Even now, AV, they remain the one immediate visual record that everyone can have access to, with no need for a projector or video player. So it is vital to allot enough time and money to finding a good photographer, since his representation of your wedding is how it will be remembered in the future.

The wedding photographer's art is a mixture between reportage (like a newspaper photographer) and portraiture. He has to work quickly and unobtrusively, with little time to prepare lighting and so on, and no room for trial and error. It is by no means easy and there's heavy pressure on him to produce good results. There are many average photographers, few excellent ones.

Recommendation, as always, is the best lead. Then make sure you like the results — the style of his photographs (misty or plain?), that they are technically good (focus, composition, framing — which refers to his position-

ing of the subjects in the viewfinder, that he hasn't cut tops of heads off/granny out of the group, etc.), that he has a creative and quick eye. Look at group shots — is everyone looking at the camera? Do they look static and uneasy? Shots of the couple — are they both looking relaxed and happy? or are those false smiles? Candid shots — has he captured an off-guard expression, a funny moment? or did he miss them altogether? Watch out for the set poses (see House style). If you are having young attendants, check he is good with children.

Ensure, too, that you like *him* — is he easygoing, cheerful, relaxing? This is important, as the last thing you want is someone pushing you around and flustering you. If you get on well, the photographer can be a boon — he's been through this dozens of times before, can give plenty of advice, and help the smooth running of events. It will also produce the best results on film as you'll be more relaxed in front of the camera.

He will need to be adaptable and remain unfazed on the day in the event of timing

45

going haywire or there being a downpour. It's good to have an alternative indoor venue lined up. One couple had to have all their formal group pictures taken in church — after marching down the aisle triumphantly, they saw it bucketing down outside and did an about turn back to the altar for the photographs, while the congregation sat twiddling their thumbs.

House style

The types of studio can be loosely divided in two. There are those that take straightforward semi-formal shots of the couple and groups, plus a general record of the day snapped at the traditional plot points. Most do candid reportage shots as an optional extra. Then there are those who do more contrived, arty photographs. They have a set routine, which includes soft-focus portraits under the weeping willow; the best man and groom exchanging the ring, handshakes and toothy grins; the misty couple at the church entrance holding hands and looking back over their shoulders. Some can produce montages of Him and Her floating in a cloud, superimposed on the Rolls Royce grill or the church steeple.

The standard of the Non-Misty studios can vary tremendously. Only you can tell if they meet your requirements by looking at their past work. But beware the ones that produce little more than snapshots. Aesthetics are important, and can be achieved without looking contrived. A good wedding photographer should assess the composition of each shot before clicking. Some, like Portman Press, manage to attain an old-fashioned quality by slightly distancing their subjects from the mêlée, giving them the importance they deserve. The portrait of Harriet Monckton at Claridge's on the morning of her wedding is reminiscent of a Cecil Beaton (see colour photograph opposite page 128).

The Non-Misties charge in two ways: either a set fee of £200–£300 for the day, including around 80 colour proofs (they take about 150 but do their own selection to cut out duds); or attendance free of charge but you pay for each photograph ordered. Some people may think these earn-as-you-print studios take less care as they are not being paid to cover the event, but in fact they are more anxious to make every photograph a winner since their earnings depend on it. They may take fewer pictures — anything from 60 to 160 — but there will be more hits.

In the old days, there would be two photographers, one of whom would take black and white shots of the guests and the couple at the church, and then nip back to the studio (or even a makeshift darkroom at the reception) and produce proofs before everyone went home. Every guest would order at least one picture of themselves and one of the couple. Sadly, this seldom happens now, because using two photographers became uneconomical and with the advent of colour photos the number of orders dropped. However, it's not an impossibility, say Portman Press for example.

The case for black and white

Colour is used almost exclusively these days. It needs no fanfare — it has obvious appeal and appropriateness and no one would dream of not having a colour record. But black and white photographs can be far superior in quality and suitability. Light and contrast can be adjusted in the printing if conditions were not ideal, whereas you are stuck with colour shots once they are processed; 'flaws' such as spots or bright red cheeks that jump out of colour snaps are flatteringly toned down in black and white — even disliked physical features can be softened out with clever use of light; and the pictures can seem more statuesque and important than snap-happy multi-colour reality. Some photographers may be reluctant to undertake black and white as well as colour because it is too demanding (an extra camera, differing lighting conditions . . .), but a good studio will cope.

If only colour is available, you could ask a friend to do informal black and whites. In this event, remember not to send the films off to the same processor as you would for colour

A tentative smile for the photographer.
(Tom Hustler)

you want is booked up on your wedding day, you will have to find someone else.

Visit the studio with your mother and fiancé for a preliminary talk. The first visit is important to establish personal contact, to assess the photographer's work and to make sure both he and you are aware of the requirements of the other.

- Make sure the photographer you see is the one you'll end up with — and not one of his minions.
- Check out what equipment he uses. An autofocus compact camera may produce adequate shots, but any guest could do that. He should have a camera that produces large negatives for the formals (the quality is far superior) and a good camera with interchangeable lenses (from wide angle to telephoto) for the reportage shots. Make sure he has back-up equipment. It's also worth asking if he sends his colour film to a professional laboratory, and checking that the set of colour proofs he produces for his fee are of album quality.
- Talk him through your plans on the day. He may have a set 'package' which covers the important moments, but this will be flexible. He will appreciate a thorough brief.
- Discuss any extra shots you want, if you want black and white as well as colour, if you want to be photographed at home before the wedding (many brides *don't*), and so on.
- Discuss fees. He may need an assistant for a big wedding, in which case there may be a small surcharge. Travel expenses are extra.

prints. Take them to a professional photographic firm, who will print a set of contact sheets very cheaply. Then you can choose the best shots and have them professionally printed on good paper. Matt looks and prints better than glossy for black and white. Colour looks richer on gloss than on a silk finish.

Booking your photographer

Book early enough to ensure the coverage that suits you. It's not like booking the dressmaker who can produce four dresses in as many months for the same day. If the photographer

After the initial visit, make a definite booking by telephone or in writing. Nearer the event, arrange a further discussion with the actual photographer assigned to your wedding about the amount of coverage he should give to each aspect. Give him a list of who should be in the group shots and of any other people you particularly want photographed, run through all the moments and poses to be covered.

Coverage

The ideal package is to have some formal shots, some candid, some colour, some black and white. You could have some photographs of you at home preparing, plus a few portraits in the garden, perhaps. Then black and white of each set of guests arriving at the church (this is a tradition in Scotland and the ideal way to capture all your guests on film — when they're looking at their best). Then colour and/or black and white of the following: the groom's and then your arrival at the church. A few in church, near the altar if permissible (see In church below), or from the back. The jubilant procession. The couple at the church entrance, various groups outside the church (with attendants, add parents, add more family; the groom, best man and ushers is a traditional shot, but ask for one with you in it too — the contrast of the bride in white against the darkness of the besuited men looks good). Getting into the car (a shiny black limousine reflecting the bride's dress can produce some stunning results). Candid shots at the reception. Informal, lively shots of young bridesmaids and pages. Speeches, toasts, cake cutting. Going away (some wonderfully surreal pictures of the couple amid a shower of confetti; the car; boisterous guests).

In church

In the church, the sanctity of the service should never be disturbed. For this reason, photos in church are few and usually done with available light — flashguns are taboo. These shots are always at the discretion of the clergy (it is the photographer's job to find out what he may take). There should be no objection to the photographer standing quietly at the back and taking photographs during the service. Most churches allow photographers to come forward for the signing of the register and the triumphal procession and occasionally the actual vows and placing of rings (taken up at the altar) but it can be felt that photography here is an intrusion.

Register Office

Photographs during the service are not permitted. The building seldom provides a photogenic setting and, as Tom Hustler points out, 'Chelsea has all those steps outside. If you pose the groups on the steps you risk being run over by a No. 22 bus and you only get nostril shots. The best solution is to go to a park and photograph the bride and groom there.'

Formal group shots

The timing on the day is very delicate. As you emerge from church, the guests will be queuing up to follow you out. There's usually time for a few quick semi-posed shots of the bride and groom before the guests start champing at the bit. Then you can take one of two courses.

If the weather is fine, you can continue your photo session outside the church. Clear the entrance to liberate the guests and then line up for a few more semi-formal shots with attendants, parents, etc. This gives scope for happy, relaxed, candid shots as well as posed groups. Family and friends appreciate being able to greet you immediately after the service. It's also inevitable that they will want to take their own pictures. This is the official photographer's nightmare (distracting cries from all directions means no one ever looks at him, and friends' photos lose him business — one photographer confesses trying to scupper others' shots by photographing into the sun with a special filter), but all in all, it's preferable to the bridal party dashing off straight after the service.

The other course is to do just that, to go on to the reception and have the formal shots taken there before the guests arrive. Some photographers will have earmarked a spot in the garden — and this setting is ideal. There should also be an indoor 'studio' set up in case of rain. Do make sure the room is suitable. Not only should there be enough space and ideally an air of formality, but the background should not interfere with the composition of the group. One couple's entire set of formal photographs came out with a white fireplace sticking out of the bride's dress (a good photographer should not, of course, fall into this trap). If you have a cooked meal lined up, make sure the caterers

have allowed enough time for the photo session.

DIY

As with other aspects of the wedding, amateur friends can be employed. Most guests take cameras as a matter of course. But even if you ask one specially to record the day, you'll find an abundance of photos of *his*

Tiptoeing through the gravestones: the photographer captures the bridal party in a marvellous unposed group, framed by a mist of trees and sky.
(Tom Hustler)

friends, that he's missed out crucial moments because he was chatting . . . and more duds. So by all means use friends as back up — *some* of their photographs will probably be *better* than the professional's and you can cream the best of the guests' snaps to make up an alternative album — but don't rely on them to cover the whole event as a professional would.

Natural daylight and black and white film give this candid shot of Michelle Cadbury (née Cooper) texture and mood. It has a spontaneity and delicacy that is often missing from more set colour portraits. (John & Annette Elliot)

Tom Hustler on . . . wedding photography

❛ A photographer has got to be a crowd-controller and fairly bossy. I do lots of candid shots but many of these I have, in fact, organized. I sometimes stick one of the bridesmaids out in front as though she's been naughty. At one of my early weddings — Pamela Mountbatten and David Hicks — Amanda Knatchbull got up, and turned her back on the camera and screamed (she was only two at the time). Everybody looked down at her and Lord Louis said, 'Amanda's had enough now, that's it.' But I took the picture and they loved it. Since then I've often recreated that situation. ❜

50

Looking your best

An experienced photographer should be able to advise you how to look your best — on angles and expressions, whether you should have your hair up or down, what sort of make-up is most successful, etc. Of course you don't want to be a slave to photography but, on the other hand, you don't want to be disappointed by the results.

One photographer points out how much easier it is to photograph good-looking couples — not, as you may imagine, simply because they are naturally photogenic — but because they are not squeamish and embarrassed in front of the camera. They stand up straight, smile radiantly and spontaneously, look confident and at ease. If you hate having your photograph taken, try a few practice poses in front of a friend's camera or the mirror. Make sure you don't hunch your shoulders, practise looking unhounded and relaxed. A good photographer should help by capturing you at your best without first cajoling you into watching the birdie and saying cheese. (See also Beauty, page 111.)

Lady Elizabeth Anson on . . .
photographs

❛ If you allow the guests to leave the church before you take the formal pictures you can end up with them arriving at the reception before the bride and groom. If the photographs are being done at the reception, the best man and bridesmaids must remember to get into a car very quickly after the service because they can't begin photographing without them. But if you have the photos after the handshaking then the bridesmaids and pages are all skew-whiff and covered in chocolate cake.

You want somebody who takes photos very quickly. It's best to start with the full group and then take away people so that you finally get down to the bride and groom. That's what my brother — the Earl of Lichfield — does. There's quite a knack to it. ❜

Photographers

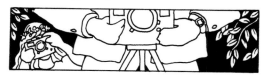

Portraits

ROSALIND MANN
Burdrop House, Sibford Gower, Banbury, Oxfordshire (029578) 8288

Queen of the pearls-and-Alice-band school of portraiture. Head and shoulders engagement pictures of the bride-to-be and portraits of the couple. If you wish, she will submit photos to *Country Life*; the Editor makes the selection for publication.

Wedding coverage

London

AARDVARK PHOTOGRAPY
3 Stockwell Terrace, London SW9
(01) 735 8901

Philip D. Durell covers the whole wedding day, but specializes in capturing the decor and floral work on film. Prices on request.

BELGRAVE PRESS BUREAU
7 West Halkin Street, London SW1
(01) 235 3227

Well-established, reliable company that covers society and other weddings in London and within a 15-mile radius. They photograph whatever is required, but generally go after the speeches unless in the country, when they may stay until the going away. Formal groups plus reportage; 60 to 150 pictures are taken in colour, plus black and white if requested. They send you proofs and contact sheets and a couple of enlargements for you to choose from. No attendance fee but you pay for each print, from £4.50 plus VAT for 8 × 6 in (203 × 152 mm) prints.

PORTMAN PRESS BUREAU LTD.
175 Vauxhall Bridge Road, London SW1
(01) 630 9560

A similar set-up to Belgrave Press, with a high standard of photography. They will go out of the London area and will do black and white, though they prefer not to. They take about 60 to 100 photos or more if required. All proofs are sent to clients to choose from. No attendance fee unless over 30 miles out of London or a small Register Office wedding. From £4.40 plus VAT for 8 × 6 in (203 × 152 mm) prints.

Country and Scotland

ABBEY STUDIOS
5 Whitworth Road, Querns Business Centre, Cirencester, Gloucestershire (0285) 3069; 23 Milton Road, Swindon, Wiltshire (0793 38815)

Friendly firm who regard each wedding as special and aim to mould into the occasion. They have a natural advantage in their locality as Cotswold country churches make appealing backdrops. Their team is trained to observe and record incidents and to meet your special requests. They are adaptable should problems arise. From £113 to £150 for 30 finished prints in an album.

BILL BATES VAN HALLAN
16 Blenheim Road, Basing, Basingstoke, Hampshire (0256) 465217

Good formal wedding coverage — he has lots of practice when covering events for Jennifer's Diary in *Harpers & Queen*. Tailors package and prices to your needs.

RICHARD CLIVE
Bedford House Studios, Nunnington, North Yorkshire (04395) 237

Does Yorkshire society weddings, mainly through personal recommendation. Formal groups and reportage; doesn't interfere with the natural progress of the day. From £200

depending on the amount of coverage, then you order enlargements.

JOHN AND ANNETTE ELLIOT
North Street Farm, North Street, Breamore, Fordingbridge, Hampshire (0275) 22250

Superb quality photographs by husband-and-wife team (he takes and she styles formal shots; he covers bride at home while she photographs guests at church — double the coverage). They like to meet the couple informally and do a recce of church and reception in advance, so that they fit in like guests on the day. Black and white work is a speciality and John has produced some marvellous candid portraits of the bride, groom and attendants (see page 50). Can do sepia prints too and, naturally, colour. All by word of mouth; £300 for the day including 250 photographs. Engagement portraits, too, usually at bride's home. Submits to *Country Life*.

RICHARD GREENLY PHOTOGRAPHY
Brunton House Cottage, Collingbourne Kingston, Nr Marlborough, Wiltshire (026485) 294

Engagement sittings (from about £100) as well as wedding coverage countrywide. He is especially good with children. The basic (all-colour) package (£255) involves taking about 150 photos, of which you keep 80 5 × 4 in (127 × 101 mm) prints. You can adjust the package as required, trading the bride's pre-church portrait for a selection of guests arriving at church, adding the church interior and flowers (plus £15) or the going away (plus £10), etc. Total coverage in black and white costs £350; partial coverage, £15 a film.

TOM HUSTLER
9 Chiltern Road, Caversham, Reading, Berks (0734) 475804

Tom loves to join in the weddings he covers and usually ends up giving lots of advice and help. He clicks away as the bride gets ready,

Relaxed smiles from Mr and Mrs Bruce Underwood, against the backdrop of a pretty Cotswolds church in the village of Rodmarton.
(Abbey Studios)

whizzes through the formal groups and takes dozens of candid shots at the reception. All informal, nothing set — though this can impose a snapshot quality on prints. For £345 a day he takes about 200 5 × 3 in (127 × 76 mm) colour prints and presents you with the best. Engagement portraits in his white-washed garden studio cost £75 to £100 for 60 prints in colour or black and white.

MOIRA LEGGAT
18 Clarendon Crescent, Edinburgh
(031) 343 2531

Weddings and portraits. She prefers capturing the mood of the day to confining her work to

53

posed groups. Plenty of candid and personal photos, from the bride's morning preparations to the going away. 'Moira Leggat has a lovely way', enthuses Mr Maxwell, the florist. 'She makes people feel important, but as if it's no bother.' About £300 for 200 to 250 5 × 5 in (127 × 127 mm) photos.

DESMOND O'NEILL FEATURES
Wychwood, Leatherhead Road, Oxshott, Surrey (037284) 2998

He covers mostly society weddings, which often appear in *Harpers & Queen*. For a wedding with 200 guests, he charges from £200 to £300, producing an album with 10 10 × 8 in

A moment captured in a stream of light (below). (Moira Leggat)

(254 × 203 mm) prints and a set of contacts of 100 to 150 shots.

VOLLANS OF KNARESBOROUGH
16–28 Cheapside, Knaresborough, North Yorkshire (0423) 862626

Old-established firm who follow their families through the years — they photographed the Theakstons as children, for their engagement, and their weddings. Friendly, speedy and unobtrusive coverage. For £135 they take 35 to 45 pictures from which you choose 15 to go in one of their handmade albums.

The bridesmaid who blossomed into one of the world's most famous brides: Sarah Ferguson (right) *with sister Jane and father Major Ronald at Jane's wedding to William Makim in 1976.* (Desmond O'Neill Features)

VIDEOS

(Tom Hustler)

'It all went so quickly and I can't remember a thing!' This is the eternal cry from both bride and groom. They race around in a euphoric cloud, determined to talk to everyone yet hardly aware of what's being said since they are simultaneously experiencing several conversations and scanning the entire gathering. That evening, they collapse on the bed from nervous exhaustion and try to piece together the day's events. By morning it's all a haze and their one wish is for an action replay.

Enter the video: a one-and-a-half to two-hour programme all about you and your wedding day. Before the event, some couples — and particularly the groom — argue against it: We're not performing seals, the equipment will get in the way, we'll feel self-conscious and fluff our lines ... But a professional video-maker should not provoke any uneasiness. He will stay in the background as much as possible, working with natural lights; he won't ask you to perform especially for the camera — he simply records the events of the day. One video-maker says he has had to talk

many a reticent groom into agreeing ('Think how you'll regret it in years to come, imagine how much your children would love it') and they're always delighted afterwards.

The final video can be a revelation. One company wires the bride and groom for sound. As one bride walked down the aisle, they recorded her busband-to-be whispering to the best man: 'I've still got three flaming seconds to get out of here' (or words to that effect). They were obliging enough to wipe the sound off that part of Mother-in-law's copy.

Booking

It's essential to find the right person, as there are video cowboys who set up with cheap equipment and do the job badly. Word-of-mouth recommendation is as important as ever. It is vital to meet and feel at ease with the cameraman — never just book over the phone. You must understand what will be involved and he must learn exactly what you do — and don't — want. Book your video as far in advance as possible and remember the following points:

- Make sure you see a complete recent tape before you decide — not a smart sample made to impress.
- Listen to the sound carefully. Be wary of stills photographers doing videos as a sideline.
- Make sure the fee is all-inclusive. Find out if there are any extras — licence, travelling expenses, etc.
- Make sure they have back-up equipment in case anything goes wrong.
- Only book someone who can stay the whole day.
- Make sure the video cameraman will be suitably dressed on the day.
- Give him your photographer's name so they can liaise beforehand and save any aggravation on the day.

Coverage

The video-maker covers the salient points of the wedding in much the same pattern as the photographer. He works through the day in sequence, recording highlights of vision *and* sound — the vows, church music, speeches — to produce a coherent whole rather than a collection of individual items. Most cameramen like to start with the bride at home, dressing and being made up (the video for a certain Miss World contestant's wedding began with her in the bath), but naturally they respect any feelings you may have against this. During the course of the day, they aim to capture every guest on film (made easier when there is a receiving line). Having discussed the coverage in advance, it's best to leave the cameraman to get on with his task on the day. 'It's like having a portrait done', explains one. 'You choose the artist because you like his work, and once he accepts the commission, you're in his hands. You have to trust him.'

In church

This is the most sensitive part of the day. If you are worried that it will be difficult to be sincere during the marriage ceremony with a camera whirring away, do find out exactly what equipment will be used and where it will be positioned to set your mind at rest (video cameras are in fact noiseless). Make sure that family and guests seated nearby know the form, too.

The Mechanical Copyright Society charge a royalty every time a video company films in church. Some churches require the company to have a licence from the MCS. A professional video-maker should ask your minister about licence requirements and if he has any objections to filming in church. Some ministers may be anti videos if they have had a previous bad experience. Others are nervous at the prospect of being filmed. One vicar forgot to marry the couple — his shaky fingers turned over two pages of the service book at once.

Register Office

Register Offices allow filming before and after, but not during, the ceremony.

DIY

There's no harm in a home video, but it won't necessarily do you or the event justice. Quite apart from the necessity for professional expertise, it is far more successful to have an anonymous cameraman than a friend; guests won't be so ready to play the fool in front of the camera or talk directly to the person behind the viewfinder. As with amateur photography, friends tend to film people they know to the exclusion of other guests; they often miss highlights because they're too busy having fun themselves.

57

James Forbes spent three hours briefing his Aberdeen video-maker before his Highland wedding. The chief instructions were: no slushy music dubbed over, don't film the whole service — just pan the congregation and then use the music as a soundtrack for the rest of the video. 'Yes, yes', said the frustrated movie director and promptly disregarded all orders. As the couple drove away from church, he tailed them and captured The Kiss on film, then dubbed over 'True Love' from *High Society*. At the première, James and Kerry squealed in horror, but now they love the Mills & Boon-ness of it all. The video was a three-hour success, and even after the ninth screening, James can't wait to see it again.

Video-makers

Country

LES COVERDALE
83 Shrub End Road, Colchester, Essex
(0206) 67339

Expert wedding coverage, highly recommended by Desmond O'Neill, Tom Hustler and other photographers who often meet him at the same events (anything within a reasonable day's travel). He enjoys English country weddings and likes to film the bride first to add an extra personal touch, so that the video begins and ends with the bride, first single and then with her husband. He generally films the service tucked away at the back of the church — most people find it too schmaltzy to see close-ups of faces and rings. He did the video for Baron Thyssen's wedding in Gloucestershire and received orders for hundreds of copies. He has also done smart Chinese weddings at Register Offices followed by tea ceremonies. He takes the finished

video to the couple after the honeymoon, along with his own player in case theirs is bad quality. From £350 plus VAT.

London

SHIREEN RITCHIE
20 Henderson Road, London SW18
(01) 874 2265

Many brides feel more relaxed with Shireen, particularly when it comes to filming at home, than with male video-makers. She's there to film the fixing of the veil and bridesmaids gathering before rushing to church to capture the groom and best man arriving. She notes how the pace quickens as guests arrive later and later and switch from ambling up the path to quickstepping, with the church bells ringing frenetically. Shireen usually wears a grey dress which blends in with the church. At the reception, she thinks it important to include young friends as so many photographers concentrate on aged relations. She's used to looking for special moments such as the bridesmaids and pages receiving their presents. In the evening, she comes back if there's a dance and films the first dance to round off the video. She has covered most types of wedding from society (she did Jane Gilmour's wedding) to Greek Orthodox, Jewish, West Indian and Irish weddings (complete with jigs). She works mainly in London and the home counties; will go further afield at her discretion. From £160 to £195.

TOPS VIDEO
4 Locket Mews, Locket Road, Harrow, Middlesex (01) 863 8864

A professional but friendly company who have done about 2,000 weddings since they started in 1976. They provide prospective clients with a sample of a current video — as they say, 'You are as good as your last job.' They film on U-Matic equipment and then edit onto VHS or Betamax, making as many copies as required. On every job they take two cameras and two recorders as back-up and use a radio microphone. It sounds daunting, but they make a point of getting to know the family to get a relaxed response when filming. They did Princess Anne's lady-in-waiting and they do nearly all the big Greek weddings in London. They always wear suits, and can wear tails if required. £300 plus VAT and travelling expenses (nationwide). Each copy of the tape is £35 plus VAT. Any licence fees must be paid by the client.

TRANSPORT

(Tom Hustler)

You will need a chauffeur-driven car (even if the 'chauffeur' is a friend) to take you to the church, and the same vehicle to take you from church to the reception. You may need another car for your attendants (Lady Elizabeth Anson sometimes hires a minibus to cart round all the little darlings, their nannies and mothers). The classic, monster black wedding limousine is a Dorchester. The other, more widely available, limo is the Daimler. Smart, smooth, purring motors with acres of leg (train) room and head (veil) room, either of these is ideal. Expect to pay about £70 (London rate) for a Daimler. The flash option is a white Rolls Royce.

You may prefer a vintage car. These look pretty and it's fun to wave from an open-top Twenties' Phantom. But you have to proceed at a snail's pace or you'll be blown to smitherines. On the way to the church, for the sake of staying unruffled and of decorum, it is wise to have the hood up. Remember too that these cars are delicate creatures, only able to cover short distances, unkeen on standing around in hot weather. One hire company admits their elderly cars sometimes need a push start, but they find 'it adds to the fun'. Book early as there aren't that many classic cars around. Look at the car before you book, and make sure this is definitely the one you'll be getting on the day, as some firms change their fleet or switch cars without warning. It is unwise to use a vintage car to go away in, as, apart from the extra cost, it is nowhere near as efficient or reliable as a modern car for reaching its destination on time. You don't need ribbons on an antique car — it's a case of lily-gilding.

A horse and carriage is another romantic option to cart you from church to reception, but can only be used for short distances, which is probably a good thing as it's not too comfortable, spacious or easy to get in and out of, and you'll get windswept. The most common choice is a Brougham, single or double (most go for the four-seater Double Brougham). A Landau is good in winter as it can be open, or completely closed if it pours. When booking, do be honest about any steep hills *en route* — it won't necessarily mean you

60

The first of many thresholds: going away by helicopter (above) *is a breeze for the couple and spectators alike.*
(Desmond O'Neill Features)

A genuine Macao bicycle rickshaw (right) *took James Arbuthnot and Emma Broadbent, daughter of Christie's wine expert Michael Broadbent, from their wedding at St James's, Piccadilly to their reception at Christie's.*
(Desmond O'Neill Features)

can't have a horse-drawn carriage, but that they may have to change the horse's shoes and make sure your carriage is one with brakes. On the day, don't be late — the horse should not have to be pushed to make up the time.

You may want to borrow a car or use your own, but do have a driver. One groom who tried to drive himself found he couldn't focus on the road. Which leads us to going away. A modern chauffer-driven car or taxi is a better idea than driving your own car. You'll avoid any witty vandalism, drunk-driving charges and other dampeners on the day, and can continue to feel relaxed and unflustered about getting somewhere in time or about traffic.

A boat, balloon, or helicopter are more exciting options. If yours is a riverside reception, then be theatrical and float off like Sally Rowbotham and Felix Schade did at Henley. As each case is so individual, you will have to arrange it locally. Balloons are dependent on fine weather and if it's too

Sally Rowbotham and Felix Schade take a slow launch down the Thames after their reception at Phyllis Court Club, Henley. They were followed up the river by a brass band blaring from a fellow boat. (Antoinette Eugster)

windy, they won't risk taking off — so be prepared to be disappointed. To obtain the address of a local pilot, see right.

The helicopter that is most likely to whisk you away from your front lawn is the four-seater Jet Ranger. Any lawn or car park in the countryside is a perfect helipad, but choppers have to avoid town centres. Most couples fly to a hotel on the edge of town or in the country, or to a nearby airfield or airport. The charter company will find out the nearest airfield, and can usually arrange a limousine to meet the helicopter if necessary. In summer, give several weeks' notice. Prices range from £320 to £370 per flying hour, plus landing fees at an airfield or airport (from £5 to £25), plus an opening fee if the company has to open their base (see below). Most flights are less than an hour — people travel only a short distance and, at 110 mph, the Jet Ranger can complete a sizeable return journey in under an hour.

For all types of hire transport, look first in your *Yellow Pages* for a local firm — there are *dozens* of car hire firms. Prices below are based on one journey from home/hotel to church, and from church to reception.

Transport

Vintage cars

VINTAGE ROLLS ROYCE HIRE
260 Knights Hill, Norwood, London SE27
(01) 761 6767

£200 plus VAT for one of their spectacular fleet of old Rollers within London.

Horse-drawn carriages

AUSDAN STUD
King's Walden, Hitchin, Hertfordshire
(043887) 754

They will travel anywhere with their car-

riages, inclusive in the price, though it's obviously more convenient if you can find a local company. £225 plus VAT.

Hot-air balloons

JAMES GREEN
Travel Gas, 122 Fazeley Street,
Birmingham (021) 643 3224

Keeps a list of hot-air balloon pilots throughout the country. Send a SAE and cheque or postal order for 50p made payable to Travel Gas Ltd for this Commercial Directory. Once you have the contacts, you will have to make arrangements personally.

Helicopters

Look for local Air Charter companies in your *Yellow Pages*.

CB HELICOPTERS
Westland Heliport, Lombard Road,
London SW11 (01) 228 3232

Charge £340 an hour (two hours' minimum in summer), plus a surcharge at weekends to open the heliport — £66 for one-and-a-half hours at Battersea; £20 at Brooklands. This must cover the whole time the helicopter is away from base.

CLOTHES

When you get engaged, what is the first thing you think? Probably not, 'Oooh, I'm getting married, let's organize the car hire.' It's almost certainly, 'Hmmm, what shall I wear?' A young woman's fancy turns to The Dress, followed by the accessories and the trousseau — underwear, shoes, jewellery, going-away dress or suit, hat, more shoes, handbag, honeymoon outfits, yet more shoes, lingerie, luggage . . . . This is a time for mega shopping sprees, for stretching mother's purse-strings and inevitably her patience. You also have to organize your attendants' outfits, and check up on the groom!

The dress

The golden rule is not to buy it or have it made too soon. Your taste, your size and fashions can change in six months. More importantly, as dressmakers have discovered through experience, if the dress is ready too early, it seems to lose its allure and you may go off it. Top designers Gina Fratini and Victor Edelstein don't complete a dress until the last minute for this reason. Pace it to be finished just before the day, so that it's part of the general crescendo of the preparations.

Dress lore

It's not only your boredom threshold to watch out for. Lore-wise, the dress shouldn't be completed until the wedding day in order not to tempt fate. It is safest to add the final stitch just before you leave for the church, to reduce to a minimum the interval between appearing as a bride and actually tying the knot. If the dress is bought ready-made, a detachable part such as a sash should be left off during the fit-tings. If such superstitions haunt you, you could do as the Princess of Wales did and have a little blue bow (for love ever true) stitched into your dress at the last minute.

This, of course, is part of the 'Something old, something new, something borrowed, and something blue' rhyme. It is one of the few sayings that most brides adhere to (although the last line, 'and a silver sixpence in your shoe', dropped off — even before decimalization). Something old and borrowed, preferably from a happily married woman, brings marital happiness and security; new represents the new life. The Princess of Wales's dress was trimmed with *old* lace, the silk taffeta was *new*, she *borrowed* the Spencer family diamond tiara and diamond earrings from her mother, and there was the *blue* bow. Taking no chances, she also had a tiny horseshoe of 18-carat gold studded with diamonds sewn into the dress.

Folklore can be tiresome, for, practically speaking, the golden rule is to try on the whole ensemble — veil, shoes, underwear, the lot — to check everything falls properly and nothing sticks out, and so on. Scuppering such sensible notions, it is said that if the veil is put on before the day, the bride may be deserted, have an unhappy marriage or even die before the wedding. Should a friend try on the veil, she may run off with her pal's new husband. You should not look in a mirror before you are dressed and your toilet completed — which, unless you have a stream of maidservants, is asking for trouble.

A stream of sayings surrounds the dress itself. It is supposed to be bad luck for a bride to make her own dress; even professional dressmakers often avoid making their own. The French say that a bride lives the same number of years as there are buttons on her wedding dress. A penny sewn into the seam

64

1. Lillie Langtry allure: duchesse
satin and Chantilly lace by Tatters.
Details, page 187.
(Mark Houldsworth)

2. Golden mane and flowing train (left): a splash of Hollywood glamour by David Fielden. Details, page 187. (Mark Houldsworth)

3. Formal Edwardiana from Chelsea Design Company, meets mignon sailor girl, from Tatters. Dewy-fresh flowers by Jane Packer. Details, page 187. (Mark Houldsworth)

4. Grace Kelly elegance: Fifties duchesse satin and Chantilly lace by Tatters. Details, page 187. (Mark Houldsworth)

of the gown brings luck wherever it goes later and to carry a coin (back to the silver sixpence) at the wedding secures future wealth. The seamstress who inserts the first stitch into a wedding dress will herself be married before the year is out. Each of the women who worked on Princess Anne's wedding dress with Maureen Baker of Susan Small sewed a hair into the dress. Ms Baker bans whistling in the workroom, observing the ancient belief that it whistles up evil spirits; and tacking with black thread is forbidden for its funereal associations. Finally, as we all know, the groom should not see the bride-to-be's dress before the wedding (or his bride on the morning of the wedding).

Colour

Married in white, you have chosen right,
Married in black, you will wish yourself
*   back,*
Married in red, you will wish yourself dead,
Married in green, ashamed to be seen,
Married in grey, you will go far away,
Married in blue, love ever true,
Married in pearl, you will live in a whirl,
Married in yellow, ashamed of your fellow,
Married in pink, of you he'll aye think (your
*   fortunes will sink).*

White signifies purity and also deters the evil eye that preys on young virgins of both sexes. Except in Norway a green dress, or even green garments in a trousseau, are unlucky. Green once represented the grass-stained dress of a girl of loose morals who was wont to make love outdoors.

Choosing your style

Be open-minded and be adventurous, take inspiration from shops, magazines, photographs and friends' weddings. Dressmaker Camilla Milton finds to her dismay that most English girls don't dare break away from traditional styles. They want to be clones. Of course, it is a valid point that your wedding day is not the best time to try out a totally new style or an outrageous idea that you would normally not contemplate. If you don't usually dress to stun, don't start now.

However, if you relish it, make the most of the one day when you are the leading lady. Most designers and dressmakers take their lead from the bride's personality and degree of self-confidence. The Duchess of York's designer, Lindka Cierach says: 'I feel my way along, get to know the bride, and it's true that most people can't cope with crazy fashions. But I love making outfits for outrageous, fun clients.' She dressed one girl in silver and white lace from head to toe, 'but with a lot missing'. Panels of unlined lace plunged to below the waist at the back and almost to the navel at the front.

Consider your audience, however. At a zany party it may be fun to shock; but if your wedding party will be full of straight old biddies, think twice. At best, your outfit may fall on fallow ground. Décolleté or diaphanous could spell disaster. Better to stun by being smart and chic in the French couture manner, or by wearing something offbeat like a white Edwardian-style riding habit, or the Raj look or some beautifully constructed period costume.

Wedding dresses are, to some extent, outside fashion. Prevailing styles have their influence, but you don't often see a Dallas pair of shoulders or an Azzedine Alaia synthetic slink. Unless you are as non-conformist as Paula Yates (who wore scarlet — but then she called her little girl Fifi Trixibelle . . .), your hands are bound by colour, length, material and mood. As Hardy Amies has pointed out, for a church wedding you must get the scale and proportions right and emphasize height. But what is most important is to study what suits you. Impress by wearing something that complements your looks and fits your personality, to draw all eyes towards *you* and not just the dress.

What suits you

Assess your good and bad points: hair, skin, chin(s), neck, shoulders, arms, bust, waist, hips, ankles. There are so many permutations of a person's features that it would be un-

The young fashion company Workers for Freedom designed all the outfits for Clare Gardner-Medwin, Michael Woolley and their bridesmaids Katrina (left) and Clare Harrison (right). Clare wore a silk shirt trimmed with lace and tiny shells, a skirt of taffeta and Nottingham lace and a white wool jacket to fend off the December chill. The bridesmaids wore lace skirts, white shirts with tie necks, black wool jackets and black suede caps. Michael's baggy black wool suit tops a silk shirt painted with flowers and embroidered with lucky charms. The monochromes were given warmth by beautiful dried flowers in autumn russets, from Robert Day of Pimlico.
(James Purcell)

realistic to give sound advice without seeing the individual. Ask your dressmaker's advice on how to enhance your best bits and skim over the others. Go shopping with a friend whose taste and opinions you respect and try on dozens of different styles. She will be able to consider you from all angles (and remember all eyes will be on your back view for the service).

Here are a few general points about shape. The if-you're-a-beanpole-wear-horizontal-stripes school of thought is, of course, nonsense: if you're a beanpole, you're laughing — you have a model figure. The sweet English pear is more the archetype, and the late Victorians and Edwardians knew how to enhance her. The basic lines they used would flatter almost anyone: a smooth, fitted and boned bodice leading to a slightly V-shaped, dropped waistline, similar to Sarah Ferguson's undeniably slimming dress. A boned bodice can miraculously flatten a big bust

(sometimes so flat that you need to pad it out again) and a V-waist gives the impression that your waist narrows, taking the emphasis off the hips. If you have a thickish waist and big hips, don't ever break up the line of the dress with a horizontal waistline and highly gathered skirt. Sashes are killers for all but the thin as they emphasize bust and hips. If you have the more traditionally Mediterranean top-heavy figure with narrow hips, look to the more Hollywood-style numbers that loosely drape over the top half of the body and smooth over a slender waist and hips.

A graceful neck and shoulders are among the most beautiful assets a girl can have. Fashion doyenne Diana Vreeland thinks anyone can look good if they carry themselves well and extend their necks. In general, scooped, or simple round necklines are usually more attractive than sweetheart, square or other harshly geometric lines. If you have poor skin, don't expose vast expanses of flesh. No plunge necks or scooped necks, but if you don't want to be totally covered up, use lace and veiling as a camouflage.

It's almost always wise to steer away from Ultrabrite white — it doesn't enhance any type of complexion, and in the sort of silky satins (particularly synthetic ones) used for wedding dresses, it can look cheap and shiny where off-white looks classy and chic.

Current fashions

Having touched on what suits you, there are, of course, trends. Within the general message of a narrower silhouette, less pretty-pretty romanticism and more boldness, there is much scope.

The fairy-tale Winterhalter look is sidling out, but will always remain in the background. Edwardian has taken over with its slimmer silhouette from the front view and lots of detail at the back, creating the typical S-shape from the side. Some brides are wearing riding habits from that era — long, waisted jackets with big leg o' mutton sleeves

tapering to a narrow waist, and skirts with lots of material at the back. Tatters, David Fielden and Sasha Hetherington understand bustles and bows.

Period bridal wear takes inspiration from medieval days onwards: avant-garde designer John Galliano recently revived a winsome Juliet with a mass of white muslin, high waist, banded sleeves and long train; Patricia Lester's pleated silk gown is pure Fortuny-meets-Guinevere. The baroque era is lavish and gives lots of scope for theme continuity — Louis shoes with flourishing bows for the bride, a brocade waistcoat and stock for the groom.

Heavily beaded or wafty chiffon Twenties' frocks will always have their following and can be picked up at most good antique shops and markets such as Antiquarius, 135 King's Road, London SW3.

Then there's the Thirties' Hollywood glamour look. In direct reaction to all the flounces and frills heralded by the Princess of Wales, lines are simple, fluid and sheath-like — really only for those with slender figures: Ellis Flyte's lean, langorous fantasies, to be

worn with long gloves; David Fielden's panelled Carole Lombardesque numbers. Some designers bridge the gap between the slink and the frou-frou: perhaps a ballerina-style frock, with a bodice of fine satin or lace and a froth of tulle spraying out from the waist.

Many brides are choosing the same sort of styles their mothers wore; some wear mother's dress itself, cleaned and altered to fit. Fifties' duchesse satin in the Charles James mould, in strong, simple styles that allow the fullness and lustre of the material to shine. The beauty is in the drape of the fabric and the play of light upon it.

Whatever style you choose, the late-Eighties' emphasis is on a stunning material and a beautiful cut. Materials: satin, from fine silk to heavy duchesse satin; brocade; various weights of silk; net; tulle; faille; lace. In winter, velvet, used perhaps in the skirt rather than the whole dress. Colours: shades of just-off-white, through ivory to thick cream.

Having a dress made

If you can afford the time and money, go to a dressmaker. There is no greater luxury or confidence-giver than wearing an original dress made exclusively for you. It is the only way in which you can combine all the design details you desire without compromising your taste. A good dressmaker will ensure her creation fits you like a glove and makes the absolute best of your looks. As one of Lindka Cierach's brides has said, 'I'm not beautiful, but her clothes make me feel beautiful, and this is how I *know* I will feel on the day.'

Don't let an amateurish friend or relation make your dress. It is a formal piece of attire and you'll need the confidence of knowing it will stay the course. There are various degrees of experienced dressmaker. The local lady (about £80 upwards) usually works from a pattern but has a high standard of craftsmanship. If she can't make a pattern herself, she can probably adapt existing ones and could concoct your design from two or

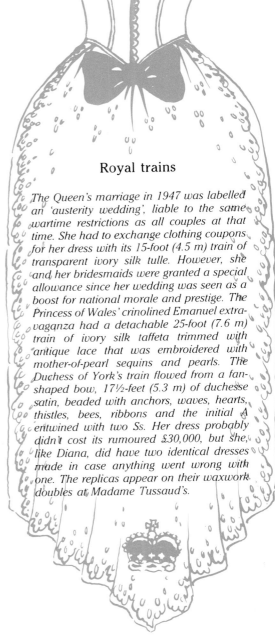

Royal trains

The Queen's marriage in 1947 was labelled an 'austerity wedding', liable to the same wartime restrictions as all couples at that time. She had to exchange clothing coupons for her dress with its 15-foot (4.5 m) train of transparent ivory silk tulle. However, she and her bridesmaids were granted a special allowance since her wedding was seen as a boost for national morale and prestige. The Princess of Wales' crinolined Emanuel extravaganza had a detachable 25-foot (7.6 m) train of ivory silk taffeta trimmed with antique lace that was embroidered with mother-of-pearl sequins and pearls. The Duchess of York's train flowed from a fan-shaped bow, 17½-feet (5.3 m) of duchesse satin, beaded with anchors, waves, hearts, thistles, bees, ribbons and the initial A entwined with two Ss. Her dress probably didn't cost its rumoured £30,000, but she, like Diana, did have two identical dresses made in case anything went wrong with one. The replicas appear on their waxwork doubles at Madame Tussaud's.

three different patterns. The professional dressmaker (about £400 upwards) can cut her own patterns and will design to order, combining your ideas with her expertise. The designer-with-a-shop (£500 to £1,000) will normally have a collection from which you choose; then he or she will have the design made to measure, perhaps adapting the odd detail. The designer proper (£1,500 upwards) is a higher plain version of the professional dressmaker and will probably have a team of seamstresses, embroiderers, beaders, etc. It is these artisans' work, as well as the cut, that sets designer dresses apart from those off the production line.

Choose a dressmaker who has been recommended to you and whose work you admire. Don't get bullied into agreeing to use the first dressmaker you see. Make sure her attention to detail and finishing off is good — hems and stitching should be invisible, covered buttons and loops neat. You should almost be able to wear the dress inside out.

To help formulate your design, cut out all the details you like from fashion magazines and build up a file of cuttings and sketches to take to your dressmaker. The professional dressmaker will inject her ideas and knowledge, do sketches and suggest material. She may have swatches and will certainly have good sources of fabric and trimmings that she can buy wholesale. If you are using a local dressmaker, you may have to buy your own fabric. The whole process will take about a month, with about four fittings.

There are two methods of cutting patterns — on the flat and on a model (known as modelling). Lindka Cierach uses the second method: 'When I work with the fabric I get an immediate response — when it's in my hands, things start happening.' Certainly the drapery and movement of a dress seem to be accentuated when it is cut in this way. The next stage is essential: the dressmaker must make up a toile, a model of the dress in calico, to see how it looks and fits, and to make any changes in style before the actual fabric is cut.

Lady Sarah Armstrong-Jones was chief train-straightener to Lady Diana Spencer, but it took many bridesmaids' hands to make light work of 25 feet (7.6 m) of taffeta as it snaked up the steps of St Paul's. (Anwar Hussein)

Lady Elizabeth Anson on . . . the dress

❛ If the bride wants help with her dress, we suggest designers or take her round to them. I think if they've got the money, Hardy Amies is the best. They have an amazing team of designers and they never tire of producing yet another bit of material or yet another drawing. I think one pictures Hardy Amies as an older person's couturier but they *are* young and they take infinite trouble. My other favourite is Lindka Cierach who is a great friend and makes very special wedding dresses of a certain kind. You always know they'll have complex detail in one way or another. She is a terribly nice person and I think this is important for your wedding — you should have a rapport with everybody concerned because it is a sensitive time. Weddings create tension and can bring out the worst in some members of the family, so the other people you have to deal with must make you feel extra special.

If there is a ball in the evening and you want to continue wearing your wedding dress, it is wise to have one that adapts so that you are not falling over your train all the time. My dress had a train that was attached at the shoulders and just undid to leave the dress itself. ❜

Designers and dressmakers

Most of the dressmakers recommended below work from home or a studio (and designers from showrooms), so do make an appointment. In general, they require at least two months' notice (four is better) and take four to six weeks to make the dress (more if doing bridesmaids' outfits too). Prices include fabric, but you can provide your own for most dressmakers and prices should drop accordingly.

Most will make attendants' outfits, ballgowns (or wedding dresses that will convert) and going-away outfits.

London

HARDY AMIES
14 Savile Row, London W1 (01) 734 2436

Made-to-measure wedding dresses, designed by Mr Fleetwood and his team. Each dress is an individual. There is no one Amies 'look' — you can be plain as plain or utterly lavish. Veils and bridesmaids' dresses are also made, though the latter is rarely requested. From £1,500 upwards.

AMANDA BARBER
59 Dorothy Road, London SW11
(01) 228 6055

Private dressmaker who designs, in collaboration with the bride, traditional dream-come-true dresses. She likes you to have what you want, as you'll be happy with the result, but she steers you in a suitable direction. Once-a-week fittings, spread over four or five weeks; the Barber procedure is fun, relaxed and boosts the bride's confidence. Amanda is noted for her sympathetic ear, and enjoys discussing all aspects of the wedding. One man noted his fiancée had withdrawal symptoms after her dress was finished. Wedding dresses from £500. Bridesmaids' and pages' outfits, too.

TATTI BOURDILLON
54 Charleville Road, London W14
(01) 381 5592 (evenings only)

Part-time professional dressmaker — she does about ten weddings a year. Her designs are classic, inspired by the past, using only good fabrics. She will trim shoes, too. Clear-thinking Tatti also offers a bridal consultancy service, which involves putting together the whole look for the bride and bridesmaids, advising on fabrics, designs, colours and suppliers. Consultancy: £50–£100. Wedding dresses: about £500.

PAM BROOKS
60 Tournay Road, London SW6
(01) 381 4037

Chinese dressmaker who can cut a pattern from a photograph or sketch. Any style of dress you want, beautifully made and finished off. Simple dresses that take about a week to make, about £150; elaborate, up to about £600.

LINDKA CIERACH
54 Hartismere Road, London SW6
(01) 381 4436

Professional, perfectionist and quick, she comes highly recommended by her long list of society brides — including, of course, the Duchess of York. Her aim is to flatter the bride, let her personality shine through. Her dresses fit like a second skin ('I like sexy but not vulgar dresses'). She made the Duchess of York's dress from the inner layers working out — the foundations are very important. She and her team have a high output of evening and wedding dresses (perhaps ten a month), and no two are the same. She likes to use top-quality fabrics (duchesse satin, silk faille, etc.) from Switzerland, France and Italy, English lace, and bags of beading — her hall-mark. Clever wedding-cum-evening dresses — she did one velvet and satin dress with a back panel which detached to create a plunge to the waist. Dresses from about £2,000, escalating according to the amount of embellishment. Veils, too. Dresses for bridesmaids — she loves doing children's outfits — from about £120.

ANNA CLOONAN
(01) 736 9080

Understated wedding dresses, for the tomboy or the sophisticate rather than the frothy romantic. She designs to order from her Fulham studio, and also supplies Tatters with a collection of sample designs, from which she makes repeats to measure. Evening wear, too, but no bridesmaids.

ROSE COUTTS-SMITH
Studio 49, 15–17 Ingate Place, London SW8
(01) 720 9807; Ansaphone (01) 720 1687

Rose trained as a costume designer at Central School and designs for London City Ballet. Her inspiration comes from costume books (lots for you to skim through) and films (*The Draughtsman's Contract* is her favourite) — Elizabethan up to Georgian are her eras. For instance, she has made a heavy cream silk Jacobean dress with laced stomacher (see colour photograph opposite page 128). She bones and lines bodices to obviate the need for bras or basques that may spoil the line of the dress. Unusual silks from France, lots of piping, masses of pearls or sequins studded over the material where suitable. She acts as artistic director and can design shoes, flowers and underwear (someone else makes up shoes and bouquets, but she makes silk camiknickers). She did a Victorian riding habit with an extravagant bustle bow, all in white with pink underskirts, a pink top-hat with veiling and pink satin court shoes. Wedding dresses from £1,000. Bridesmaids from £150 (child) or £300 (grown-up). For the groom, she makes stocks and baroque waistcoats in antique brocades and silks to complement her dresses. From £60. Also going away outfits from £300.

VICTOR EDELSTEIN
3 Stanhope Mews West, London SW7
(01) 244 7481

Many brides are already members of the Edelstein fold. They appreciate his ability to listen and interpret what they want, plus they like his restrained style. Emphasis is on cut, not short cuts. He prefers not to conceal with bows and frills. Wonderful fabrics from France and Italy — ivory damask satin, gleaming duchesse satin. For one recent bride, he designed a sleek strapless dress with long gloves that would take her to the ball in the evening. Veils made too, but you're sent to Manolo Blahnik for shoes. The showroom is by no means intimidating — it's all a bit chaotic and relaxed. Prices from around £2,000. Going-away outfits too; he designed

71

the Princess of Wales' black-dotted turquoise dress for Prince Andrew's wedding.

EMANUEL

26a Brook Street, London W1
(01) 629 5560 (by appointment only);
10 Beauchamp Place, London SW3
(01) 584 4997

Best-known for the Princess of Wales' wedding dress, the Emanuels have in fact progressed from their pioneering fairy-tale story to lean-line and other looks. Their new shop in Beauchamp Place stocks a handful of sample wedding dresses which you can have made to measure in a variety of luxurious materials and trimmings. From £2,500 up to £6,000. Couture wedding dresses designed to order cost a good deal more. They sell exquisite little blue silk hearts to sew into your wedding dress, plus their new range of shoes, bags, lingerie, bridal hosiery, veils, hats (*and* christening gowns . . .). The Emanuel ready-to-wear and couture day dresses would take you away any day.

ELLIS FLYTE

12 Greenland Street, London NW1
(01) 267 9653

Sensational one-off film-star gowns. Ellis Flyte has been designing costumes for film and theatre for ten years (she designed David Bowie's clothes for *Labyrinth*), and gets her inspiration for bridal wear from Hollywood. She has the books-of-the-films as well as photographs and sketches of her work to help you choose a look. Wonderful slithery Thirties' sheaths, lots of lace fabric, French couture silk and silk net (see colour plates 5

An exclusive design (left) *for a slender Audrey Hepburn-style bridal gown, by Victor Edelstein.*

The Emanuels' design (right) *with trademark fullness, flounce and frill, is altogether more* Gone with the Wind *than* Breakfast at Tiffany's.

and 12). The dress can take from three to ten months, with a minimum of ten fittings; about £1,000. She has no stock except those dresses made for press features, which she will eventually sell off. Also bridesmaids' dresses (around £150) and anything for the trousseau. Her luscious collection of lingerie is available at Harvey Nichols and boutiques around the country — bias-cut, film-star slips, pyjamas, camisoles and knickers of silk satin, chiffon and lace.

GINA FRATINI
Studio 7, Marvic House, Bishop's Road, London SW6 (01) 381 8759

Gina Fratini has been designing for more than twenty years and still may fit the bride herself. Her romantic classics have plenty of flounces and lace and can be made to order or bought off-the-peg from shops (these designs can be adapted slightly). Wedding dresses from £1,000; bridesmaids' £400. She always supplies her own veils to shops, in tulle, usually surrounded by fine lace (about £120).

SOPHIE HALE
10a Lower Sloane Street, London SW1 (01) 630 2567

Sophie's main work is in going-away outfits which she prefers to design especially for you, though she will discuss ideas and make variations. Her favourite design is a drop-waisted, crêpe de Chine frock with gored panels and scooped back with a bow; ideal for going away and flattering to most figures. She has a collection of couture magazines from the Twenties and Thirties and loves to recapture the fluid lines of that era. Occasional wedding dresses, too, designed with the bride. All her work is impeccably lined. From £100 for a going-away outfit; £200 for the wedding dress.

CAMILLA MILTON
39 Colehill Lane, London SW6 (01) 736 0652

Camilla loves to design a whole look, including bridesmaids' and going-away outfits; also outfits for guests. She finds brides' tastes somewhat limiting, but always designs to suit the individual. Two favourite outfits were a long peach skirt of layer upon layer of cotton net with a riding-style jacket; and a slinky Lana Turner-style gown. Her bridesmaids' dresses are about £100 for small children to £250 for grown-ups. Neat Chanel-type suits and dresses for going away — everything is classic, so you will be able to take it out of your wardrobe in ten years' time and still wear it. Matching hats, too, from £30.

THE SILK HOUSE
47 Stewart's Grove, London SW3 (01) 351 0044

Made-to-order wedding dresses from around £450 in any style you want. Coat-dress-ish going-away outfits about £250.

TOMASZ STARZEWSKI
21 Fulham High Street, London SW6 (01) 731 7202

Young designer whose ready-to-wear collections sell mainly to the States. High-glamour wedding dresses designed to order. So far, most of his jetset brides have married on exotic private islands ('I'm dying to do a traditional English country wedding', he sighs). Chantal D'Orthez, Moira Lister's daughter, married Texan Glenn Burke on the island of Mustique. She wore a strapless ankle-length tulip-petal dress in organza and taffetta, which fluttered as she moved. For Miranda Nicolle's South of France wedding, he designed a figure-hugging dress in cotton voile; it had a round neck at the front and an open rounded neckline at the back sweeping into a long trail of voile dotted with flowers and bows (see page 28). She wore no veil, only cornflowers and tuberoses in her hair and bouquet, also designed by Tomasz. From about £600, rising to about £3,000 for a beaded dress. Ballgowns are his speciality.

SARA STUDD
14b Albert Bridge Road, London SW11 (01) 720 6312

No wedding dresses. Private dressmaker who

makes classic suits or coat and skirt ensembles suitable for going away, for mother and for guests. You supply fabric (or she will help you buy some) and choose a design from her portfolio or she will create something new. Brushing the six-foot mark herself, she is a dab hand at dressing tall girls, full of advice *and* compassion. Prices from £200–£300.

Country

GRACE ELLIOTT
Worcester Office Complex, 14/16 Newtown Road, Worcester (0905) 29336 (workroom); (0905) 358659 (home — for private commissions)

Grace will design wedding and bridesmaids' dresses to order from her home showroom. Her many off-the-peg designs, stocked in bridal shops nationwide, show her style --- from Edwardian regality to Twenties' demureness with scalloped and ragged hems. Some frocks have tailcoats, some cathedral-length trains, some are awash with detail — Austrian embroidery, lace, bows, pearls. From around £300 in the shops. She also makes flower and tiara head-dresses and veils. She can dye dresses (10 per cent extra on the price) and has good ideas for party adaptations.

MELANIE FISHER COUTURIERE
11 Grape Lane, Petergate, York (0904) 646174

Each dress is individually designed and made in fine-quality fabrics — Melanie believes if you are going to the expense of having a dress made especially for you, it's worth using the best materials. Chantilly lace is one of her favourites. Prices from around £260. Bridesmaids' outfits too. Her speciality is ballgowns and smart outfits to dazzle at the York races, going-away outfits and outfits for the bride's mother. She teams up with her friend Georgina Blorr (see page 100), who makes hats to match.

Material

Use natural fabrics. They look and feel superior to man-made fabrics, they fall better, colours are generally more subtle, the texture more delicate. If you intend to recycle your dress, natural fabrics also dry-clean and dye better than man-made. However, there are some good imitations of silk, particularly in the heavyweight duchesse satins, and these are, of course, cheaper.

Below are some of the best — and cheapest — sources of fabric, veiling, lace and beading. The best silks in the world, incidentally, come from Italy (the Duchess of York's duchesse satin was supplied by Taroni, via Morazzone 8, Como, Italy) and France. The Far East is the place for dupion, slub and shot silks, and if you happen to be passing through, you can buy silk there at a fraction of the UK price.

London

BOROVICK FABRICS
16 Berwick Street, London W1 (01) 437 2180

In the heart of Soho, beside Berwick Street market, is this jolly shop crammed full of wild lamés and nets for the theatrical world, plus silks in up to 65 colours. Streetwise, laddish assistants have a good line in marketeer banter while they cut: 'You're from Australia? You're not Adelaide from Perth, are you? Did you go out on the scheme? £10 it was — don't try and make out you're posh . . .' Indian silk dupion costs £10 a metre, silk taffeta £11.50, French moiré £8.50, fine silk satin £16.50. Also cheaper, top-quality synthetic slipper satin (heavy and shiny), and duchesse satin (more lustre than shine), organza, lace, grosgrain and lining silk.

C. I. DAVIES
94-6 Seymour Place, London W1
(01) 723 7735

Friendly establishment that sells to the trade, but will make exceptions for individuals. Silk at competitive prices: dupions £7 a metre, taffetas £30, silk satin £20, silk crêpe £20 and anti-static lining £2. They supplied the linings for the latest Royal Wedding entourage.

DICKINS & JONES
224 Regent Street, London W1
(01) 734 7070

An inexpensive range of synthetic bridal fabrics stocked all year round and a special bridal counter where they are happy to advise. A large range of polyesters in silk, satin or matt finishes, crêpe de Chine, organza, embroidered satin, etc. Their sell-out colour is ivory and pastels for bridesmaids. Silk and nylon veiling, too.

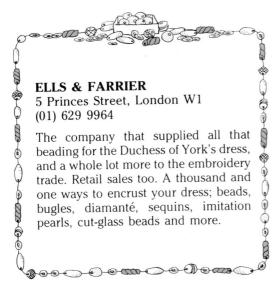

ELLS & FARRIER
5 Princes Street, London W1
(01) 629 9964

The company that supplied all that beading for the Duchess of York's dress, and a whole lot more to the embroidery trade. Retail sales too. A thousand and one ways to encrust your dress; beads, bugles, diamanté, sequins, imitation pearls, cut-glass beads and more.

JOEL & SON
77-79 Church Street, London NW8
(01) 724 6895

A terrific source of unusual silks, imported from Italy and France. Wide, original choice of fabrics at low prices, as they stock ends of rolls and trial rolls. Over-the-top designer silks — textured and embossed, jacquards, duchesse satin in various weights, fine silk satins, crêpes, organzas, chiffon — the list goes on and on. Chirpy young salesmen and pattern books on hand to help you choose. Their next-door shop sells cheap, high-quality furnishing fabric and brocade suitable for winter wedding dresses.

JOHN LEWIS
Oxford Street, London W1
(01) 629 7711

A wide range of taffetas, lace, jacquards, organzas, guipures (heavy cotton lace), embroidered or appliquéd satins, etc., in shades of white and cream; and a spot net in pastels for bridesmaids in peach, yellow, pink, blue, lilac and turqoise. Nylon tulle in cream and white for veiling costs from £1.25 a metre. Silk tulle is £22 a metre. Nylon dress netting (for underskirts) comes in various colours at 55p a metre.

LIBERTY
Regent Street, London W1
(01) 734 1234

Famous for their printed lawns, they have a baronial dress-fabric department on a galleried floor overlooking the rest of the store. A good choice of silks and cottons, plus pattern books and long mirrors to see the material against you; pleasant girls on hand for advice. Summer sales can be hell, but bargain-worthy. Also an Oriental department in the basement for lavish, rustly silks.

MAISON HENRY BERTRAND
324 Euston Road, London NW1
(01) 388 8866

Wonderful wholesalers whose official minimum length is 20 metres (for long-trained Edwardiana?); with a bit of persuasion they might sell you a smaller amount. Twenty different qualities of silk from £2.65 to £33 a metre.

PONGEES
184 Old Street, London EC1
(01) 253 0428

Silk importers whose minimum sale is 23 metres (30 per cent extra cutting charge if you want less). Good if you intend to dress your attendants in the same material as your dress, but in any case the prices are so much lower than in the stores, it is probably still worth placing a small order. Sixty different qualities of silk in light and heavy weights, from £1.50 to £7.50 a metre.

THE SILK HOUSE
47 Stewarts Grove, London SW3
(01) 351 0044

Philippa Mackinnon imports silks from India, Korea and Italy and sells by the metre — silk brocade, printed crêpe de Chine, taffeta, organza, dupion (£12.50 a metre).

SILVAN
12 D'Arblay Street, London W1
(01) 437 6418

Silk tulle in white or off-white 173 cm (72 inches) wide at £14.95 a metre, 274 cm (108 inches) wide at £19.95) for your veil. Many antique-style lace fabrics and trims — cotton lace edgings from 30p to £6 a metre.

Country

GEORGINA VON ETZDORF
The Avenue, Odstock, Salisbury, Wiltshire
(0722) 26625

Dazzling array of fabrics for stunning going-away outfits or for wedding guests' outfits. Georgina and her partners, Martin Simcock and Jonathan Docherty, design and hand-print beautiful silks and wools in their nineteenth-century barn. Some jazzy abstract designs, some pastel and swirly, printed on soft crêpes, floaty chiffons and organzas, mohair, wool and crushed velvet. From £13 to £25 a metre. Also a small selection of trendy, off-the-peg clothes for men and women — shirts, jackets, dressing gowns, scarves, gloves, ties — any of which would add pizazz to a going-away outfit. Available in London at Harvey Nichols, Liberty, Paul Smith, Whistles and the latest Whistles shop in the basement of Lord's, 41 Burlington

Arcade, Piccadilly, London W1 (01) 493 8939. The Odstock shop/workshop is open Wednesdays 2–6 pm and Saturdays 10 am–1 pm and 2–5 pm. Look out for Christmas and late spring sales.

Designer shops

London

BELLVILLE SASSOON
73 Pavilion Road, London SW1
(01) 235 3087

Designer/director David Sassoon is best known for his lavish ballgowns — he was among the first to go back to the big taffeta splash. Similar wedding dresses, as well as leaner ones with bustles and lots of back detail. Ready-to-wear wedding dress, £400–£1,000. Made-to-measure (Sassoon's designs, with adaptations), from £1,500. Going-away outfits: ready-to-wear, £300–£500; made-to-measure, from £1,000. Matching bespoke hats.

BIDDULPH & BANHAM
Stand Y5, Antiquarius, 135 King's Road, London SW3 (01) 351 9463

Susan Biddulph and Sarah Banham have recently branched out on their small stand from trendy evening wear into bridal wear, too. A fashionable range of dresses in silks and synthetics at more realistic prices than you normally find in this neck of the woods. A good deal of bows, bustles, boning, ruching, off-the-shoulder, flamenco, and some convertibles, from long-sleeved modesty into minimal party-time shock-wear. Also veils with satin or pearl trim. From £99 (for example, an acetate flamenco-style wedding dress, figure-hugging to the knee then flaring out with a big bow) up to about £250 for more expensive materials and styles. Will make to measure.

CATHERINE BUCKLEY
302 Westbourne Grove, London W11
(01) 229 8786

Wedding and going-away outfits of antique lace. In the early 1970s Catherine bought a ton and a half of Victorian/Edwardian jacquard lace at 1/9d a yard and her stock (the only lace like it in existence) is still going strong. Delicate but dramatic dresses, blouses and long skirts (separates can be worn afterwards) in period and complementary designs. Along with a team of beaders, she produces replicas of Twenties' dresses with beading on net. She can tint lace to any shade. Dresses, £600–£800; blouses, about £300. Although this is a shop, it's wise to make an appointment.

CHELSEA DESIGN COMPANY
65 Sydney Street, London SW3
(01) 352 4646

A calming shop with white tiles, well-spaced clothes and gentle, helpful assistants. High calibre, made-to-order dresses from Catherine Walker's designs. In rare cases she will create a whole new look for you, in preference to adjusting an existing design. A few samples in the shop and lots of photographs. Some traditional styles, some more fashionable — for example, a grosgrain gown with pointed twists at the shoulders, bare back, a small train and tulip front; a peplum jacket cut on the cross and full-length skirt in Edwardian riding-habit style. From £550 to about £2,000. Also Register Office outfits, such as a classic white suit with long jacket, and going-away outfits in plain and polka-dotted silk. (See colour plate 3.)

DAVID FIELDEN
137 King's Road, London SW3
(01) 351 1745

Fielden designs fashion-conscious dresses of substance — boned and heavy in duchesse

Ivory silk jacquard shawl collar jacket with deep peplum, and matching 'waterfall' skirt with tiered train, by David Fielden.
(Avid Images)

78

satin, thick soft silk, scrunchy slub silk, shot-silk dupion; other gowns take long, sweeping lines — Thirties-type dresses with diamond panelling, or drop-waisters with balloon skirts of net. Many dresses mix two or more fabrics. Everything is made to order from samples, and there's a two- to three-month waiting list. Styles can be made up in any material from the range available and the design can be adjusted as long as it doesn't require a new pattern (bustle or drapy details could be adapted to suit you). From £450 for a silk bustle suit, for example, or £750 upwards for really elaborate dresses. Also head-dresses of satin roses and net, and petticoats. (See colour plate 2.)

GALLERY OF COSTUME AND ANTIQUE TEXTILES
2 Church Street, London NW8
(01) 723 9981

A small selection of fine Edwardian and Victorian lace blouses, collars, bloomers, petticoats and wedding dresses. One silver lace wedding dress cost £3,000. Petticoats range from about £15 to £125, depending on the fineness of the lace.

MR GUBBINS
135 King's Road, London SW3
(01) 351 1513

Small shop next door to David Fielden's, with about 50 samples. Mr Gubbins was one of the forerunners of the romantic pretty-pretty look. Frocks in fine creamy silk with lots of little threaded ribbons, silk rosettes, lace and bead trims — some cover-up Victoriana, some sailor-style drop-waisters, some more boned, ballgown-style. Worn with hooped petticoats or underlayers of net (also sold here), all the dresses take on stature. From £220 for simple styles to £750-plus for extravaganzas. His designs are stocked throughout the country at good bridal shops.

SASHA HETHERINGTON
289 King's Road, London SW3
(01) 351 0880

About a dozen wedding dresses to buy off-the-peg, plus many seasonal designs that can be made to order and altered as you wish. Silk, particularly dupion, is a speciality, but Sasha will use cheaper cottons or synthetics. Styles are fun and modish. Prices from £250 to £850. A limited hire service, too. (Hint if you're skint: look out for hire dresses which get sold off when they begin to look worn.) Head-dresses can be trimmed with handmade silk flowers and veils made to match your dress. Satin wedding shoes from Italy — flatties, courts and some more unusual styles with buckles or scalloped edges — cost about £65, plus £12 to be dyed to any shade. Brightly coloured ballgowns and party dresses of many designs, too. For going away, classic little silk suits have added razzmatazz — bows down the back of skirts, flouncy peplum jackets, etc. A handbag of the same fabric and a natty hat designed by Sasha or Viv Knowland trimmed to match will complete the ensemble.

TATTERS
74 Fulham Road, London SW3
(01) 584 1532

Owned by Missie Crockett, and Graham Hughes, this is one of the best-loved caches of luscious silk dresses. A shopful of samples for church and Register Office weddings and balls, plus ballgowns and some daywear. Nearly all their own designs and a few by Anna Cloonan, Beverly Summers and others. A *mélange* of trad, streamlined, Edwardian and Fifties' looks (inspired by Charles James and Christian Dior). A wedding dress takes three or four months to complete; they don't like to change any design details but will scale down certain things to suit your figure. Trains are an optional extra on most designs. Wedding dresses from £300 to £1,200. Hatter Stephen Jones' head-dresses include one with a huge single rose to be worn with swathes of veiling. Samples of Elizabeth Stuart-Smith's shoes are stocked, plus hooped and net petticoats at about £40, lace gloves and silk sashes. (See colour plates 1 and 4.)

Marina Reese (née Killery)'s wedding dress was made to her own design. The skirt is of ivory duchesse satin and the bodice of heavy corded lace, both found in New York by Marina. Her veil is made from extra-fine silk tulle from Liberty's. Her ivory satin shoes were made to measure by Elizabeth Stuart-Smith and elaborated with beading. The jewellery is by Theo Fennell (see page 16) and the bouquet of roses and ivy by Michael Howells. Marina's hair was styled by Kevin of John Frieda.
(Michael Howells)

RITVA WESTENIUS
153c Fulham Road, London SW3
(01) 581 3878

This Finnish designer fills her shop with classic evening and bridal dresses. Dupion and silk-satin gowns detailed with beading, pleating, tucks, piping or silk rosebuds; several designs involve embroidered lace on fine cotton net with guipure trim. Allow three months for a dress. Average cost is £700. Head-dresses available if you have ordered a dress. A circlet of 14 handmade, soft silk flowers costs around £86 or £6.50 for individual blooms. Veils of lace, plain silk tulle or embroidered with pearls cost around £86, too. Bridesmaids' dresses stocked at about £100 for a child and £156 for grown-ups. (See colour plates 10 and 12.)

Country

ANNABELINDA
6 Gloucester Street, Oxford (0865) 246806

Where many an Oxford undergraduate has found a get-up for a May Ball — and many return to be dressed for their wedding. Some trad silk styles with their familiar piping, binding, smocking, embroidery or appliqué, all hand-finished, and some breakaway fashion frocks; from £400 to £800. Bridesmaids' dresses, from £150, can be made in Thai silk — plain, candy stripes or prints. Liberty prints, too. All designs are made to order, and they can adapt or design from scratch. Veils and head-dresses, too, which can be made from silk to match the dress; also little bags and Alice bands. Dresses are stocked by Liberty and Roberta Buchan in Edinburgh, but the best selection is here at Oxford. Closed in August.

ROBERTA BUCHAN
176 Hope Street, Glasgow (041) 332 6060;
104 Morningside Road, Edinburgh
(031) 447 8549

The main bridal shop is in Glasgow; Edinburgh is part-bridal, part-daywear, suitable for the mother of the bride. Silk and satin dresses, some with trains, by David Fielden and others, starting at £200. Masses of hats, veils, head-dresses and wedding shoes.

CHRIS CLYNE
66 Dublin Street, Edinburgh
(031) 557 1903; also upstairs at 55
Beauchamp Place, London SW3
(01) 589 1429

Wedding dresses designed and made to order, from about £1,000. Lots of panache and many different looks; like Bellville Sassoon, Chris was in at the beginning of the taffeta ballgown phase, and has progressed accordingly. Veils, head-dresses and deliciously original bridesmaids' frocks. Ready-to-wear collection suitable for going away, mainly silk or silk mixes, dresses and two-pieces, from £400. Hats to match, designed and trimmed by Chris.

DESIGNING WOMAN FOR BRIDES
33 Walton Street, Oxford (0865) 54241

Newish shop devoted to brides, owned by Carol Grant of Designing Woman (see page 96). Pretty and relaxed, it has massive mirrors, good lighting and room to swing a train. Dresses and suits for Register Office and church weddings available off-the-peg or made to measure. Choose from existing designs or have an original designed for you. £350–£900. A typical suit may have a calf- or full-length dress with shoestring straps and back kick pleat and a jacket with pointed peplum, satin lapels and cuffs. You could have a huge detachable satin bow with long tails that act as a train. Bridesmaids' outfits from £69 to £150 for an adult size which doubles up as a ballgown. Sally Cochrane head-dresses, Anello and Davide shoes which can be dolled up, Anne Philippson veils and Chantal Thomass lacy-topped stockings and motif tights.

DROOPY & BROWNS
20-21 Stonegate, York (0904) 21458 (shop and HQ); 60 Petergate, York (0904) 37115 (bridal wear only); 37-9 Frederick Street, Edinburgh (031) 225 1019; 21 Milsom Street, Bath (0225) 63796; 16-17 St Christopher's Place, London W1 (01) 935 3198

Ruches and ruffles: silk dupion Edwardian Lady suit (left) *by Designing Woman for Brides.*
(Photograph courtesy of Designing Woman for Brides)

The silk rose brocade dress (right) *was made to order for a bride by Chris Clyne of Edinburgh. Fitted, boned and swathed, the gown has a bustle and huge bow falling into a short train. The frivolous headgear is of rose silk net with a brocade crown.*
(Tony McGee)

Designs by owner Angela Holmes for the bride, attendants, going away and guests. Bridal wear veers towards Victorian and Edwardian, from £275 to £900. Day dresses are simple and old-fashioned with full skirts, puffed sleeves and sashed waists, about £70.

LACE
51 Winchester Street, Salisbury, Wiltshire
(0722) 333371

A pretty boudoir full of partners Carol Brace's and Lyn Lundie's designs (Lyn's dresses are slim-fitting and flapperesque, some in antique lace and some beaded), plus others by Mr Gubbins, Fiorito, Beverly Summers, Allison Blake and Patricia Miller (including her new range of budget dresses). From around £150 to £800. Everything is reduced in July for their sale. Carol designs lacy bridesmaids' dresses (from £75 for a child) and all accessories: silk flower head-dresses, silk-trimmed veils to match the dress can be made to order, silk shoe-clips with flowers or bows. A full range of satin shoes by Gamba is stocked. Hooped petticoats are hired out to customers. Also silk dresses and separates from £100. Matching hats can be made for £30 £80. Lyn also has a shop at 47 South Row, Covent Garden, London W1 (01) 379 7335.

MONKS' DORMITORY
31 Sir Isaacs Walk, Colchester, Essex
(0206) 577188

Owner Judith Brew lives in a nearby eleventh-century abbey, from which the name of the shop derives. Upstairs is a bridal room with enough space to accommodate your back-up team _and_ to swan around in pleasingly untatty sample dresses. These are by Andrea Wilkin, Gina Fratini, Country Bride and Caroline Charles, from £250 to £900. Alterations can be made. A range of head-dresses, veils, underskirts and crinolines. Downstairs are special-occasion dresses for mother, guests and going away, by Jasper Conran, Betty Jackson, Gina Fratini, Sheilagh Brown and Caroline Charles. Bermona hats, silk lingerie by Lejaby. Fashion shows are held twice a year with a wedding finale.

PROPOSAL

18 Catherine Street, Salisbury, Wiltshire
(0722) 29810

Wedding and bridesmaids' dresses and going-away outfits designed and made to order by Margaret Lee. They stock a wide range of silks and synthetics — satin, taffeta, crêpe, etc. — and lace, including some antique lace (all good stuff for DIY brides). They also make head-dresses and veils, hire out hoop petticoats, and sell shoes and jewellery.

SMITHS OF BATH

11 Beaufort Square, Bath, Avon
(0225) 27376

Large, rather old-fashioned, boudoir-type shop lined with finery by Lyn Ashworth, Gina Fratini, Andrea Wilkin, Catherine Buckley, Janina Zuba, Jane Grey, Allison Blake and Sue Rangeley, whose exclusive £1,000-plus dresses are encrusted with hand-embroidery and appliqué. Smiths make veils to match the dresses; some are hand-painted. Going-away and guests' outfits by Arabella Pollen, Catherine Buckley, Jean and Martin Pallant; hats by Philip Somerville and Kirsten Woodward.

TIZZIE DEE

8 Montpellier Arcade, Cheltenham, Gloucestershire (0242) 584188

Ready-to-wear silk wedding dresses. Their own exclusive designs range from £300 to £700; also dresses by Mr Gubbins, Lyn Ashworth and Gina Fratini, but nothing over £1,200. They are attempting to oust crinolines and go sleek, but appreciate the provincial fashion time-lag. The provincial service certainly makes up for it — every dress is pressed before collection. Bridesmaids' dresses can be made to complement the dress; veils, silk-flower bouquets and head-dresses are sold, and you can hire a hooped petticoat. They have designer mother-of-the-bride outfits, and a thriving millinery business (they made five hats for the last Royal Wedding).

Department and chain stores

If you are on a tight budget, brave the stores and shops at sale time (January and July). Sale dresses will be old samples and end-of-season stock and some look shabby, but you will get more for your money. Most shops cater for Register Office brides, including those who have a blessing in church afterwards and want something moderately formal.

LAURA ASHLEY

9 Harriet Street, London SW1 (01) 235 9796, and branches throughout Britain

Perhaps the most reliable source of pretty-but-cheapish bridal wear. Inspirational catalogue with *Tess of the D'Urbervilles*-style photographs of country brides in organza, moiré taffeta, voile and cotton (see colour plate in colour section beginning opposite page 96). A small selection of styles, ranging from Ashley hallmark, high-necked Victoriana to lower-cut, rustic, romantic ruffles. From £125 to £185. Cotton sailor-suits for pages (from about £27) and sprigged or stripy dresses for bridesmaids (from around £30 for children and £60–£95 for adults). Accessories include realistic flower garlands (around £30) and combs (about £6) for the hair, bobbin-net veils (£19.95), hooped petticoats (around £3), lace gloves, hats and cream damask pumps (£29.95).

HARRODS

Knightsbridge, London SW1 (01) 730 1234

A large bridal department with all the gear — mostly traditional wedding dresses from designers such as Grace Elliott, Andrea Wilkin and Beverly Summers, silk-flower head-dresses, veils, bridesmaids' and pages' outfits. Wedding dresses of all prices (average around £600), bridesmaids' about £125. Lofty

No frills infallibility: Laura Ashley's wild silk scoop-neck wedding dress (Lavinia) resembles Fergie's, minus the beads. The cotton damask dress (Diana) has a graceful V-neck at front and back.
(Laura Ashley)

changing rooms, a sofa and magazines for heavy-duty dressing-up sessions with mother. Helpful, patient staff will find shoes and veils for you to try out the whole look.

JOHN LEWIS
Oxford Street, London W1 (01) 629 7711, and branches of the John Lewis group throughout Britain (though stock will be more limited)

Off-the-peg dresses at the cheaper end of the market by Ellis, Columbine, Bridget Black, Mr Gubbins and Country Bride. Prices from £125 to £699. Veils (no silk), head-dresses (one of the largest collections in London) and brides-maids' dresses too.

LIBERTY
Regent Street, London W1 (01) 734 1234

The bridal department stocks samples from many designers, including Sujon, David Fielden, Patricia Miller, Caroline Parry-Jones, Annelise Sharp, Anna Cloonan, Janina Zuba, Karen Ashton and Annabelinda. Orders take six to eight weeks and they will make altera-tions at a small surcharge. Delicate silk or lawn underwear. Bridesmaids' dresses can be made to measure in a number of styles and colours. The hat department has an in-house milliner who will design headgear and veils to your requirements.

Second-hand and hire dresses

(For antique dresses, see pages 79, 88, and 90.)

JANE BUCKLE BRIDAL WEAR HIRE
Victoria House, 62a Unthank Road, Norwich (0603) 623991

Most of Jane's dresses are silk and antique lace, from designers such as Andrea Wilkin, Grace Elliott and Mr Gubbins. The average original cost is £800, but to hire costs from £125 to £350 (the upper end would retail at around £1,000). She stocks a few man-made-fibre dresses, from £40 to £80 to hire. A dress lasts looking new for about five weddings and is then sold to the last bride for a nominal extra. Price includes cleaning, altering length and delivery nationwide (but you must return it back to her by Red Star — about £6). You can view and try on dresses (silk ones only) by appointment at a Kensington hotel which Jane visits during the week. She hires out petticoats (£7.50 for a hoop; £10 for silk tulle), veils (from £5 man-made to £35 silk) and a small selection of bridesmaids' dresses — £25 for children's, £35 for grown-ups'.

SASHA HETHERINGTON
289 King's Road, London SW3
(01) 351 0880

Hires out a few dresses and sells off old hire and sample dresses cut-price.

LYN STANDBROOK
Squirrels Leap, 12 Elmhurst Drive, Dorking, Surrey (0306) 889272

Lyn buys and sells second-hand wedding dresses in good condition from top designers such as Gina Fratini, Andrea Wilkin, Beverly Summers, David Fielden and Tatters. She will buy outright or act as agent. Sometimes designers themselves ask her if she wants to buy their stock and brides often contact her before buying a dress to see if she will be able to sell it afterwards. Occasionally she ends up with a new dress when a wedding has had to be called off. She only takes dresses that cost under £500, and her cheapest dresses are around £22.

WEDDING DRESS EXCHANGE
At One Night Stand, 44 Pimlico Road, London SW1 (01) 730 8708

Joanna Doniger deals in fashionable styles that have been worn once only and originally cost at least £500. These sell for a third of the original price plus £50 commission. She stocks around 75 dresses. Second-hand veils are also sold, plus new satin shoes which can be dyed to match dresses. One Night Stand is the hire part of the shop, for evening gowns and cocktail frocks from £40.

To clean, pack or recycle?

Tradition decrees that it is unlucky to sell, remodel or dye a wedding dress, lest married happiness be imperilled. Designer Tomasz Starzewski certainly believes a wedding dress is 'to be put in a box and taken out ten years later to reminisce — but never to wear again'. Americans take this to the extreme. Thousands of brides send their dresses to a Los Angeles laboratory for ultrasonic dry-cleaning and restoration, which guarantees the dress' life for a century. It is then laid to rest in an airtight casket.

However, the more practical-minded have no hesitation in transforming their dresses into ballgowns, christening robes or cami-knickers . . . and one bride even made her brocade dress into lampshades. It seems to justify the expense if you can get more than one afternoon's use out of it. Dressmakers can advise you how to adjust a dress to wear afterwards and on dyeing. Always have it dyed professionally. Rose Coutts-Smith makes her dresses with all natural fabrics and threads so that they will dye consistently. For the second appearance of Harriet Monckton's Jacobean dress, at the Rose Ball in London,

Rose slipped the sleeves down off the shoulder, removed the bustle, added a pink underskirt, caught the skirt up at intervals around the base, twisted the train round and secured it with a pearl brooch and silk rose (see photograph below).

Whatever afterlife you intend for your dress, always have it dry-cleaned as soon as possible after the wedding. Champagne, white wine, scent and perspiration are invisible to the eye, but will yellow with time. If you do stain your dress, the experts advise you not to touch it, but bring it to them as soon as possible. Be sure to use a hand-

Harriet Ross (née Monckton) shall go to the ball: wearing her wedding dress in its alternative mode (see text above).
(Mark Houldsworth)

finished process (which means extra care is taken and the dress will be ironed, not machine-pressed). After cleaning, wrap the dress in tissue paper to avoid creasing and pack it in a box away from daylight.

Cleaners and dyers

(For restoration of antique dresses and veils, see page 90.)

CHALFONT CLEANERS AND DYERS
222 Baker Street, London W1
(01) 935 7316

Wedding dresses dyed individually to the exact colour you choose, £54.50. Allow two to three weeks. They can also do alterations such as removing trains.

CONCORD
105 Walton Street, London SW3
(01) 584 0784; 9 Pond Place, London SW3
(01) 589 4939

Excellent dry-cleaning, all dealt with individually. Tatters send all their customers here and you can always see sumptuous gowns hanging in the window. Cleaning of this kind of dress will cost from £45 up to £100 and takes about two weeks.

JEEVES OF BELGRAVIA
10 Pont Street, London SW1
(01) 235 1101

Hand-finished cleaning from £25 to £45 depending on how delicate the work is (they like to inspect things first, and to know just what you've spilt on them). On Saturdays, there are ballgown-and-wedding-dress-laden queues up and down the pavement. They clean satin shoes and veils, too, and will box dresses for £5. Allow about four days.

The veil

The bride's ensemble is incomplete without a cloud of veiling. Some girls profess they want to look 'natural' and so dispense with the veil, but it is a vital accoutrement. Having outgrown its original function (in ancient Greece and Rome it protected the bride from the wicked eye of a jealous suitor), it serves today to balance the total image, tying up with the shade and splendour of the dress. It adds importance and stature to the bride at this formal event and, more enticingly, there is the mystique of the concealed face, demure but alluring, on entering the church and the triumph of the walk back down the aisle, veil thrown back and wafting on a breeze.

A good veil is not cheap. You could follow the tradition of borrowing an old veil, or hire one from your dress shop. Otherwise, ask your shop or dressmaker to make you a veil to match the dress. Fine silk tulle is expensive, but it is the only veiling to fall really beautifully. All you need to do is secure a doubled length onto an Alice band — good veiling needs no trimmings. You could also look for cotton net, but nylon really is too stiff and scratchy unless you want a dramatic spray effect. Most good bridal shops (see pages 70-75, 77-86 and 88-90) have a selection of veils, silk-flower and other head-dresses, or you could anchor the veil with a fresh-flower head-dress (see page 121).

New and antique veils and head-dresses

London

LUNN ANTIQUES
86 New King's Road, London SW6
(01) 736 4638

A small stock of well-preserved antique veils

and wedding dresses. Veils average £200. A nineteenth-century dress would cost from £300 to £600. They will try and meet any special requirements. Also, for bridesmaids, a few Edwardian white voile dresses with lace inserts, from £60 to £90.

MELANIE O'TOOLE
90 Chasefield Road, London SW17
(01) 672 8916

Melanie makes both simple and extravagant head-dresses of silk flowers, velvet or satin ribbons, shells, diamanté, sequins, feathers, etc. and veils to go with them. Depending on the level of intricacy, they cost from £50 to £100. She can send a brochure if you can't visit her and also sells a head-dress kit which includes silk flowers, ribbons, beads, wire, etc., for £35. Little hats with veils and bows cost from £45 to about £100. She also makes theatrical masks, should you be having a masked ball after your wedding.

ANNE L. PHILIPPSON
8 The Causeway, Teddington, Middlesex
(01) 977 9688

Wholesale only, but she supplies all leading bridal shops and can send a catalogue and list of stockists. This charming German woman has been making veils for 35 years. A fount of knowledge, she sees a return to long, long veils. Her designs are mainly of silk tulle embroidered with pearls or sequins, of Chantilly lace, plus a few synthetic ones. She also produces handmade circlets of flowers or pearls, and silver-dipped tiaras and coronets with fake stones.

Country

BARTLETT STREET ANTIQUE CENTRE
9 Bartlett Street, Bath (0225) 330267

Anne Edmondson's stall on the ground floor is groaning with exquisite antique lace. She has a constant supply of lace veils, some on display and some carefully stored away in paper. Prices vary. She also has some period

Your veil doesn't have to trail conventionally down your back or sit on the crown of your head. Twist it, pin it, pile it up on top. Make it into a huge bow, wrap it into a toque or catch it at the sides, Twenties-style. Place it in different positions on your head to see which suits you best. Veil by Ritva Westenius, dress and gloves by Ellis Flyte (details, page 187, plates 11 and 12).
(Mark Houldsworth)

wedding dresses and lacy honeymoon négligés.

SALLY COCHRANE
9 Grand Parade, Brighton (0273) 674089

Handmade, embroidered or silk-flower head-dresses. From £15 for a simple Alice band up to £65 for something more elaborate. She takes about ten days and can use your dress material. She supplies Liberty, Designing Woman for Brides in Oxford (see page 81) and The Happy Bride, 26 Spring Street, Brighton.

Restoration

ROYAL SCHOOL OF NEEDLEWORK
25 Princes Gate, London SW7
(01) 589 0077 0181- 943 - 1432

A repair and restoration service for antique lace veils and wedding dresses (they restore all antique lace used by Tatters). You can send or deliver a precious veil or dress here and they will give you an estimate for the work. The average price for cleaning an antique veil is £15 plus VAT and for basic mending, from £25 plus VAT. They can dye a veil to match the dress, too.

The trousseau

The word trousseau derives from the old French *trousse*, a small bundle of valuables, originally paid to the husband. Nowadays that bundle is a wifely perk. It refers to her outfits for going away and the honeymoon. Most brides splash out on some new lingerie and a naughty nightie, and perhaps one or two outfits for the honeymoon, some shoes and a handbag.

Lingerie

Don't underestimate the importance of your underwear. Unless you are utterly sylph-like, your brief is to find something supportive yet pretty that won't spoil the line of the wedding dress. Of course, if your bodice is boned, you won't need a bra. If not, the good news is that the old-fashioned contraptions that spontaneously combusted throughout those misguided years of 'liberation' are back with a vengeance. Heard of the 'eighteen-hour girdle'? The 'cross-your-heart bra that lifts and

---

RIGBY & PELLER
2 Hans Road, London SW3 (01) 589 9293. Also at Croydon (Contour, 1021 Whitgift Centre; (01) 681 1153)

The best place to buy your wedding day underpinnings. Consider this: owner Mrs Kenton believes that 78 per cent of all women wear cheap, ill-fitting bras that lose their shape after *six weeks*. Her bras last *ten years*.

'When a girl is preparing to be married, it is a good stage in her life to start afresh with the basics and to realize that well-fitting underwear will set her up for years. All your clothes will look better and your figure will be enhanced if only you'd wear decent foundations.'

Quite so. Mrs K's selection of off-the-peg bras, basques, corselettes, etc. come in sizes you didn't know existed, from 30AA to an F-cup. These can be altered to fit, or made to measure from scratch, taking the style of your dress into account so that nothing untoward shows. A made-to-order basque-for-life takes about a month and costs from £125 to £200 depending on how elaborate it is. Rigby & Peller are aware that not every bride can afford this sort of service and ensure that everyone is fitted with something they like and can afford. For £2, you could buy their patented attachment to adjust your bra to a backless one.

They also stock pretty camisoles, knickers, French knickers, petticoats, nightwear, stockings and tights. The Croydon branch specializes in hosiery, including wedding designs with motifs. They can give you longer suspenders if you're the sort who ends up with more leg than stocking. And for the honeymoon and beyond, there's swimwear that lasts five years.

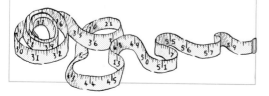

---

separates'? They're not just for mothers. Figure-clenching basques and brassières are actually *comfortable*, help posture, smooth out spare tyres and give you the supreme confidence of knowing you'll stay in place all day.

Frilly French knickers and camiknickers are undoubtedly delectable, but best saved for playtime on honeymoon as they can bunch up under your dress. There is nothing worse than self-evident straps, lace, dark colours or a visible panty line. Make sure underwear fits like a second skin; consider a strapless bra and make sure it is cut low enough at the back. Flesh pink, apricot ·or creamy tones show through the least. A heavy dress on a hot day can be punishing, so minimize the layers and wear lacy or dotty stockings rather than tights. (Pop socks may be practical but how unsexy can you be?) A garter is for fun and for flashing at the reception; it should be worn above the knee.

Lingerie shops

Liberty, Next and Selfridge's are good sources of off-the-peg lingerie. (See also page 71 — (See also page 71 —) Rose Coutts-Smith and Ellis Flyte are but two who make silk underwear.)

London

BRADLEYS
83 Knightsbridge, London, SW1
(01) 235 2902; 26, Marylebone High Street, London W1 (01) 935 1216

For brides, they do a roaring trade in corselettes, smooth all-in-one lace bodies and hold-up stockings. Their bras go from 30AA cup (why bother?) to a 46DD and a 44F (*bother*). Also special wedding tights and stockings by Chantal Thomass with motif and lace designs and traditional silk stockings. Their broderie anglaise négligés cost around

£35 and their most expensive silk ones £1,200.

JANET REGER
2 Beauchamp Place, London SW3
(01) 584 9360

Her legendary lingerie with silk and lace trimmings and top-quality workmanship has become a tradition for brides to wear on honeymoon. Mostly off-the-peg bras, camisoles, suspender belts, etc., but a made-to-measure service is available at a price.

THE WHITE HOUSE
51 New Bond Street, London W1
(01) 629 3521

An old-established shop specializing in high-quality linen and exclusive lingerie and nightwear. Ravishing silk négligés slither from £375 up to £1,130. Some brides have already been filling their bottom drawers with their bed- and table-linen.

Country

LINGERS
8 Grape Lane, York (0204) 23426

A feast of stripped pine and lace, lingerie tumbling enticingly from drawers and cupboards, soft-lit lamps: trousseaus without tears. Everything is made in natural fibres, by Dior, Perla and some new young designers. Silk camiknickers, £40–£50; négligés, £90–£200. Stockings and tights by Perla.

Shoes

Whether you blow out on a Blahnik or plump for a pump, the happy day will be the happier if your feet are comfortable. Don't buy shoes with a different heel height from normal (but if you're a stiletto queen, be prepared to get stuck in the grass). Wear shoes in around the house for several days. Choose a substantial style that gives support, with at least a small heel — ballet shoes can be agony. Fabric looks better than leather (try Scotchgarding satin against the elements), in a shade that matches your dress (most shoe shops and

makers can dye). Avoid sandals and peep-toes. You don't have to spend a fortune on shoes — common or garden satin courts can be dressed up with ribbons, rosettes or silk flowers.

Children's shoes

Children's feet are fine in ballet shoes. They look sweet and are cheap enough for it not to matter if they get scuffed and muddy. If shoes tend to slip off, tie them on with a flourish of ribbons. You can, in any case, embellish them with flowers and so on. Very little boys can wear ballet pumps too. Buckle shoes can be found at Scotch House (see page 106). Otherwise any plain little sandals will do, but make sure all attendants will be shod in the same design.

Shoe designers and shops

(See also pages 70-72, 79, 81, 83, 84, 85 and 86, and investigate leading shoe shops countrywide, such as Bally and Russell & Bromley, who stock some designs suitable for weddings.)

London

ANELLO & DAVIDE
92-4 Charing Cross Road, London WC2
(01) 836 5019 and London branches

Theatrical and ballet shoes in satin and leather, scalloped button boots, laced boots, Edwardian mules, Twenties' shoes and courts in various heel heights. You can have them made in your own material, dyed and appliquéd, with a dolly bag or pochette to match. The shoes sit at the cheaper end of the market (around £30 to £40), but can look clumpy.

Manolo Blahnik's fairy-tale wedding slipper design.

MANOLO BLAHNIK
49-51 Old Church Street, London SW3
(01) 352 3863

Lauded as the best shoe designer in the world, his glorious little shop off the King's Road is togged up as a Roman villa. The maestro's designs can be made to order in the fabric of your dress, and hand-embroidered with thread, pearls or beads. They take from five to six weeks to make. There is a stock of exquisite winter or summer wedding shoes in satin, grosgrain, silk ottoman, brocade and velvet. Prices from £150, escalating into thousands for particularly elaborate creations.

FREDERICK FREED
94 St Martin's Lane, London WC2
(01) 240 0432

A firm of theatrical shoemakers. Ballet shoes start at £9, ballet operas with leather sole about £14 and heeled ballet operas, £17. These shoes can be covered with your own material (allow four weeks), but there is no dyeing service.

GAMBA
3 Garrick Street, London WC2
(01) 437 0704

Satin flatties through to three-inch-heel courts for around £30 (see satin ballet pumps in colour plates). Other styles include a Twenties' shoe with instep bar and Louis heel (£38.50), a bridesmaids' flat shoe with bar (£18.50) and satin ballet shoes, from about £7. Their dyeing service takes ten days and costs £6. Shoes can be made in your dress fabric — if it is heavy enough — for about £40.

GLANVILLE-SHARPE
London House, 26-40 Kensington High Street, London W8 (01) 938 2222

Lisa Sharpe made the bridesmaids' shoes for the latest Royal Wedding, on the strength of one previous commission from Lindka Cierach. She designs classic pumps and

93

courts in a variety of heel sizes with puffy bows or silk flower trims. She will also design to order. All made by outworkers to order from her stock of 50 different coloured silks, or in your dress fabric. You can have a last made or buy a standard size. About £120. Hair and shoe bows and handbags, too.

MARY GOODMAN
7a Duncan Terrace, London N1
(01) 833 2367

Young designer whose long, narrow, flat, medieval shoes in silk, petersham or leather look as though they should peep from under ermin-trimmed robes. She can make the shoes in your dress fabric from a smallish range of existing designs or will design and make to order. Heels can be incorporated. From £40 to £60 ready made; around £100 made to order.

TREVOR HILL
12 Greenland Street, London NW1
(01) 267 1036

This Australian shoe designer makes baroque-ish shoes with high tongues and bows, elfin pumps and slippers, all with his own vampy touch. No set wedding shoes, but will sketch and make designs to order and can use your dress fabric. Two to three weeks; from £60.

EMMA HOPE'S SHOES
7a Duncan Terrace, London N1
(01) 833 2367

Based in a garden studio in Islington, shared with Mary Goodman, she has a range of baroque and rococo shoes and mules with medium to highish heels. Styles can be made in satin, brocade, moiré, crushed velvet, suede, leather or your own material, plus bows and pompons. From £65 to £80 ready-made, or about £100 handmade to order. About a month to make.

DAVID IRELAND
Portobello Market, Portobello Green, London W11, on Friday mornings

Antique silk and tapestry shoes to offset a period wedding dress (provided you have small, narrow feet). Very delicate, beautifully crafted designs, for around £30. He occasionally has antique wedding dresses and waistcoats for sale in various states of repair.

RAYNE
57 Brompton Road, London SW3
(01) 589 5560 and branches countrywide

Rayne stock classic, elegant courts in satin which they can dye to match the dress. They come in three heights — 1, 2½ and 3½ inch heels. About £90.

ELIZABETH STUART-SMITH
129 Curtain Road, London EC4
(01) 729 3365

When she's not making shoes for James Bond or *The Wizard of Oz*, Elizabeth produces lavish Louis shoes, showered with cotton lace, seed pearls and diamanté — shades of Madame Pompadour — and simple courts or slippers in taffeta, brocade or your own fabric. About £100 a pair, up to six weeks to make, though she is doing less and less bespoke work. (See colour plate 1.)

Going-away gear

The going-away outfit is your second excuse to knock 'em out on the day. Although it will be glimpsed only fleetingly, most brides do splash out on a new dress or suit and hat plus, funds permitting, new shoes, bag and even gloves. It will be especially worthwhile if you choose a classic style that you know suits you and will get plenty of subsequent wear. On the practical side, make sure it will be comfortable for travelling, preferably uncrushable, and not made of a fine material that could be damaged by the inevitable spray foam. It is *de rigueur* for the groom to depart looking dapper in a suit or blazer, perhaps with a handkerchief in his top pocket and wearing a trilby or a panama. Some couples dress to complement each other — one pair swopped roles, she departing in charcoal, he in white. Another couple went away dressed indentically in loud grey check suits.

Compatability is . . . his 'n' hers going-away outfits. Identical, almost, but you can tell them apart by their shoes.
(Moira Leggat)

For dressmakers and shops see pages 70-75, 77-84 as most cater for going-away outfits as well. Other sources are Laura Ashley and Monsoon everywhere and — for switched-on designer wear in London — Liberty (Regent Street, London W1 (01) 734 1234), Chic of Hampstead (Heath Street, London NW3 (01) 435 5454) and The Dressing Room (81 George Street, London W1 (01) 935 4772).

Designer shops and department stores

London

THE BEAUCHAMP PLACE SHOP
55 Beauchamp Place, London SW3
(01) 589 4155

Going-away silk dresses and suits. Sleek tailoring and modern silhouettes. Ever-changing designers such as Ventilo and Emmanuelle Khanh. Viv Knowland hats, Accessoire shoes. P.S. While you're in Beauchamp Place, check out Jasper Conran (no. 37) and Bruce Oldfield (no. 27).

CONSTANT SALE SHOP
56 Fulham Road, London SW3
(01) 589 1458

End-of-line designer clothes at half the price. Mainly Italian — Krizia, Ungaro, Erreuno, Armani — and British — John Rocha, Jacques Azagury, etc. Chic little suits, printed silk dresses, a small range of hats and shoes, ball dresses.

HARRODS
Knightsbridge, London SW1 (01) 730 1234

Of course. Virtually every international designer under the sun. Oldies and sophisticates can scour Evening & After Six, Separates, the Designer Room and International Room; youngies, Young Designers (Paul Costelloe, Ally Capellino, John Rocha . . .) and Way In.

HARVEY NICHOLS
Knightsbridge, London SW1 (01) 235 5000

For going-away and guests' outfits, one of the most appealing stashes of British and international designer wear in town. Azagury,

95

Conran, Oldfield, Krizia, Chloe, Lagerfeld, Roland Klein, Montana, Betty Jackson and many more.

ANOUSKA HEMPEL
2 Pond Place, London SW3 (01) 589 4191

An enchanted world of midnight blue and gold, rippling with silk dresses in classic, drop-waist designs. Around £500 off-the-peg and £600 made to measure. Puffs of ball-gowns, sumptuous in more midnight blue and jewel shades, can be remade to order in ivory as wedding dresses (from around £1,500). Understated but luxurious hats and shoes co-ordinate, from about £150.

LUCIENNE PHILLIPS
89 Knightsbridge, London SW1
(01) 235 2134

One of the finest selections of British designer wear, promoted by the heavily French Lucienne, an Anglo-fasho-phile ever since she discovered Jean Muir. 'Our shop', she pronounces, 'is like Ali Baba's cave.' Some grand wedding dresses, ballgowns and going-away wear by Gina Fratini, Lyn Ashworth, Anna Cloonan, Penny Green, Victor Edelstein, Jacques Azagury, Tomasz Starzewski, Salmon and Green, Jean and Martin Pallant, Jasper Conran . . . . Lots of big shoulders and nipped-in waists, masses of hats, and ''uge, 'uge 'eadbands'.

WHISTLES
14 Beauchamp Place, London SW3
(01) 581 4830 and London branches

Constantly changing supply of young designers' work. Nouvelle couture Parisian chic, with the accent on beautiful body-conscious tailoring. Also shoes, bags and hats.

Country

DESIGNING WOMAN
31 Walton Street, Oxford (0865) 513266

Designer wear by Georges Rech, Ally Capel-

lino and MaxMara plus Carol Grant's own collection of classic mix-and-match silk day and evening wear. The basement is devoted to ballgowns.

Hats

Weddings are hat occasions. Whether you're going away or staying put (as a guest), you'll need a hat. 'Apart from the Duchess of York', ventures one rag trader, '*everyone* wears a hat when they go away. I think she slipped up there.' Fashion has never been more accommodating to hat lovers: wide-brimmed stunners, madcap shockers or chic little toques — any hat goes except *no* hat.

Sally Schade (née Rowbotham)—no hat—kisses a row of hatted guests goodbye.
(Antoinette Eugster)

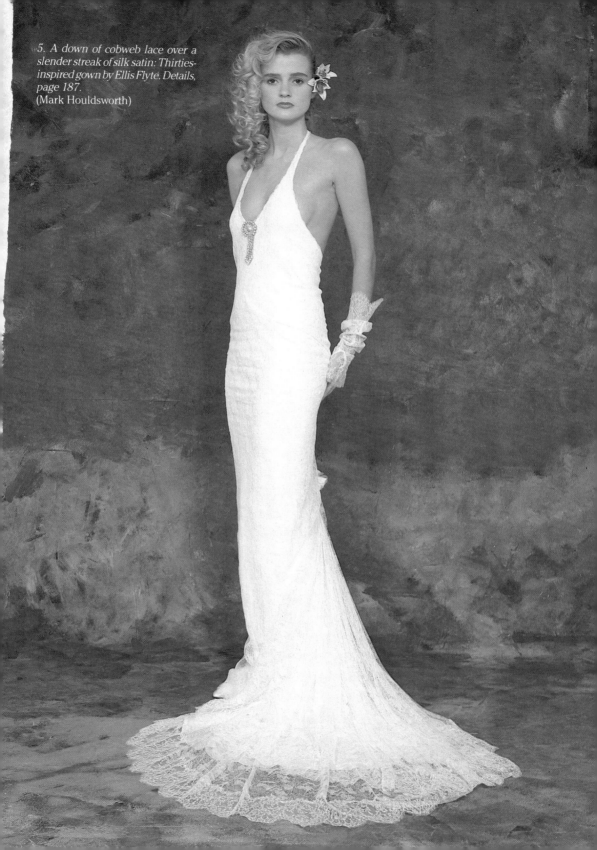

5. A down of cobweb lace over a slender streak of silk satin: Thirties-inspired gown by Ellis Flyte. Details, page 187.
(Mark Houldsworth)

6. Improvisation and imagination:
clouds of frou-frou net,
an antique camisole,
a smooth satin sash,
a creamy lace stole.
Details, page 187.
(Mark Houldsworth)

7. Colonial crispness: a jacket of fine white linen and Brussels lace, a veil of diaphanous muslin, a skirt of Indian silk. This page and left show what DIY brides can do by scouring antique markets, chain stores, fabric shops and mother's wardrobe. Details, page 187. (Mark Houldsworth)

8. *Prithee pretty maiden, will you marry me? Maid and page, dressed by Chelsea Design Company, dally awhile at Claridge's. Details, page 187.*
(Mark Houldsworth)

Pretty in pink (right): *Laura Ashley's floral printed cotton for grown-up and baby bridesmaids alike, topped with a summer straw hat tied with pink silk sash.*
(Laura Ashley)

9. *Red velvet for a winter wedding. Max and Cosima, in Chelsea Design Company sailor suits, looking relaxed and happy for the press photographers. Happy, that is, until the young stars' patience wears thin, and Cosima declares: 'No more'. Details, page 187.*
(Mark Houldsworth)

10. *Tutu divine* (right): *a froth of innocent ivory and a spray of daring red, by Ritva Westenius. Details, page 187.*
(Mark Houldsworth)

11. *Sheer beige and soft rouge for a perfect skin — but these last moments are apprehensive ones . . .* Details, page 187.
(Mark Houldsworth)

12. *Ellis Flyte's cowl-neck dress dips low* (left), *but modesty preveils — Ritva Westenius' beaded tulle veil.* Details, page 187.
(Mark Houldsworth)

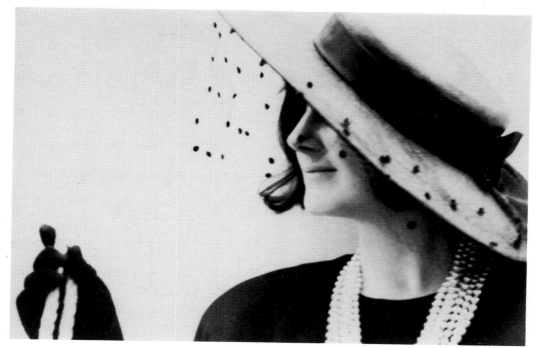

Milliners and shops

Wedding guest Gilly Forge wears one of her own creations in straw with superfine dotted veiling. (Jock Macdonald)

London

ACCESSIBLE TOO
12 Soudan Road, London SW11
(01) 720 4031 or (01) 582 7696

Trendy young hat biz run by partners Clare Wentworth-Stanley and Janet James who used to make hats for the Royal Opera House. Their collection includes Edwardian styles in fine or coarse straw with silk trimmings. From £60 to £80. Fabulous cotton polka-dot hat-boxes at £20.

PAUL CRAIG
14-15 D'Arblay Street, London W1
(01) 437 5467

Soho Mecca of the millinery trade. Many designers have their creations blocked here. Established for about 40 years, Paul Craig sells all the raw materials to make or trim a hat. The basic 'hood' costs from £2.50 to £10 for straw and £6.50 to £12 for felt, and they will block and trim it to order (prices vary). Ready-to-wear hats, too, from £12 to £200.

GILLY FORGE
Unit 14/10 Park House, 140 Battersea Park Road, London SW11 (01) 627 8751

Gilly recently set up on her own with a covetable collection of original blocks, yards of antique lace and net and boxes of fabulous feathers. She is one of the few young designers who painstakingly blocks her own hats. Styles encompass huge *Out of Africa* straw hats with overblown silk roses and velvet trims, to little *Murder on the Orient Express* asymmetrical astrakhan pill-boxes with a wisp of French veiling. Also a range of witty little cocktail hats, such as lobster claws on a deep blue sea of velvet. She has clients of all ages, and will adapt designs to suit. Prices from £60 to £80.

FREDERICK FOX

87 New Bond Street, London W1 (01) 629 5706 (by appointment); 169 Sloane Street, London SW1 (01) 235 5618

Well-known royal hatter whose not-too-expensive collection is stocked nationwide; his handmade couture models (from £150) can be ordered at New Bond Street. Bridal head-dresses, too, individually made. Many top dress designers send clients to him.

THE HAT SHOP

58 Neal Street, London WC2 (01) 836 6718; 9 Gees Court, St Christopher's Place, London W1 (01) 629 1347

A wide range of designer hats — Frederick Fox, Philip Somerville, Jane Lambert, Kirsten Woodward, Julie Elliot, Andrew Wilkie, Fred Bare. From simple hats at £10 to elaborate ones in the hundreds. They can make to order (allow two weeks) and trim to your whim. Mail-order service, too. They can make bridal head-dresses on request.

MARINA KILLERY

(01) 727 3121

Holland Park-based designer with buckets of imagination and talent, much admired by dress designer Chris Clyne. She has designed hats for the Princess of Wales and the Duchess of York. Marina bandies words like 'fantasy' and 'frippery' and loves big picture hats. She will dye straw to match your outfit or make a hat from your dress fabric (though putting fabric round the hat cheapens it). She corresponds the size of hat to (a) your personality, and (b) the width of your shoulders rather than your overall size. From £80 to £120 for a big brimmer, complete with hatbox.

PAMELA FURS AND THINGS

Unit Y4, Antiquarius, 135 King's Road, London SW3 (01) 352 5234

Famous for making Fergie's furry Davy

Marina Killery's design (left) *for a rough straw hat with organza ribbon tied under the chin.*

Striking wide-brimmed hat with black trim (right) *by Philip Somerville.*
(Mark Houldsworth)

Crockett hat, Pamela makes exotic white-mink or fox-fur hats for winter weddings. About £50. She also stocks small fur jackets and capes, plus a small selection of virginal white cotton, antique wedding dresses.

GRAHAM SMITH
2 Welbeck Way, London W1
(01) 486 1522 (by appointment)

Special occasion couture hats that have graced the heads of Princesses Diana and Margaret. As design director of Kangol, he covers the field of styles (available in all top stores).

JANE SMITH STRAW HATS
131 St Philip Street, London SW8
(01) 627 2414

Jane Smith and her three milliners used to make hats for television dramas such as *Brideshead Revisited* and *Pygmalion*. Now she designs hats for Laura Ashley, Alistair Blair and Paul Golding, as well as for her own Battersea shop. Expect to find Edwardian-style sweeping summer hats in fine straw and trendy little squashy hats like parcels. Untrammelled by fashion, Jane will design to order. A plain straw hat is around £70. They also make bridal head-dresses to order — silk flowers, beads, lace on garlands and circlets.

PHILIP SOMERVILLE
11 Blenheim Street, London W1
(01) 629 4442

A recent addition to the run of royal hatters. Classic shapes, including wide-brimmed straws in various colours that you can trim yourself, around £30, and a wealth of more expensive, trend-setting designs. Makes to order from existing designs. Stocked at Harrods.

KIRSTEN WOODWARD
Unit 26, Portobello Green Arcade, 281 Portobello Road, London W10
(01) 960 0090

Off-beat, witty, cock-eyed creations with bundles of glamour. It was she who designed the pâtisserie and upholstery collections for Karl Lagerfeld in Paris (croissants, *chaises-longues* . . .). Prices from £60. Off-the-pegs are stocked at major stores and hat shops around the country; she makes to order by appointment. Also unusual head-dresses for brides, such as Thirties' Hollywood caps with draped cowls under the neck.

Country and Scotland

ALEX MUIR
9a Mid Shore, Pittenweem, Fife
(0333) 311479

Grand hats from skilled hands that will also fit a veil beautifully. Expert handling of layer upon layer of tulle.

Alex Muir crowns unflustered Camilla Ferrand with Juliet cap and veil before her Scottish wedding. (Moira Leggat)

NETHERWOODS
9 Grape Lane, York (0204) 644257

For weddings and the races, Georgina Blorr works in conjunction with Melanie Fisher (see page 75) to create a complete look. She stocks most major designers (Frederick Fox, Viv Knowland, Philip Somerville, Stephen Jones, Herbert Johnson . . .), which saves a trip to the Big Smoke. She can have a hat made to order for you or can trim one herself. Simple unadorned hats cost as little as £10 but serious designer hats start around £30. A selection of hatboxes include original French oval ones and her own hexagonal ones. Also brides' head-dresses and veils to order.

100

Gloves

'Take away the 'g' and give us a pair of loves.' Wedding guests would exchange these words along with pairs of gloves, which used to symbolize maidenhood. Greek brides carry a lump of sugar in their gloves to promote sweetness all their married lives.

Long silk or short lacy gloves suit certain styles of wedding dress — the sleeveless Hollywood vamp, the Scarlett O'Hara layer-cake. And gloves doll up any going-away outfit. Look for splashy silk and wool gloves by Georgina von Etzdorf (see page 77) and second-hand kid gloves at Portobello Market and Antiquarius.

CORNELIA JAMES
53-5 New Bond Street, London W1
(01) 499 9423

The best hands slip into Cornelia's handsome, made-to-measure gloves and gauntlets of silk, satin or leather — quite plain or ornamented. To complement the wedding dress she has a wide range of stretch lace gloves, from wrist- to elbow-length, some fingerless. There's also a collection at Liberty and Harrods. (See pages 84 and 85.)

Jewellery

Bridal jewellery should be minimal but exquisite. It doesn't have to be real, but avoid the vampy, gaudy, chunky looks of too much diamanté or metal. Diamonds are divine, but pearls are more popular — such lustrous droplets complement the sheen of ivory silk. Or wear delicately hued stones such as amethysts or aquamarines, perhaps toning in with flowers and/or bridesmaids. Necks look bare without some small adornment — a gold chain, a string of pearls. If the dress is quite plain, you could wear more stunning jewellery; if there is already plenty of bodice detail, don't crown it with out-of-control jewels. The prettiest earrings are small pearl or precious stone studs or diamond and pearl drops. Drops have more impact if hair is away from the jaw. Leave hands free of chunky watches/bracelets/signet rings — stick to a fine chain or pearl bracelet and the engagement and wedding rings.

See pages 16-18 for precious jewellers. If you're broke and can't borrow the real thing, go for costume jewellery. No longer merely copying authentic pieces, this is the modern face of jewellery, a trendsetting art in its own right.

Costume jewellery

BUTLER & WILSON
189 Fulham Road, London SW3
(01) 352 8255; 20 South Molton Street,
London W1 (01) 409 2955; also at
Harrods.

A delectable treasure trove at the head of the fashion field. Pearls have always been their biggest sellers for brides: chokers (£40–£60), strands (around £10) and earrings such as diamanté hearts with drop pearls. (See colour plates 1, 5, 6, 7, 10 and 12.)

HARVEY NICHOLS
Knightsbridge, London SW1
(01) 235 5000

For a wide range of pearly jewellery and glittering knick-knacks at reasonable prices. (See colour plates 3, 4, 6 and 10.)

Attendants' outfits

The bride is responsible for her bridesmaids' and pages' outfits. Traditionally and properly, her parents should pay. However, it is not unusual now for attendants' mothers to stump up for their clothes or at least for material and shoes. It would be courteous to

wait for the mother to offer, but if nothing is forthcoming, you could suggest sharing costs. This is an area where money can be saved, however, by recruiting a dressmaking friend or member of the family. Attendants' outfits, less formal than the bride's, should be safe in amateur hands.

Bridesmaids

There are three good reasons why bridesmaids' dresses should be made specially: for the fit — every child at their different stage of growing up is a completely different shape; for continuity — to tie in with the bride; for style — there is limited off-the-peg choice, particularly for grown-up bridesmaids. Most dressmakers cater for the whole bridal entourage (see pages 70-75).

It is a good idea to choose an adaptable style that can be used again as a party frock. Liaise with older bridesmaids over their outfits; take their inevitably different figures into account as well as their taste, and make sure they don't look little-girly. The total look of the bridal party will be most pleasing if the line of the dresses follows that of the brides', and the colour tones in. The same creamy colour, or a deeper shade, with coloured trimmings is always successful, as are pastels. Plain tends to look smarter than patterned, especially on grown-ups; the recent splash of chintzes and silk ginghams looked sweet on the little ones, but spriggy prints can look twee. Avoid dark colours, even in winter. Small children can appear swamped and out-of-place in deep velvets.

Remember that children's dresses will almost certainly be rough-and-tumbled up, so avoid full-length frocks that they'll trail along the ground or trip over and use a stalwart fabric — nothing fine and chiffony that will rip. Waist petticoats are destined to slip down, so go for one with a bodice.

Last minute adjustments: maid-of-honour Justine Schouller (far right) with bridesmaid Victoria Howard-Vyse. The dresses, in pastel cotton chintz from Peter Jones, were made by Justine for the wedding of her sister, Clare Reilly to Barnaby Faull. (Mischa Thompson)

Bridesmaids just wanna have fun: having discarded their head-dresses and posies Sophie Faull **(left in both photographs)** *and Victoria Howard-Vyse dismantle their outfits.*
(Mischa Thompson)

Red velvet trimmed with fur and shiny black shoes **(right)** *keep these attendants looking crisp and even at this winter wedding.*
(Tom Hustler)

Pages

The pages' attire conforms to a number of set formulas. Since mid-Victorian times, it has been a tradition for small children, particularly boys, to be train-bearers. The little darlings would be got up as Little Lord Fauntleroys, wee kilted Highlanders (echoing their Queen's love of things Scottish), and later as mini sailors — as reintroduced by the Duchess of York. All these styles are still current and can be made by the bride's dressmaker — although people are wisely

A big day for a small girl: Naomi Gummer **(left)** *was Sally Schade (née Rowbotham)'s tiniest attendant.*
(Antoinette Eugster)

A brood of bridesmaids and pages **(right)** *kitted out by Amanda Barber.*
(Desmond O'Neill Features)

playing down the chocolate-boxy knicker-bocker story. Military uniforms are *de rigueur* if the groom is an officer and wearing uniform (available through his regiment's master tailor, who can make up miniature uniforms or lend out any he may already have); both the Princess of Wales' and some of the Duchess of York's pages wore period Royal Naval uniform. Or you could break with tradition, like Nick and Arabella Ashley, who dressed their two pages as Teddy Boys in drape coats, drainpipes and bootlace ties, with slicked-back hair.

Children's shops

(See also Laura Ashley, page 84.)

CHELSEA DESIGN COMPANY
46 Fulham Road, London SW3
(01) 581 8811

A few wedding designs (billed as party wear) for tinies up to teenage — although they reckon their large sizes fit a (small) grown-up. Their big seller, for two to twelve-year-olds (£118 or £130) is a silk dupion frock in pale pink, corn yellow or ivory, with deep lace trim. Weenies are sashed, teens cummer-bunded. Other teenage styles start at £225. No head-dresses or shoes. For little boys they sell sailor suits — in navy blue and red velveteen for winter (around £55) with piped hats (about £14), or in cotton for summer. Velvet shorts, taffeta knickerbockers and frilled silk shirts too for pages. (See colour plates 8 and 9.)

MEMBERY'S CHILDREN'S CLOTHES
1 Church Road, Barnes, London SW13
(01) 876 2910

Sally Membery creates beautifully detailed frocks in silk, cotton, Liberty print, etc. Her own look is classic, traditional and proper; she has set designs or will follow that of the

Madcap maids Clare (left) *and Katrina Harrison* (right) *in their Workers for Freedom outfits (see also page 66).*
(Michael Woolley)

bride's dress. Elizabethan, Twenties' and mini-Sixties' bridesmaids and a troop of little sailor boys are among those that have emerged from her workshop. Made-to-measure dresses from £75 to about £200. She makes net petticoats and hair bows, can get head-dresses from a Liberty supplier and will dye ballet shoes to go with your silk. Sally did Henrietta Spencer-Churchill's attendants for her splendid wedding at Blenheim Palace.

THE SCOTCH HOUSE
Knightsbridge, London SW1 (01) 581 2151

The full Highland kit for pages (and for brides-maids too). Children should be measured at least four months before the wedding. The complete outfit doesn't come cheap, but will last for generations. It consists of the kilt, £120 (using about five yards of your clan's

106

tartan); Argyll velvet jacket, £126; jabot blouse, £14.50; Montrose belt, £24; socks, £4.50; garter flashes, £1.50; Cromwell buckle shoes in sizes 6–13, £15; sizes 1–5, £24.50; day sporran, £9.50–£18; long tie, £4.50; and, to overdo it completely, the tartan waistcoat, £21.

The groom

It's a cinch for the groom. *All* men look good in morning suits (provided they fit). There are set conventions as to the exact form of attire, and the smartest, most formal look is undoubtedly the old traditional one. Make sure the best man and ushers will be wearing the same shade of suit as you, the groom, and let it be known to guests that morning dress will be the order of the day (but never state this on the invitation).

Dark suits are infinitely preferable to modern pale grey ones: black coats and charcoal trousers with a vertical pattern. You shouldn't wear a handkerchief in your breast pocket — it detracts from the smartness of a carnation or rose in the lapel. Waistcoats are traditionally black and single-breasted, although old-fashioned double-breasted ones in grey or buff are equally smart (Prince Andrew has been seen in both). Brocade waistcoats complement the sumptuousness of the bride's dress and can match in colour. Pale, stiff, single-breasted modern waistcoats are the sort most to be avoided.

Taking stock: Tad Ross with best man and ushers, all dapper in dark suits.
(Portman Press Bureau Ltd.)

A gleaming black silk top hat is traditional (along with chamois-leather gloves in the left hand and a cane or umbrella in the right . . .), but its funereal associations have led most people to go for the grey felt variety. However, experience shows that *any* top hat is cumbersome to carry and can look comical on the head, so it might be more sensible to dispense with it.

The shirt should be white with a stiff Eton collar, though any plain white shirt will do; cufflinks beat buttons for dash. It's nice to break the monotony with bright braces and a jolly silk tie — coloured stripes or paisley instead of grey/black brocade. Or you can wear a stock, which looks good in creamy silk to match the bride rather than grey cloth. Stock pins are in, tie-pins out. Feet should be clad in charcoal socks (clean) and black plain leather lace-up Oxfords (polished). And if your bride is going to the effort of wearing pretty underwear, you could at least return the compliment by chucking out your holey, old-school nylon Y-fronts and investing in a pair of dashing cotton boxers.

Full Highland dress is the form if you have your own tartan. But unless you're a royal, exempt from many of life's agonies, no underwear is the absolute rule. If you're set on Highland kit, don't get married in winter. Officers can wear regimental, naval or air-force kit from their own outfitters. If the wedding is informal or you don't have or won't hire morning dress, a plain grey or dark suit is acceptable.

James Forbes in the Forbes' tartan and Kerry Toms. (Alan Donald)

Bargain-hunting

Old morning suits never die, they seldom even fade away. Made to last for ever, they are usually far superior in quality (the cloth, the cut) and more stylish than modern ones. You should be able to find one in good condition for around £50. Check that armholes and the trouser seat are not too worn or unappealing before buying, and dry-clean in any case before wearing. On Friday and Saturday mornings, Portobello Road Market (Portobello Green, London W10) has rows of second-hand stalls that often sell morning suits and waistcoats at bargain prices. Several trips and some mix-and-match know-how may be needed to obtain the complete ensemble. Oxfam shops and second-hand clothes shops countrywide are likely sources. The Country Gentlemen's Association magazine, *Country* (from the CGA, Icknield Way West, Letchworth, Herts (0462) 682377), is a smart *Exchange & Mart* worth scouring for well-preserved morning suits (and dinner jackets), available by mail order.

New, second-hand and hire sources

GIEVES & HAWKES
1 Savile Row, London W1 (01) 4343 2001

Made-to-measure and ready-to-wear morning suits (black coats are the norm), single and double-breasted waistcoats and grey cravats. Last summer, Bob Geldof wore a £1,000 bespoke morning suit from Gieves when he collected his honorary knighthood from the Queen and a month later at his wedding. He teamed it with patent leather pumps with bows. Gieves do not normally dress pageboys — that they made the period Royal Naval uniforms for the pages at both the Princess of Wales' and the Duchess of York's weddings was an exception.

HACKETT
117 Harwood Road, London SW6
(01) 731 7129

The English gentleman's Mecca. Second-hand morning suits in black and grey (although they consider grey more appropriate for racing), new morning suits in black only; new and second-hand trousers in stripe or a dog-tooth; buff or grey double-breasted waistcoats, plus a few brocade and spotty ones. White or stripy collarless shirts, stiff collars and collar studs, ties but no stocks. Their second-hand wear is scrupulously spring-cleaned and in good condition; a complete outfit is about £97 second-hand or £195 new. Top hats are £45 second-hand and £85 new; shoes — brogues and Oxfords — about £40 to £50 second-hand and £70 new.

LIPMAN & SONS
22 Charing Cross Road, London WC2
(01) 240 2310

A vast array of morning suits in three different shades of grey, or black; grey waistcoats, stripy trousers, top hats, shirts, ties, cravats and gloves. All new or second-hand in a large range of sizes. Black morning suits start from £70 ex-hire; new from £165 (identical to but cheaper than Moss Bros). Suits are hired for only £20 plus deposit, with no stipulation as to when they must be returned (some men collect outfits a month in advance). Open 8 am to 8 pm during the week and 9 am to 6 pm on Saturdays.

MOSS BROS
Bedford Street, London WC2
(01) 240 4567 and country branches

The best-known source of hire clothes, although a suit costs £35 with black coat (curiously, it's £40 for pale grey). Reserve seven to ten days before the day and return the following week. A deposit of £50 for non-credit card payments. A new off-the-peg, three-piece morning suit costs from £245 (heavyweight) to £265 (lightweight, more tailored).

TOMMY NUTTER
19 Savile Row, London W1 (01) 734 0831

Extravagant, double-breasted, silk-brocade waistcoats that dandies about town cannot resist. A good present from the bride.

THE SCOTCH HOUSE
Knightsbridge, London SW1 (01) 581 2151

A braw collection of tartans — all 300-plus in existence — and all the accessories (see page 107). Men's off-the-peg kilts cost from £170; made-to-measure from £210 (give at least four months' notice).

BEAUTY

(John & Annette Elliot)

A part from The Dress, a prime pre-occupation in brides is to change their appearance in some way. You've heard the one about 'he wouldn't have asked you to marry him if didn't like the way you look', but it doesn't help the wedding photographs, or your bikini'd figure on honeymoon. If you really are concerned with losing weight, highlighting your hair and so on, do it: diet and dye it.

You will probably be extra-active and a bit jittery with all the wedding preparations, so use it to your advantage. Add some other form of exercise such as swimming or bicycling, only eat when you're really hungry (and stop as soon as you've satisfied the hunger). In the month prior to the wedding, you could spend a few days at a health spa, perhaps with Mother or your chief bridesmaid, which should free a few extra pounds. Have a sauna or steam bath and massage a day or two before the wedding (though be careful if you are prone to spots — the steam may coax them to the surface). A facial certainly will bring spots out, so make it two

Above *Michelle Cooper, attended by her hairdresser Hugh Green.*

weeks before. If you choose, have eyelashes dyed, legs waxed and a pedicure in the week before the wedding.

Hair

All sorts of people will advise you not to change your hairstyle just for the day. This is valid up to a point, in that you don't want to create an unknown persona for one day, but some styles look better than others with a head-dress and veil. The Princess of Wales did very little to her hair on her wedding day, and it fell lankly about her face, doing nothing to uplift her features or complement her outfit. She later learnt about the value of setting lotion and hairspray for formal occasions. Princess Anne, on the other hand, looked more striking than ever at her wedding, with careful hair styling and make-up. And the Duchess of York compromised with a tamed, ringleted version of her usual free-flowing mane.

110

The best policy is to try out new styles; go to your hairdresser with a mock-up of your head-dress and veil and see what suits you best. In general, long hair without much body looks better up or back rather than straggling around your face. If you decide on a dramatic cut, colour change or perm, do it several weeks in advance so that you, your husband-to-be, family and friends can get used to it.

Make-up

Aim for a natural daytime make-up rather than a party make-up with lurid blusher and loaded-on mascara, since unforgiving daylight exposes every bit of warpaint. On the other hand, do bear in mind that to look your best for the camera, and particularly for video, you do require a heavier make-up and blue-mauve tones are best avoided on film. It is a tricky balance to be achieved — not too pale and washed out in all-white, yet not too colourful and artificial. A light tan gives a healthy glow to your complexion and you will need less make-up. Catch a few rays when possible, or spend a few sessions on a sunbed (which also prepares you for your holiday) but don't go overboard — a hardy nut-brown skin does not look good with delicate ivory silk.

Use pan stick and then a golden foundation to cover up blemishes, etch out dark shadows under eyes, and tone down rosy cheeks. Your make-up won't look caked as long as you buy good-quality cosmetics and apply them correctly. Ask advice at the cosmetics counter of any big store. Make-up should be matt and not shiny, as you will appear sweaty in pictures that use artificial light. Brush loose translucent powder over the foundation. Accentuate and enhance your good features, from bone structure to eyes and lips, but with tone rather than colour. Contour your face with neutral mocha shader and apply a stroke (not a china-doll blob) of peach or caramel-toned blusher, but watch out for demarcation lines which glare out on video.

Use light browns, caramels and greys on eyes. You can blend in a little muted colour, but never garish shades like turquoise. Avoid any defined edges to the shadow, and don't highlight up to the eyebrow — it makes you look in a state of permanent surprise. Go easy on the eyeliner (never use black inner liner) and mascara unless you want to create a particular look à la Monroe or Madonna. Match lipstick roughly to your natural lip colour — warm pinks through to honeys, not too pale or too dark. The message from one photographer is: 'Try and look like you do in real life, but glammed up a bit.'

The golden rule is to practise first. Look at yourself with the head-dress, in various lights including daylight, and wearing white. Your appearance will alter under different conditions.

Beauty routine on the day

Have a warm bath with scented bath milk which is neither drying, like foam bath, nor too oily. Don't make it too hot so that you go red or stay in for too long so that you feel like going back to bed. Have a manicure — paint nails with clear or pale pearly varnish (and leave *plenty* of time for them to dry thoroughly) or simply buff them up. Put on foundation, powder, shader and blusher. Make sure you blend foundation over jawline, but don't bring it so far down that you'll get a tide-mark on your dress. Shade eyes and put on mascara if you choose. Do all this before going to the hairdresser's so that you don't spoil your hair by scraping it out of the way to do your make-up. If the hairdresser is coming to you, he will style your hair before you dress and then put on your head-dress and veil afterwards. When everything is in place, apply lipstick and touch up eyes. Protect your dress with a cloth if you put on any extra powder.

Lady Elizabeth Anson on . . . hair and make-up

❝ We supply make-up and hair people. My hairdressers — Hugh at 161 — go out to brides on the morning; they are very calming. The bride should go to the salon for a run-through beforehand. I have two make-up people who do very natural make-up. There's nothing worse than looking in the mirror and thinking it's not you — it's often because the eyes are made up differently. Your dressmaker will usually help you with your hair and head-dress if you can't afford a hairdresser; she'll help to relieve the panic, give you confidence and can always slip into the front of the car and help you arrange the dress when you arrive at the church. The bride nearly always forgets she will probably need her make-up later in the day. It's best if Mother has it in her bag to take into the registry during the signing and for the reception. ❞

Health spas

London
THE SANCTUARY
11 Floral Street, London WC2
(01) 240 9635

Not a spa, but a jungly all-female club where you can have a pamper day in the pool, whirlpool, sauna, steam room and sunbed for £19.50. Extra charges for massage and beauty treatments.

Country and Scotland
CHAMPNEYS HEALTH RESORT
Nr Tring, Hertfordshire (04427) 3351

Dynasty-style resort where stars go to buff up their bodies. All the latest equipment and therapies — you'll feel (and have spent) a million dollars when you come out. From

about £60 a night including basic treatments, but there are endless tempting extras. Day of Health and Beauty, £54.95.

CHAMPNEYS AT STOBO CASTLE
Stobo Castle, Borders (07216) 249

Small, secluded set-up in the (not quite) wilds of Scotland. Up-to-date therapies include underwater, seaweed and deep-heat, volcanic-mud treatments. This and the clear air will make you feel tinglingly cleansed. Mothers and daughters tend to go together for about five days, and they'll tailor their facilities to your needs. Basic price is £63 (single room) or £49 each (double), plus extra for some beauty and health treatments. A pamper day, including lunch, is £45.

FOREST MERE
Liphook, Hampshire (0428) 722051

Pretty austere stuff if you want to shed weight, but it works. Bundles of therapies and facilities including indoor and outdoor pools. From about £330 a week including massage, sauna, etc., plus extra for beauty treatments.

SHRUBLAND HALL HEALTH CLINIC
Coddenham, Suffolk (0473) 830404

Perhaps the most highly regarded spa in Britain. A lovely country house and gardens, with emphasis on beauty via health from the inside out. Therapies, treatments, sports and exercise classes to set you on the straight and narrow. From about £250 a week, including main treatments.

Hair and beauty

In the country visit your local tried-and-trusted hairdresser to discuss styles. They will normally be happy to come to your house on the morning of the wedding.

London

JOHN FRIEDA

75 New Cavendish Street, London W1
(01) 636 1401

A stylist will come to your home on the morning of the wedding or they can work in the salon. They will braid flowers into your hair.

HARI & FRIENDS

30 Sydney Street, London SW3
(01) 352 2295

A nice, relaxing salon to drop into on the morning of your wedding if you live nearby. Hari has subtle ways of making your hair do what you want it to do and can incorporate flowers and silk bows.

HARRODS HAIR AND BEAUTY SALON

Knightsbridge, London SW3 (01) 730 1234

All hair and beauty treatments you may desire — nails, waxing, massage — plus, for about £15, they will show you how to apply your wedding make-up. Ring first for an appointment.

HUGH AT 161

161 Ebury Street, London W1
(01) 730 2196

Past masters at tending grand heads — or making lowlier ones look grand for the day. They'll go to your house.

MICHAELJOHN

23a Albemarle Street, London W1
(01) 499 7529

It was Denise MacAdam from Michaeljohn that tamed Sarah Ferguson's tresses for her big day. One of the stylists will come to your home if you live out of town, although the distance they are prepared to travel is up to

them. Some of them work specially with brides and will advise on styles, head-dresses and veils. They will also do manicures and pedicures on the day.

NEVILLE DANIEL

175 Sloane Street, London SW1
(01) 245 6151

They will come to your home, can work with fresh flowers, fit the head-dress and do a practice run with the veil. They also offer a manicure and pedicure on the morning of the wedding and can do make-up, too. A make-up costs around £15, manicure £6.50 and pedicure £12.

Scotland

ANGUS GORDON

53 Frederick Street, Edinburgh
(031) 225 1978

The best hairdressers north of the border, revered for their professionalism. They often work in conjunction with Flowers by Maxwell (see page 128), liaising over the style, colour and angle of the flowers. Mr Gordon suggests you have two or three trials before the wedding at the salon, trying out different styles and discussing which suits you best. About a fortnight before the wedding they check on the dress, flowers and colour scheme. They also encourage Mother and even Mother-in-law-to-be to come in and try on their hats. It is not unusual for Mr Gordon to arrive at the bride's home early on the wedding morn to tend to the heads of the bride, mother, bridesmaids plus any close relations. He will revive the bride's hair with fresh flowers before the reception and, in the evening, he will look after Mother's hair once she removes her hat and can give the bride a restyle before she goes away or for an evening dance. Their beauty therapist will do a facial, full make-up and manicure. Make-up, like the hair, requires a trial.

FLOWERS

Flowers are a key part of the wedding. Decorator-flower arranger Michael Howells would go so far as to think they are more important than the dress. Disagree as you will, it is worth planning them just as carefully. Flowers are needed for the bride's and brides-maids' bouquets and head-dresses, buttonholes for the groom, best man and ushers, corsages for the mothers (optional) and to decorate the church and reception. Used cautiously or carelessly they may *do*, but with thought and imagination, they alone can create atmosphere — vibrant, colourful and fragrant.

Of course, your pocket may not match your imagination, which leads many brides to skimp on flowers or get friends and relations to play florist. This may work in churches and marquees, but it is worth getting a trained florist to make up bouquets and head-dresses.

It's a time-consuming and skilled job and one that has to be carried out immediately before the wedding when there are a dozen and one other things to get paranoid about.

Personal recommendation, as with all services, is the best way to choose your florist. Look at other local weddings and ask around. Using a local florist is more convenient and saves delivery costs, but some can be dated and unadventurous. Ask to see photographs of past work. It is a good sign if the shop looks fresh, pretty and organized.

Choosing your flowers

Most brides do need guidance. They may have one or two favourite flowers plus a colour theme; they will almost certainly have a

114

mother who can visualize exactly what *she* wants. Don't be pressurized into settling for someone else's choice. Look at lots of magazines as well as the florist's portfolio; ask your dressmaker's advice and ask the florist to sketch her ideas. Consider practicalities, too — what you will be happy carrying, for example. Neatly bound stems are holder-friendly, but can look twee. A sheaf can be clumsy to carry, but looks fresh and countrified. Remember, too, your bouquet has to be something your chief bridesmaid can take over easily in church.

Your florist will need a visual idea of the dress to make the bouquet and head-dress complementary in style, shape and colour. Take snippets of material of the dress and bridesmaids' outfits, sashes and ribbons and drawings or photos of the design. Discuss your hairdo for the head-dress and the whole look. Florists try to suit the style of bouquet to your character, which is why a personal visit is so important. Most brides visit their florist at least twice and some five or six times.

Given enough warning, almost any flower can be obtained and some florists will cultivate a plant specially — but this could mean up to a year's notice. Arrange an alternative choice of flowers in case of bad weather or unavailability. One bride had a near disaster. She had chosen off-white Madonna lilies for a sheaf tied with cream ribbon and a dramatic head-dress of lilies. Her mother supplied the flowers from her own garden and sent them, the heads as yet unopened, to the florist in good time. On the morning of the wedding, the flowers had still not opened and so the florist made up a head-dress and sheaf with the only other lilies available — lurid orange ones. The bride was horrified and distraught, but mother, no mean flower arranger herself, stepped in, coaxed the original lilies open with hot water and remade the head-dress.

Joanna Lascelles (née Philipson) carries an impressive bouquet of mixed creamy white flowers and foliage, designed by Moyses Stevens.
(Philip Durell, Aardvark Photography)

Artificial flowers

Many brides feel happier in silk flower head-dresses. Even bouquets can look good using the fine fakes available, such as giant tiger lilies from the General Trading Company (see page 43). The advantages are no wilting, no seasonal worries, no hay fever — and you can keep them. Feathers and ribbons can be incorporated. Dried flowers and leaves look gorgeous in autumn and winter, particularly at the church and reception and, for example, carried in baskets by the bridesmaids.

The symbolic flower

Since ancient times, certain flowers and foliage have been dredged in symbolism. The Saracens connected orange blossom with fertility, for the plant is abundant in flowers, fruit and lustrous dark leaves. Still the most traditional bridal flower today, it is maddeningly difficult to obtain and — symbolically speaking — artificial blossom should be avoided lest it bring bad luck.

Tudor brides favoured marigolds, broom, rosemary and wheat, all gilded and dipped in scented rosewater (lilies, one imagines, were left ungilded). Wheat, naturally, symbolized fertility and rosemary remembrance, while rosewater was a fragrant love potion to unite the couple. In attendance were no brides-maids, but a lone boy carrying garlands of wheat and rosemary. The bridal chambers would be decked in yet more of the same.

It was customary for a bridesmaid to plant a sprig of myrtle from the Victorian bride's bouquet at the bride's door. Its future blossoming heralded the next wedding, but if it died, the planter would become an old maid. Happily, myrtle propagates with ease. Cuttings of myrtle and veronica from Queen Victoria's wedding bouquet have flourished into bushes at Osborne House on the Isle of Wight, and subsequent royal brides take sprigs for luck.

White roses mean virginity. In Normandy

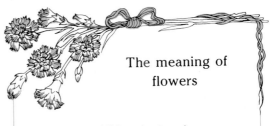

The meaning of flowers

Buttercup — *childhood memories, childishness*
Camellia (white) — *unpretending excellence; (red) — loveliness*
Carnation — *pure love, deep love*
Cornflower — *hope*
Daisy (white) — *innocence*
Forget-me-not — *true love*
Gypsophila ('baby's breath') — *fertility*
Honeysuckle — *bonds of love, sweetness of disposition, fidelity*
Ivy — *friendship, fidelity, the unbreakable bond of marriage*
Jasmine — *amiability*
Lily (white) — *purity and modesty*
Lily of the valley — *love charm, return of happiness*
Myrtle — *love*
Orange blossom — *bridal festivities, fertility, marriage luck, love*
Orchid — *beauty*
Rose — *.love; bridal rose — happy love; white rosebud — girlhood and a heart ignorant of love (the Victorian interpretation of virginity); red rosebud — pure and lovely; white rose — I am worthy of you*
Stephanotis — *you can boast too much*
Tulip (red) — *declaration of love*
Violet (blue) — *faithfullness*

Beware:
Lavender — *distrust*
Yellow rose — *decrease of love, jealousy*
Striped carnation — *refusal*
Yellow carnation — *disdain*

the bride wore in her hair a white rose and a small mirror framed in green silk. Both were laid at the head of her bed on her wedding night, showing that maidenhood, the fading rose, was over.

When the Victorians arrived on the scene, the language of flowers blossomed and flourished. Almost no flower was left unlabelled. Floral conversations ensued: He offers her myrtle for love, she rejoins with lavender for distrust, he pleads with burdock for persistence, but she reads the wrong book and thinks it means 'touch me not' and that is the end of that little romance.

The bride's bouquet

A good bouquet should be featherlight and well-balanced both in appearance and to carry. Fresh flowers should look like fresh flowers. As you walk down the aisle your hair moves, your veil floats and your dress billows, the train swishing out behind. The whole image flows — and so should the flowers. There should be a fresh, natural movement to the bouquet rather than a static, sculpted shield of blooms, wire strangling the life out of them.

It was Constance Spry who said: 'Let the flowers breathe and let the butterflies in.' If a stem swept to the right, she let it be. She never manipulated flowers into an unnatural position. Though her own work ended with her death in 1960, her influence today — over every apect of floral arrangement — is felt more strongly than ever.

A century of bouquets

The shower arrangement, the traditional triangular, trailing bouquet first became fasionable in the 1890s. The Edwardians carried totally-out-of control bouquets that, in photographic line-ups, looked as if they were sporting a whole herbaceous border. In the late Twenties, brides rested bouquets or sheafs of unwired flowers in the crook of one arm. By the Forties, bouquets had grown once more to gargantuan proportions, with big blooms such as roses and carnations, masses of asparagus fern and trailing foliage. Such flowers — few types were available — couldn't be wired into neat little posies; instead, all the stems were left on and wired into a moss ball.

CASCADE

VICTORIAN POSY

SHEAF

In the Sixties, with more sophisticated floral technology, bouquets shrank to tight little embroidered pin cushions of flowers. The Seventies and early Eighties were characterized by the more elegant, formal shower until, in 1981, the Princess of Wales broke the trend with her enormous bouquet — a cascade of highly scented gardenias, golden Mountbatten roses, white odontoglossum orchids, stephanotis, lily of the valley and white freesias, set among a profusion of foliage including the traditional myrtle and veronica.

Dynamic and bold: lilies and fern form strong shapes in Jane Packer's design.

The country bride had arrived. The romantic Victorian crinolines, floaty fairy-tale ballgowns and Laura Ashley frills that swept across the country were accompanied perfectly by loosely wired showers with masses of foliage, or swathes of unwired flowers tied with ribbon that looked like you'd just raided the garden; swarms of little bridesmaids with baskets of fresh garden flowers completed the image.

The Duchess of York's bouquet, in keeping with its bearer's somewhat anti-fashion image, harked back to the neatly packed bed of blooms of earlier years, but its graceful curving lines and the bold lilies gave it a 1986 feel. Ivory gardenias, cream lilies and clusters of lily of the valley were sculpted into the shape of an S. No foliage, highly scented flowers and the S-shape were the bride's commands, perhaps not what designer Jane Packer would have created if given free rein. As to whether this has started a trend for initials, Jane Packer sincerely hopes not. 'An S worked because it was a flowing shape, but imagine an H or an F! You may as well be carrying a placard with your name on it.'

The new style of bouquets

While the effusive country look is still flourishing, starker, more striking bouquets complement the new sleek, sophisticated bride. There is a wider use of exotic flowers and unusual foliage and more colour. Almost anything goes — anything, that is, but contrived, plastic-like arrangements.

For the natural look, use wild and country garden flowers such as cow parsley, clouds of gypsophila, honeysuckle, lily of the valley, pinks, roses, herbs, twiggy and trailing foliage. Smaller blooms give a dotty, feathery, frondy, light effect; larger flowers add impact. If the dress is heavily decorative and detailed, the bouquet can be simpler.

Clean cut, elegant, slender dresses allow for more flamboyant, exotic bouquets. If it's a knockout Hollywood-glamour gown or something tomboyish and simple, go for a bold, more modern arrangement, less fussy and frou-frou, with a sparing selection of flowers Orchids or lilies set in spiky foliage, or even just one lovely lily. Movement is still crucial, be it flowing or dynamic — there is nothing static or neat and tidy about the new bouquets.

Bedecked with flowers

Victorians used to deck the whole dress in flowers — garlanded around the hem, echoing flounces and other details, corsages on the bodice. This could easily be done today, wiring flowers and ivy, say, into a fine garland and pinning or tacking it in swags above the hem of the dress, or wearing it as a long sash in Miss World style. Clusters of little flowers can be pinned on the dress, cuffs can be encircled by flowers. Past brides have carried a floral muff, fan, or a prayer book with flower bookmark, although these are rather neat and contrived.

Bouquet lore

Just before the bride leaves in her going away clothes, she throws the bouquet among the bridesmaids and her friends. The one who catches it will be the next bride. On the Continent, the bride's bouquet is said to have medicinal virtue — three leaves from it will cure any fever.

Budget bouquets

Save florist's bills by choosing a loose arrangement (not too many blooms) of flowers that are in season. Cut costs completely by carrying a single flower from the garden or an armful of roses or lilies tied together with ribbon. One spring bride dressed up a bunch of daffodils with a foppish white bow. The country look of bundles of mixed flowers gathered freshly from the garden can be just that. And the advantage of flowers on their stems is that they can be kept in water until the last moment. As for wired bouquets, don't be deceived by the loose, natural look — they require careful construc-

tion. Professional florists remove stems completely from some flowers and wire the heads lightly onto a false stem to give that natural effect. The morning of Prince Andrew's wedding saw Jane Packer and five cohorts wiring 600 stems of lily of the valley for hoops and head-dresses. So only DIY if you KIA (know it all).

Preserving the bouquet

Straight after the wedding, bouquets that weren't jettisoned into the crowd should be lightly dusted with silica gel and laid on more silica gel in a box. The box should be sealed in an airtight bag for a few days.

PRESSED FOR TIME
58 Acorn Avenue, Braintree, Essex (0376 28201)

They press and frame bouquets. It's a nail-biting business getting bouquets to them fresh, by Special Delivery, but they make a fine job of it. From about £70.

Foliage

Foliage is more fashionable now than ever. Shapes vary from spikes and spires to tendrils and trails, textures from downy soft to shiny gloss, colours from silvery grey through greens and yellows to natural wheat and autumnal russet. Seasonal availability is of no great concern. You could work almost exclusively with foliage in winter when the selection of fresh flowers is limited.

All year

Most evergreen foliage, with the bonus of

flowers	scented	white	ivory	yellow	peach	pink	red	orange	blue	purple	seasonal availability
azaleas		~	~	~	~	~	~	~		~	spring–summer
bluebells									•		spring
buttercups				•							summer
camellias		●	●			●	●				winter–spring
carnations		●	●	●	●	●	●	●		●	summer ⎫ all
carnations–spray		~	~	~	~	~	~	~		~	summer ⎬ year
Christmas roses		●									winter
chrysanthemums		●	●	●	●	●	●	●		●	all year
crocuses		~		~						~	spring
cornflowers						~				~	spring–summer
daisies		•									summer
delphiniums		•							●	●	summer
forget-me-nots									•		spring–summer
freesias	✿	~	~	~	~	~	~	~		~	winter–spring
fruit blossom	✿	~				~					spring
gardenias	✿	●	●								summer
grape hyacinths	✿								•		spring
guelder roses		●									summer
gypsophila		•									summer–all year
heather		•		•						•	spring–summer–autumn
honeysuckle	✿	~		~		~					summer
irises	✿	●	●	●					●	●	early summer–all year
jasmine	✿	~									spring–summer
lilacs	✿	●								●	spring
lilies–belladonna	✿					●					early autumn
–Easter		●									spring–summer
–madonna	✿	●									summer
lily of the valley	✿	•									spring–summer
magnolias	✿		●								summer
michaelmas daisies		~	~							~	autumn
myrtle	✿	~									all year
narcissi–daffodils, etc.	✿	●	●	●				●			spring
orange blossom	✿	~									spring–summer
orchids		●	●	●	●	●		●		●	summer–all year
paeonies	✿	●	●			●	●				summer
primroses				~							spring
rhododendrons		●				●	●	●		●	spring–summer
roses	✿	●	●	●	●	●	●	●		●	all year
snowdrops		•									winter–spring
statice		•		•		•				•	summer–all year
stephanotis	✿	~									summer
sweet peas		~	~	~	~	~	~	~		~	spring–summer
tuberoses	✿	~									summer
violets	✿	~							~	~	spring–summer

Key ✿ scented • small flowers ~ medium flowers ● large flowers

flowers and berries in season. Dark glossy leaves — holly, laurel, bay and cotoneaster; variegated — euphorbia and ivy (particularly hedera 'needlepoint' and *H. caneriensis*). Ferns — asparagus, maidenhair and hare's foot. Dried foliage — ornamental grasses, reeds, seeds, pods and fruits. Herbs such as the traditional rosemary.

Spring

Twigs of new foliage such as small, freshly opened birch leaves on the branch, light-weight sprays of mimosa, Solomon's seal.

Summer

Natural foliage from the abundant selection of flowers in bloom. Hedgerow plants — cow parsley, elder, etc. — and cottage-garden sprays of lavender and goldenrod.

Autumn

Deciduous leaves turning colour for reception and church: all manner of foliage in rich shades of bronze and gold, such as copper beech and acer. Harvest fruits — wheat, barley, berries and currants. Green foliage — bells of Ireland, varieties of mahonia and hosta.

Winter

Conifers and shrubs such as holly, pteris (especially *Pteris japonica*) and spotted laurel give a show of colour with berries. Glossy evergreen bouquets with lipstick-red berries can be stunning against a silk satin dress.

The head-dress

(See also pages 88-90.)

A fresh flower head-dress can be the bride's crowning glory. Don't be put off by the thought of it wilting. Roses (though not their foliage), lilies, tuberose, honeysuckle, freesia and many other flowers will last. Just how much impact the head-dress has depends on

your personality. Bear in mnd that it must anchor the veil.

Fresh flowers can be used in a multitude of ways — a frondy garland; a halo laden with large blooms; a flower tiara like the Duchess of York's; a floral Alice band; slides with sprigs of flowers; a single exotic bloom fastened behind one ear in South Pacific fashion; a semi-circle of flowers at the back of the head; a dramatic evergreen wreath of bay, myrtle, rosemary, ivy, etc.; flowers entwined in the hair, Pre-Raphaelite style. Liaise with your hairdresser and florist.

Head-dress lore

A floral wreath represents maidenhood, which dies along with the flowers. The circlet can be thrown among the guests — to secure a fragment ensures early marriage. In Switzerland the wreath is set alight and the brighter it burns, the more luck it brings. Greek brides wore an evergreen wreath, expressing the quality they hoped their marriages would achieve.

Bridesmaids

The bridesmaids' flowers can be beautifully spontaneous, with splashes of colour. Bouquets for grown-up bridesmaids can follow the line of the bride's, with less extravagance, more colour. Fidgety little ones want nothing too cumbersome or intricate that can be strangled by intent, hot little hands. They can't fail to look adorable with beribboned posies, baskets or trugs laden with country flowers, pomanders looped over a wrist with ribbon, hoops twisted with flowers, or one long garland fastened to the wrist of each bridesmaid — like a slave train. This may keep them together for the service, but there will be histrionics later if you don't liberate them.

The head-dress could echo the bride's, topknots can be circled with flowers or half-circlets worn at back of the head like the Duke and Duchess of York's. You could try

Julia Blackburn and her bridesmaid in clouds of gypsophila.
(Philip Durell, Aardvark Photography)

making garlands for the little bridesmaid's heads, using flowers that represent childhood innocence — buttercups and daisies — plus pretty, wild and garden flowers such as cornflowers and honeysuckle. Some flowers that are prone to droop, such as lily of the valley, should have their stems plunged in boiling water. Wire flowers to a circlet of cotton-covered wire from a haberdashery or hat department (make sure it is an exact fit — an uncomfortable head-dress will be ditched early on in the proceedings). Flowers can be pinned to young bridesmaids' shoes but, again, don't expect them to last for long.

Buttonholes

It is the groom's or best man's responsibility to organize buttonholes for themselves and the ushers. Non-droop carnations are most popular; roses, gardenias or sprigs of lily of the valley are sweeter-scented alternatives. Choose flowers in white or to match the bride's colour scheme. The mothers of the bride and groom sometimes wear a corsage — a spray of flowers in a colour to match their outfit.

The church

The first step is to ask your minister who is in charge of church flowers. If you have a professional florist, she should liaise with the church. However, this is one area where you can cut down on expense by organizing the flowers with amateur helpers. There is normally a rota of volunteer flower arrangers from the parish, who will advise you on where best to place flowers and whether there are any rules about the decoration of the altar. They may be happy to assist or take over arranging the flowers. Discuss your scheme with them and decide what flowers you will need to buy in addition to the usual church supply. Check there are suitable containers.

Alternatively, if you know someone from a local flower-arranging society, they might decorate the church for you, for just the price of materials. The flowers in Westminster Abbey for the Duke and Duchess of York were arranged by 42 women from NAFAS, the National Association of Flower Arrangement Societies, who drew straws for the privilege.

Decorate the church the day before and ask the head arranger to check them and top up vases on the morning of the wedding. If there is more than one wedding on the day, liaise with the other bride(s) to agree on colours and perhaps share the cost. The flowers are normally left in church afterwards.

As a general rule, place flowers high up, where light falls on them and they are most visible. A few large arrangements are better than lots of small ones, apart from posies at pew ends. Pale creamy or silvery tones are the most striking — dark colours, particularly blue, get lost.

You don't have to stick to conventional arrangements. If pews face the aisle, swag garlands along the front pews. Flowers can be festooned around the font and any pillars. An example of a good and imaginative flower arrangement was Michael Howells' design for an early summer wedding: he lined the aisle with scented white broom and potted apple trees in full blossom.

The reception

In hotels, restaurants and some hired halls, flowers will be part of the wedding package, arranged at their discretion. You should be able to choose the colour scheme as long as there isn't another reception that day.

Private houses and marquees can be decorated by your florist, caterer or you and your friends. Continue the colour theme. The main focal points are at the entrance where you receive guests and the cake — place a posy on top and arrangements or festoons at the base. Put small arrangements on tables.

In the house, place large pedestals where they can best be seen. Garlands can be hung over fireplaces and paintings, and twisted around bannisters. In autumn and winter, swags of dried flowers, foliage and fruit look

flowers (allow extra, to be on the safe side). Order those you don't have in the garden from a florist or wholesaler. Buy Oasis, rose wire and tape, borrow buckets.

Two days in advance: Leave Oasis to soak in the evening. Have ready a table, secateurs, scissors, step-ladder, Oasis, wire, containers and pedestals.

One day in advance: Pick flowers early in the morning after the dew has gone. Choose half-closed blooms, nothing full-blown. Keep them cool, in water, and spray with moisture. Flowers with thicker (not papery) petals, hold moisture and last longer. Rose stems should be hammered, dipped in boiling water, soaked for some time in warm water and stripped of thorns. Collect other flowers from the florist. Put everything into deep buckets of water and leave in the shade.

Arrange flowers in Oasis as desired. Leave garlands until last. Use flowers and foliage with strong but flexible stems. With fine rose

sumptuous above mantelpieces and pictures. Rich brocade can be draped as part of the design.

Marquees give masses of scope for flowers — spiralling down poles, baskets hanging from support points, festoons along the top of the tent wall, decorated chandeliers, stone urns filled with flowering plants, trellis work, ornamental trees, pedestals and flower trees (place a broomstick into a large pot of flowers, pack flowers into a ball of Oasis and fix to the top. Small flower trees with plain bases can be used for the table.

Florists' ideas include using fruit, vegetables, moss and lichen wired in among the flowers, sculpted arches, topiary, an umbrella of flowers over the top table and mosaics of petals in the bride's path. One garden was completely replanted for an extravagant reception.

DIY countdown

One week in advance: Work out quantities of

wire, fasten one flower to another like a daisy chain. Lay the garland outside overnight in a shallow tray of water and cover.

The day: Pin garlands in place. Make sure Oasis is still damp. Spray flowers with moisture.

Florists

Unless otherwise stated, the following florists cover the entire floral aspect of weddings. If decorating the church/reception, they will probably want to see the venue beforehand, and most will travel within a reasonable day's work. Give at least three months' notice to avoid any problems. Charges vary, but a reputable London florist will cost from £40 for just the bride's bouquet.

The Cadbury cake (left) *for Michelle Cooper and Justin Cadbury.*
(John & Annette Elliot)

London

MARY ADAMS FLOWER DESIGN STUDIO
4 Kinnerton Place South, London SW1
(01) 235 7117

Bouquets from the dainty, natural, flowing school and a team to transform your wedding space. Mary Adams' book, *Natural Flower Arranging* (published by Batsford, 1981) covers her style and may help guide yours. Lace and hand-painted ribbon sometimes feature in her bouquets and she will work with silk or dried flowers. She also runs career courses in wedding floristry and short courses on flower arranging from her pretty Edwardian mews studio.

CURZON LAWRENCE FLOWERS
20 Motcomb Street, London SW1
(01) 235 6317

Interior and garden designer David Hicks' favourite florist: 'It smells the best, the flowers

Searcy's organized this reception (right) *and Anne Tweed filled the frame tent with flower trees and other floral arrangements.*
(Philip Durell, Aardvark Photography)

are top quality — would go so far as to say it is the best flower shop in the world.' Individual design by Lynne Lawrence, a good fixer who can produce flowers at very short notice — even 24 hours. Excellent with head-dresses — she can weave flowers into your hair and combine fresh flowers with tiaras, fabric, bows and rouleaus (hair rolls). Her style is loose but bold.

CAROLINE EVANS
49 Atalanta Street, London SW6
(01) 381 5494

A team of skilled florists, not a shop, which means personal attention can be given to clients. Natural style, using unusual garden flowers and coloured foliage. Also handmade silk flowers from Italy and beautifully preserved dried flowers. For receptions and churches they do pedestals, candelabra arrangements and flower trees such as an orange tree with daffodils growing from the base.

FABULA FLOWERS
29 Chester Square, London SW1
(01) 730 8898

Susan Storey is inventive and attentive to colour and texture. She'll use cheaper flowers if requested, but won't compromise artisti-cally. She made a flower muff to complement one bride's cossack-style outfit, and once reconstructed a spectacular orchid tree — a skeleton Sumat tree covered in moss, set with orchids — for the bride and groom to stand by at the receiving line.

MICHAEL HOWELLS
42 Bloemfontein Road, London W12
(01) 749 7414 (See also page 159.)

Artist Michael Howells creates theme weddings, designing flowers and decorations on as lavish a scale as you desire — from a dramatic wreath and bouquet (he swathed one bride in bay and myrtle, after a Sergeant portrait, filling her crown with roses and lilies at the back) to completely replanting your garden) which he did for John Aspinall's exotic country ball). For a big country wedding based on *Tess of the d'Urbervilles*, he had about 20 friends cutting cow parsley for three days just for the church. A wedding for a bride called Rose was all roses, swags of ivy and sheaves of corn. Theatrical vision and execution — he can create grand effects from very little and uses clever devices like mixing paper flowers with fresh ones where they will not be seen closely, so that all appear genuine.

CAROLINE JACKSON
60 High Street, Wimbledon Village,
London SW19
(01) 947 9722

Ex-Pulbrook & Gould, she does the flowers for Juliana's (see page 148) and the Pie Man Food Company (see page 144). Her marquee decorations include flowers around poles, trellis greenery, hanging baskets and flower trees. At a Christmas candlelit wedding, she decorated trees with fairy lights and, in pursuit of the natural look, she has used lichen branches from Wales.

MOYSES STEVENS
9 Bruton Street, London W1
(01) 493 8171

Well-established firm with strong seasonal styles devised by designer Michael Matthews — though they can adopt any look. Excellent at period work, as they design flowers for BBC productions such as the Dickens series. For one marquee they created a herbaceous border and chandeliers of flowers and they will spray baskets and containers to match your colour theme.

SARAH O'CONNOR
132 Broomwood Road, London SW11
(01) 585 0609

Decorations close to Constance Spry's heart — Sarah learnt from her mother, Ann Ord, who used to arrange the flowers at Mrs Spry's demonstrations. Lightweight, feminine style,

Joanna Philipson's bridesmaids (**left**) *surrounded by dewy dollops of creamy waxen flowers by Moyses Stevens.*
(Philip Durell, Aardvark Photography)

My carriage overfloweth: Georgina Booth and Mark Rowse (**below**) *went away in a horse-drawn carriage brimming with country blossom.*
(Sue Carpenter)

using lots of garden flowers and foliage. She particularly enjoys making bouquets.

JANE PACKER FLORAL DESIGN
56 James Street, London W1
(01) 935 2673

Inventive, fashion-conscious florist chosen by Sarah Ferguson to design her flowers and those for her entourage. The floral hoops were inspired by the children's Edwardian outfits and Jane likes to vary her look according to the concept of the wedding. She loves to be adventurous and is always trying new ideas — often used in *Brides* magazine. Strong, stark, unpretty-pretty bouquets are one current direction. (See flowers in colour plates.)

JOHN PLESTED AND DAVID JONES
Unit 14, Battersea Business Centre, 103-9 Lavender Hill, London SW11
(01) 223 4327

Lavish floral arrangements and decorations for receptions and parties with up to 2,000 guests. All the top party organizers swear by them, including Lady Elizabeth Anson of Party Planners, and Chance Entertainment. They specialize in themes — period, colour or extravaganzas such as a circus.

PUGH & CARR
26 Gloucester Road, London SW7
(01) 584 7181

Tricia Colson and her colleagues love the country look, using garden and wild flowers — cow parsley, lavender, buttercups, etc. Flexible and full of ideas. They like the continuity of a theme, be it colour or a particular flower.

PULBROOK & GOULD
181 Sloane Street, London SW1
(01) 235 3186

A pillar of the floral realm, highly recommended by those in the know, though perhaps lacking the personal touch of smaller-timers. A training ground for bright young florists (many girls from Rosemary

Gray's Eggleston Hall course start here), with a high standard of artistry. Imaginative, up-to-date designs; they'll pull out all the stops for grand affairs.

CONSTANCE SPRY
25 Manchester Square, London W1
(01) 486 6441

Continuing the tradition of the great pioneer of the natural look. Primarily a training establishment and not a flower shop, they can do the whole wedding shebang given lots of notice (it's the teachers who'll arrange your flowers). Many of their blooms are grown in the late Mrs Spry's gardens at Windsor.

Country and Scotland

THE CONSERVATORY
The Drive, Hove, East Sussex
(0273) 731759

Old-established firm who will launch into weddings of any scale with enthusiasm. They did one three-day wedding in London that cost £ 50,000. Their style is adaptable to suit the event.

FLOWER GARDEN
10 Manchester Road, Wilmslow, Cheshire (0625) 525255; 65 Park Lane, Poynton, Cheshire (0625) 874543

The country, cloudy look comes to Cheshire. They specialize in bouquets, and take a great deal of time and care over organization.

FLOWERS BY MAXWELL
32b Castle Street, Edinburgh
(031) 226 2866

The top florists in Scotland, brimming with ideas and advice. Mr Maxwell has wonderful sources of garden flowers which have longer stems than those commercially grown, providing a better shape for arrangements. He likes to use blooms and foliage with strong seasonal associations, that will bring nostalgic memories in years to come. Grand decorations, making important use of lighting. At

Old family friends may have been confused at the wedding of Harriet (née Lizzie) and Tad (né Alexander) Ross, but the couple were in no doubt as to whom they were marrying. Harriet spent the eve of her wedding at Claridge's, where she was photographed next morning preparing for the ceremony (top right). A mystical cloud of silk tulle (centre right): Harriet, with Mother and bridesmaids, arrives at the Church of St Bartholomew the Great at Smithfields. The wedding theme was cream. Harriet (above) wears a Jacobean-style dress of French silk, designed by Rose Coutts-Smith, who also made Tad's matching stock and brocade waistcoat. The cake was made by Searcy's and the floral decorations are by Pulbrook & Gould. Going away (right): bound for Claridge's, Rome and Portugal, Harriet looks crashingly smart in a black suit from Whistles and fine straw hat. (Portman Press Bureau)

Fergie may have promised to obey, but the grand young Duke of York already has his role cut out for him. Here, glowing in Lindka Cierach's masterpiece (fittingly, in duchesse satin), the Duchess waves from the balcony of Buckingham Palace while Prince Andrew gathers up the tail end of her 17½-foot embroidered and beaded train. For her bouquet, she chose gardenias, lilies and lily of the valley for their heady scent, and Jane Packer sculpted them skilfully into the desired 'S' for Sarah. (Anwar Hussein)

Spontaneous smiles of relief at the end of a nerve-wracking ceremony and the official photo session: the Prince and Princess of Wales are captured on film by Patrick Lichfield. Diana is enshrouded in her Emanuel extravaganza, complete with crinoline and 25 feet of lace-edged, detachable, taffeta train. Her bouquet contains a mass of creamy white flowers and trailing foliage, including orchids, stephanotis, lily of the valley, freesias, and the royal tradition of myrtle and veronica. (Patrick Lichfield)

*Sir Bob and his scarlet lady: Bob
Geldof, heavily medalled and
fashionably not shaven, in Gieves &
Hawkes tailoring, and Paula Yates,
dazzling in Jasper Conran's Sixties-
style satin, tie the knot officially at
their home in Kent. They did it once
before in Las Vegas, but nothing
could beat a traditional English
country wedding.*
(Brian Aris)

one event, a sweep of yew trees was tented over, covered with gypsophila and lit up.

CAROL FOSTER
40 Middlecroft Drive, York (0904) 490385

Carol Foster is known for her marvellous use of natural garden flowers and greenery at smart Yorkshire thrashes. She masterminded the flowers for Simon and Annette Howard's wedding at Castle Howard and for Lord and Lady Ingleby at Ripley Castle.

ROSEMARY GRAY
Eggleston Hall, Barnard Castle,
Co. Durham (0833) 50378

The Principal of Eggleston Hall Finishing School, Rosemary Gray demonstrates flower arranging; many of her ex-pupils are now reputable florists. She also runs Partners Flowers at 27 Horsemarket, Barnard Castle, where you can buy unusual foliage grown in her gardens and greenhouses. She dislikes stereotyped arrangements, preferring to use fewer flowers and more foliage, pods, seed heads and berries. She covers Durham, Northumberland and North Yorkshire.

AVVY ROPNER
Dalesend, Patrick Brompton, Bedale,
N. Yorkshire (0677) 50207

Church and reception only. In church, she does vast formal pedestal arrangements, flower balls hanging from the arches and decorated columns. She loves roses, lilies and sweet peas in season, but can obtain any exotic type of flower. Mainly big weddings in Yorkshire and a few in London and the South.

SECTION IV

CATERING

There is a school of thought that considers food at a wedding reception of minor importance as long as the wine is good and plentiful: if bubbly be the food of love, swill on. Whether you celebrate your nuptials with nibbles, noggins or a Bacchanalian feast, it is certainly one of the most important aspects of your wedding. As photographer Tom Hustler points out, 'People forget that, above all, a wedding has to be a good party. Better to have fewer guests than not enough drink.' And people are unlikely to remember the glory of your lily of the valley or the resonance of the *Trumpet Voluntary* above the misery of dog-eared sandwiches and one lone glass of Harvey's Bristol Cream/Asti Spumante/Pomagne.

The factors determining your style of catering are budget, the number of guests and the time of the wedding. If the guest list exceeds 100 or so it is wise to use an outside caterer, unless you are a professional with plenty of staff on hand. If your budget and numbers are modest you could prepare the food yourself with the help of trusted friends.

What time of day?

Most people choose a time — as far as is possible in fitting in with the church — that corresponds to the type of reception they wish to have and can afford. An afternoon cocktail party with bite-size eats is cheaper than a full lunch or dinner, although it does depend on drink — if cocktails means non-stop champagne, it could match the expense of a mere wine-washed lunch. Everyone you talk to will advise you differently as to the ideal time. It boils down to personal preference.

Morning marriages could be followed by a wedding breakfast/brunch of, say, creamy scrambled eggs, kedgeree, devilled kidneys, hot croissants, Buck's Fizz and steaming real coffee. In practice, this only works well for a small party, as scrambled eggs × 200 will be unpalatably hard and watery, croissants soggy and so on. Far-travelled guests may feel a bit flat if the party ends at lunchtime. But if the catering is reliable and it's a smallish informal crowd, brunch is a scrumptious, cheapish option.

If you marry around noon, lunch is on the menu. Increasingly popular and one of the most successful options, it's hampered only by budget and space. There is a focal point to the party — particularly for guests who have come a long way — and everyone departs feeling well wined, dined and happy. It avoids rushed pre-wedding lunches and guests getting over-drunk (too much alcohol on an empty stomach). Lunch could be a served, sit-down affair or a buffet — or somewhere in-between (starters on the table, buffet main course, served pudding). Hotels tend to cater for sit-down lunches with a top table, seating plan and full service. Most people agree this is too formal and inflexible and there's the horror of being placed on a boring table (top table can be top yawn, particularly if it's facing the reception with the bridal party in a row — no one can mix and young bridesmaids and pages often get stuck next to unknown grown-ups).

The ideal set-up, in the eyes of James Forbes of Spats, is a buffet lunch. It doesn't have to be too extortionate as you can save on champagne by serving wine during lunch, just topping up the glasses with champers for the speeches. Don't lay tables, he suggests, as people can't then join friends at tables with their full quota of diners. Just put cloths on the tables and have knives, forks, napkins and plenty of chairs readily available.

Making merry: a slap-up sit-down lunch and an afternoon reception delight young and old alike.
(**Above:** Belgrave Press Bureau)
(**Right:** Tom Hustler)

However, it is worth designating a few tables for relations and making sure grannies and great uncles aren't pushed out in the fray.

The traditional reception, and the one Lady Elizabeth Anson recommends for economy's sake, is an afternoon cocktail-cum-tea party. It's a two- to three-hour bash with plenty of booze and a finger buffet: short and sweet. The only disadvantage is that it can leave guests rather drunk, disorientated and hungover at an awkward time of day. But it does mean the bride and groom can depart for their hotel, change and have dinner in an unhurried fashion. If there is no party in the evening, guests often make their own arrangements to go out to dinner somewhere nearby.

The mid-afternoon wedding slot is not the best if you *are* having a dance. One well-worn guest thinks there should be no gap between wedding and dance because everyone feels deflated and hungover by evening. It also means you are giving two parties in one day, tanking people up with drink twice. Ideal timing is a late-afternoon wedding leading into a drinks party, dinner and dance.

Finally, your late-afternoon wedding could be followed by a drinks party and/or dinner.

Drinks-only works well in London, where most guests live locally, but isn't very suitable for country weddings where guests may have travelled a long way and may have to stay in the neighbourhood overnight. Dinner with no dance suggests a degree of formality and haute cuisine — impressive but expensive. The most obvious venue for this would be a hotel, restaurant, club or large private house (rather than a hall or marquee). A buffet is usual if there is a dance as well.

Caterers

A good, experienced caterer is a boon. Not only will they take all the hassle of providing victuals out of your hands, but more often than not, they will have the knowledge and contacts of a party planner and will impart the information for free. This is because they take commission from all services they subcontract to, but don't charge *you* for their time. They can advise you on venues, marquee hire, toastmasters, florists, photographers, and more. Often these wedding services will have worked together before, so they are well informed and can justly recommend each

F I N G E R   B U F F E T

132

The Toastmaster with the mostest

IVOR SPENCER
12 Little Bornes, London SE21
(01) 670 5585

The diminutive red-coated toastmaster is a legendary figure at weddings. President of the Guild of Professional Toastmasters, he also runs a school for toastmasters and another for butlers. On top of announcing guests as they enter the reception and introducing the speakers, he acts as liaison officer between bride and her parents and the head waiter, photographer and so on. He also organizes the whole shooting match, as he did for Mark Thatcher and Diane Bergdorf. If you can't secure him (price negotiable), he can send one of his graduates for £100 plus VAT in London (outside costs a little more).

However, Freddie Meynell of Searcy's suggests you only need a toastmaster if it's a large formal do; otherwise, the head waiter can introduce speakers and announce the cake-cutting and going away, although this is not ideal.

(Art Zeesman Photography)

other (although it may be wise to double-check with past clients for impartial reports). A few caterers charge extra for their party-planning service — make sure you are aware of such fees.

It is most important to shop around a little for your caterer. Personal recommendation has to be the best introduction, but obtain several estimates. You can work out a menu together if their set ideas don't suit. Note the following points:

- Ask for a detailed breakdown of charges, since they can cover any combination of services (delivery? overtime? tips? service charge? equipment hire? corkage? travelling expenses? party planning? etc.)
- How many staff will you need for your number of guests?
- Are they prepared to stay if the reception runs over the estimated time?
- Will staff expect to be paid after the reception?

- Exactly how much food is included in the price — how many canapés calculated per head?
- Do they re-plate left-over food for you, or take it away?
- Will they need access to kitchen facilities and for how long?
- If in a marquee, will they need a water supply? A service tent?
- Do they provide all equipment (including, for example, a cake knife even if they are not supplying the cake)?
- How long will they take to clear up? Are they known to leave everything in excellent order?

Drink

Compare wine prices — it could well be more economical to buy your own (on a sale or return basis), but you may have to pay a corkage fee. Clear this with your caterers and make sure they will provide ice, glasses and bar equipment. If you are going to have a pay bar, find out whether the caterer has a licence to sell drink. They should organize the licence themselves, and get an extension if you are having a late-night party.

A question of bubbles

Some people wouldn't dream of throwing a wedding bash without a good — and they may insist on vintage — champagne and champagne alone. This would normally be for a drinks-party reception. If you are providing lunch, you suffer no loss of face in serving a good wine with the meal. Or you could have both champagne and wine on tap (Searcy's find that when they serve both, a quarter of the guests choose wine). Pink champagne, is *très* à la mode and no longer dismissed by wine buffs (not that it's any cheaper than the ordinary stuff). Other party-givers insist on proper champagne for the toasts, but don't mind still wine throughout the reception (there is certainly no point in having both real champagne and sparkling wine — one just shows up the other). Others

Nuptial fizz. But which one popped the question? (Tom Hustler)

like the bubbles but would settle for a *méthode champenoise* or sparkling wine. There are some fine sparklers available, but do choose carefully. Caterers will supply or recommend wines. Or go to a reputable wine merchant or off-licence (Oddbins, Peter Dominic, Victoria Wine are well regarded) and ask their advice.

Avoid cheap, sweet, fizzy wines which will induce throbbing hangovers. Avoid, too, sticky-sweet sherry — guests will want a clean-tasting, refreshing drink, not a cough cure. Good, interesting, sparkling wine buys are Clairette de Die (about £4.50) and Crémant de Bourgogne Rosé (about £5), both from Waitrose; G. F. Cavalier Blanc de Blancs Sec (under £3) and Jean Perico Brut (a Spanish *méthode champenoise*, about £4), both from Oddbins. The best supermarket chains for wine are Waitrose, Sainsbury's and Tesco, in that order. If you go for their house champagne (under £8 a bottle) or *méthode champenoise*, you won't go far wrong. Another cheaper alternative is to serve Buck's Fizz, mixing the orange juice with a dry sparkling wine instead of champagne.

For a drinking wine, a light, fruity, non-acidic, medium-dry German or Alsace white glugs down well. As a fun alternative for country weddings, Searcy's suggest English wines from Sussex, Kent and Hampshire, which have a similar style to a Moselle or Hock. You may want something drier, plus a red, to go with food. At an evening party, you could offer spirits. A bottle of whisky costs the same as a bottle of champagne but goes much further. Searcy's find that Admirals and Generals always ask for a whisky on the sly, so they recommend secreting a bottle or two for special guests. If you do have spirits, be sure to ask for left-overs back. The staff may open several bottles, pour one or two tots, and then charge you for the whole bottle. One man who married in the Seventies is still living off his wedding booze. Always have soft drinks available — mineral water and orange juice (pure, not powdered, tinned or squash, which is a nasty shock to carton-weaned tastebuds).

At Naval weddings they drink more than average, at Army weddings slightly less.

Freddie Meynell of Searcy's suggests:

- Serve white wine in goblets and champagne in tulips so that waiters can top up appropriately without forever asking which drink.
- Stinge hint: If you have a 1:30 or lower staff-guest ratio you save money on staff *and* drink — less wine will be consumed as it won't ever reach those thirsty mouths, but be prepared for grumbly guests. For a good party, it's essential to circulate the drink.
- Guests eat more at country weddings — allow up to 18 canapés each instead of the abstemious townies' 12.
- For winter weddings, try a hot punch on arrival (the tastiest uses cheapo red plonk and brandy and spices), which warms the cockles and weakens the knees, followed by wine, Kir or champagne.
- If you are having a self-service meal, place small buffet tables all round the edges of the room/marquee with enough food for about four guest tables each, rather than a big table at one end — it cuts out queues completely and means everyone can be eating within about 15 minutes.
- Seating plans: for informal bashes, reserve some tables near the cake for VIPs and let the rest arrange themselves. For smallish, semi-formal affairs (around 100), have a plan pinned up with everyone's table number (though he thinks it unnecessary to have individual placement at the table). Large parties mean congestion round the table plan, so give each guest a card with their table number on it when they leave their coat.

DIY catering

If numbers are manageable and you have a reliable, keen team of helpmates, you and/or mother could organize and prepare the catering for your wedding. The golden rule is to make a detailed plan of action and to dish out the duties from stage one, so that everyone knows exactly what is expected of them. Make a countdown checklist, and stick to it rigorously.

You will almost certainly need to borrow or hire cooking equipment, china, cutlery, extra chairs, an urn for boiling water, heated trays, etc. (see your local *Yellow Pages* for hire companies). You may also have to book fridge and freezer space with the neighbours. That you can freeze food will reduce most of the last-minute panic, but do leave ample time for defrosting and for presentation and arrangement (a task which is best delegated, as it must be done on the day). Do check which foods freeze well and will not suffer in the defrosting.

Have staff posted to serve, clear and wash up on the day. Unless the reception is at home, it may be wise to stick to cold food. If you *are* having hot food, delegate all kitchen duties. The bride's mother is the hostess and must be free to introduce guests at the reception. For cocktails and buffets you'll need people in the kitchen, handing round, and manning the bar and buffet table. Have each course cleared and washed up as it is finished, so that there is no pile-up at the end.

Catering calculations

Stand-up afternoon cocktails

7 sq ft (5.85 m^2) a head
1:20 staff–guest ratio
12 canapés a head (London) ⎫
18 canapés a head (country) ⎭
Half to two-thirds bottle a head

Sit-down buffet lunch

15 sq ft (12.54 m^2) a head
1:20 staff–guest ratio
Two-thirds to one bottle a head

Sit-down served dinner

15 sq ft (12.54 m^2) a head
1:10 staff–guest ratio
Two-thirds to one bottle a head

What food?

Don't be too ambitious: avoid elaborate recipes from your French cookery books; nothing too rich, spicy, sauce-ridden, fiddly or over-decorated — just good, fresh, top-quality food in ample quantities. Magazines, cookery books and caterers' menus offer inspiration. Test out any new recipes beforehand, and work out quantities carefully.

A finger buffet is the most informal arrangement and gives you scope to try all manner of canapés. This is no soft option — a good deal of care needs to be taken. As guests will be standing while they eat, probably without a plate, food should be one-bit-size, non-drip and non-crumbly. On the other hand, there is nothing so unappetizing as dry, stodgy foods such as sausage rolls that are all chewy pastry and no sausage, bridge rolls and sandwiches

that are all stale bread and no filling, unforgiving quiche. Hot canapés such as angels on horseback or sausages must tread the fine line between scalding and lukewarm; a platter of cold, congealed, greasy titbits is enough to turn any stomach. And things spread on biscuits can turn them soggy.

Hot little quiches, tartlets, baby pizzas, choux puffs, feta-filled filo parcels, stuffed mushrooms, herby sausage, scampi, chicken satay sticks and so on are delicious provided they are served at the right temperature and have enough filling/dip. Successful cold eats are asparagus wrapped in fine brown bread, cream cheese wrapped in ham, ditto in smoked salmon, dates filled with cream cheese and walnuts, crudités (carrots, cauliflower, cucumber sticks, baby tomatoes) with dips (Sainsbury's and Marks & Spencer make life easy with taramasalata, hummus, and fresh mayonnaise), wedges of Brie, jumbo prawns and crab claws with dip, tiny springily fresh sandwiches, mini meringues and éclairs — the list is endless, the message is *freshness*.

Lunch is less fiddly. You can't go wrong with a cold buffet — a whole succulent salmon, joints of rare beef and ham, turkey, a Coronation Chicken-style dish, quiches, easy-to-eat salads — potato (jazzed up with spring onions and crispy bacon) and a hundred-and-one permutations of rice, pasta, beans, crispy lettuce, radicchio, mange-touts, grated carrot, cucumber, radishes, tomatoes, apple, celery, nuts, coleslaw, etc. Follow with strawberries and cream, biscuits and cheese, coffee. Take advantage of garden produce — one father of the bride was so well organized that he was able to plant vegetables and fruit in the spring that were just ready for picking by the time of the wedding. You could pick your own fruit at a local farm and freeze it if necessary. The advantage of a hot meal is you can make casseroles and goulashes in advance, freeze them, and then just heat them up on the day. You could serve salads, rice, pasta and/or hot bread with them.

If the wedding is small and informal, you could ask friends to provide a dish each. One bride provided the main course and asked all her friends to contribute either a summer pudding or a chocolate mousse for dessert.

Drink for DIYs

Most off-licences will provide wine on a sale-or-return basis and many will hire out glasses, too. They may not be the cheapest suppliers of ice, so check in your *Yellow Pages* for local ice suppliers and compare prices. If you have champagne or white wine, you will need plenty of ice and somewhere to put it (make sure everyone has a bath before the ice is delivered!). The general rule for quantity is half-a-bottle a head for a stand-up-and-shout,

and a bottle a head for a sit-down-and-swig — people drink more with food and when they're sitting down. Experience shows that the more there is the more is drunk. Things run more smoothly if wine is handed round rather than freely available at a bar. If you *do* have a bar, make sure you have a responsible ally behind it.

Lady Elizabeth Anson on . . . budget catering

' It is difficult when you can't afford to drink champagne all through the reception but you want to toast with bubbles. What you need is a double set of glasses — wine throughout, and champagne handed out during the speeches. You can cut down tremendously on the food side. Financially, it is better to get married in the afternoon than the morning. Between 3 and 6 pm, you can get away with hot sausages done in honey and herbs, small eggs, cucumber or tomato sandwiches in brown and white bread alternated on the plate and tiny little cakes — meringues, brandy snaps, Florentines and éclairs.

For lunchtime receptions you really have to have a buffet. The cheapest way is to decide on one or two main courses — a lovely chicken salad and a fish mousse, for example — plus some salads, and not endless different dishes; the more variety you have the more wastage you will get. I did one lunchtime wedding where the couple were giving a party with dinner that evening, so they served very extensive and extremely good canapés for lunch — a meal of titbits. I got Anton Mosimann from the Dorchester to do them.'

At Hollywood-actress Lana Turner's wedding reception, there were life-size statues of the bride and groom carved in ice and giant baked hams with 'I love you' written in pimentos.

The cake

'Society cakes', proclaims *The Tatler*, 'unlike Society brides, are dressed in white, stark-white.'

You can take a colour theme too far. But white trimmed with pale pink roses or peach icing swags could hardly offend and Harriet Monckton's cake (by Searcy's) in a buttery cream that matched her dress was nothing if not tasteful (see colour photograph opposite page 128). Square or round in three tiers is the norm, leaving room for a little or a lot of creative licence. The cake and its table are customarily further adorned with fresh flowers (see photograph on page 124).

Colin Cowdrey's three tiers were surrounded by sugar cricket balls, bats and stumps. Ronald Reagan's wedding cake was a life-size sugar cast of himself. Paula Yates and Bob Geldof had masses of kitsch mauve rosebuds on a white cake — both times. Helena-Jane Romer chose a post-modernist pyramid cake with blue 'snooker balls' holding each tier. Anna Thompson had two cakes — a fairty-tale castle (for her, a landscape architect) and a sports car (for him, a motoring maniac). Another bride played the violin and her beau was a sci-fi fan, so their cake was decorated with notes from the theme music of the film *2001 — A Space Odyssey*.

DIY cake

Your mother or a friend may be able to make your cake (it is supposed to be bad luck to make it yourself). It's wise to ask a professional to ice it. Start about three months in advance of the day: a rich fruit cake, with brandy or another spirit lovingly applied (the Duchess of York's cake was laced with rum, brandy *and* port), will mature irresistibly (but never freeze it). In calculating the size of cake, remember: (a) an extra layer is usually made for cutting before the reception, to avoid a delay in handing it round; (b) it is traditional to save the top tier of the cake for the christening of the first baby (if you completely seal it in tin foil and then in an air-tight tin, it will keep for many years). As well as accounting for guests at the reception, don't forget absent friends — especially present-giving ones — to whom you may want to send slices (you can order cake boxes from a

Baby you can drive my car: Anna Thompson and Al Joyce's red sports car cake.
(Clare Faull)

Home sweet home: the bride's weekend retreat rests atop the groom's house. The bride's mother was horrified but the bride insisted there was no suggestion of female domination.
(Moira Leggat)

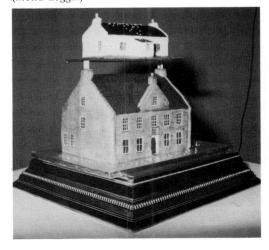

stationer). Estimate eight to ten portions per pound of cake.

Tiers must be balanced in size — good proportions for a three-tier cake are 12 in, 9 in and 6 in (30.5 cm, 23 cm and 15 cm); two-tier, 12 in and 8 in (3.05 cm and 20.5 cm), 11 in and 7 in (28 cm and 18 cm) or 10 in and 6 in (25.5 cm and 15 cm). The bottom tier should be deeper than the. rest. Some bakers and confectioners will hire out cake tins and boards (which should be at least 2 in (5 cm) larger than the cake).

Good Housekeeping's classic rich fruit cake recipe

Square tin size		6 in (15 cm) square	7 in (18 cm) square	8 in (20.5 cm) square
Round tin size	6 in (15 cm) diameter	7 in (18 cm) diameter	8 in (20.5 cm) diameter	9 in (23 cm) diameter
Currants	8 oz (225 g)	12 oz (350 g)	1 lb (450 g)	1 lb 6 oz (625 g)
Sultanas	4 oz (100 g)	4½ oz (125 g)	7 oz (200 g)	8 oz (225 g)
Raisins	4 oz (100 g)	4½ oz (125 g)	7 oz (200 g)	8 oz (225 g)
Glacé cherries	2 oz (50 g)	3 oz (75 g)	5 oz (150 g)	6 oz (175 g)
Mixed peel	1 oz (25 g)	2 oz (50 g)	3 oz (75 g)	4 oz (100 g)
Flaked almonds	1 oz (25 g)	2 oz (50 g)	3 oz (75 g)	4 oz (100 g)
Lemon rind	a little	a little	a little	¼ lemon
Plain flour	6 oz (175 g)	7½ oz (215 g)	12 oz (350 g)	14 oz (400 g)
Mixed spice	¼ level tsp (1.25 ml)	½ level tsp (2.5 ml)	½ level tsp (2.5 ml)	1 level tsp (5 ml)
Cinnamon	¼ level tsp (1.25 ml)	½ level tsp (2.5 ml)	½ level tsp (2.5 ml)	1 level tsp 5 ml)
Butter	5 oz (150 g)	6 oz (175 g)	10 oz (275 g)	12 oz (350 g)
Sugar	5 oz (150 g)	6 oz (175 g)	10 oz (275 g)	12 oz (350 g)
Eggs, beaten	2½	3	5	6
Brandy	1 tbsp (15 ml)	1 tbsp (15 ml)	1–2 tbsp (15.30 ml)	2 tbsp (30 ml)
Time (approx.)	2½–3 hours	3 hours	3½ hours	4 hours
Weight when cooked	2½ lb (1.1 kg)	3¼ lb (1.6 kg)	4¾ lb (2.2 kg)	6 lb (2.7 kg)

Square tin size	9 in (27 cm) square	10 in (25.5 cm) square	11 in (28 cm) square	12 in (30.5 cm) square
Round tin size	10 in (25.5 cm) diameter	11 in (28 cm) diameter	12 in (30.5 cm) diameter	
Currants	1 lb 12 oz (775 g)	2 lb 8 oz (1.1 kg)	3 lb 2 oz (1.5 kg)	3 lb 12 oz (1.7 kg)
Sultanas	13 oz (375 g)	14 oz (400 g)	1 lb 3 oz (525 g)	1 lb 6 oz (625 g)
Raisins	13 oz (375 g)	14 oz (400 g)	1 lb 3 oz (525 g)	1 lb 6 oz (625g)
Glacé cherries	9 oz (250 g)	10 oz (275 g)	12 oz (350 g)	15 oz (425 g)
Mixed peel	5 oz (150 g)	7 oz (200 g)	9 oz (250 g)	10 oz (275 g)
Flaked almonds	5 oz (150 g)	7 oz (200 g)	9 oz (250 g)	10 oz (275 g)
Lemon rind	¼ lemon	½ lemon	½ lemon	1 lemon
Plain flour	1 lb 5 oz (600 g)	1 lb 8 oz (700 g)	1 lb 13 oz (825 g)	2 lb 6 oz (1 kg)
Mixed spice	1 level tsp (5 ml)	2 level tsp (10 ml)	2½ level tsp (12.5 ml)	2½ level tsp (12.5 ml)
Cinnamon	1 level tsp (5 ml)	2 level tsp (10 ml)	2½ level tsp (12.5 ml)	2½ level tsp (12.5 ml)
Butter	1 lb 2 oz (500 g)	1 lb 5 oz (600 g)	1 lb 12 oz (800 g)	2 lb 2 oz (950 g)
Sugar	1 lb 2 oz (500 g)	1 lb 5 oz (600 g)	1 lb 12 oz (800 g)	2 lb 2 oz (950 g)
Eggs, beaten	9	11	14	17
Brandy	2–3 tbsp (30–45 ml)	3 tbsp (45 ml)	4 tbsp (60 ml)	6 tbsp (90 ml)
Time (approx.)	6 hours	7 hours	8 hours	8½ hours
Weight when cooked	9 lb (4 kg)	11½ lb (5.2 kg)	14¾ lb (6.7 kg)	17 lb (7.7 kg)

139

1. Grease and line the cake tin for the size of cake you wish to make, using a double thickness of greaseproof paper. Tie a double band of brown paper round the outside.

2. Prepare the ingredients for the appropriate size of cake according to the chart. Wash and dry all the fruit, if necessary, chopping any over-large pieces, and mix well together in a large bowl. Add the flaked almonds. Sift flour and spices into another bowl with a pinch of salt.

3. Put the butter, sugar and lemon rind into a bowl and cream together until pale and fluffy. Add the beaten eggs, a little at a time, beating well.

4. Gradually fold the flour lightly into the mixture with a metal spoon, then fold in the brandy. Finally fold in the fruit and nuts.

5. Turn the mixture into the prepared tin, spreading it evenly and making sure there are no air pockets. Make a hollow in the centre to ensure an even surface when cooked.

6. Stand the tin on newspaper or brown paper in the oven and bake at 150°C (300°F, Gas Mark 2) for the required time (see chart), until a fine warmed skewer inserted in the centre comes out clean. Cover with greaseproof paper after about 1½ hours.

7. When cooked, leave the cake to cool in the tin before turning out onto a wire rack. Prick the top all over with a fine skewer and slowly pour 2–3 tablespoons (30–45 ml) brandy over it before storing.

8. Wrap the cake in a double thickness of greaseproof paper and place upside down in an airtight tin. Cover with foil to store.

NB: when baking large cakes, 10 in (25 cm) and upwards, it is advisable to reduce the oven heat to 130°C (250°F, Gas Mark ½) after two-thirds of the cooking time.

Every two or three weeks, unwrap it and apply more brandy. Two to three weeks before the wedding, it's time to cover the cake with almond paste and, a few days later, to start icing. This is a skilled business, and should only be attempted if you are experienced.

When President Nixon's daughter, Patricia, married in 1971, the White House chef made a lemon sponge cake with white icing. He published the recipe so that all America could eat the same cake on the day, but he made a mistake in the calculations and the whole country nearly drowned in a flood of lemon goo.

This cake represents the three rings that Paul Berrow has given his bride, Miranda Nicolle. Tier one is the ring he gave her when they met, tier two the engagement ring and tier three the wedding ring. Each ring, designed by Paul, was made in a different gold. (Richard Taylor)

Cakes through the ages

In the early sixteenth century wedding cakes were little more than dry biscuits, baked for the ritual breaking over the bride's head. Elizabeth I's reign saw the rise of eggs, sugar, currants and spices, although the cakes were still used as missiles or crumbled over the poor bride's head. Carolean cakes, influenced by the flamboyant French, became richer and were lavishly decorated with marzipan and icing. At first, the icing was put over a mound of little cakes to give the impression of one extravaganza, but underneath still lay the lethal little weapons. The seventeenth century brought the custom for two cakes — a groom's cake that was rich and fruity and a bride's cake that was light, with spun sugar ornaments. Present-day cakes are a combination of the two.

Cake lore

To taste the cake before the wedding will cause a bride to forfeit her husband's love (though whether this applies to dipping into the raw mixture, we do not know). The bride must cut the cake, with the groom's help, or she will be childless. She should then preserve some cake, to ensure her husband's lifelong fidelity. And for luck, the couple should exchange and eat a morsel, after which every guest must join them in eating the cake. Single guests used to indulge in 'cake threading', which involved threading a piece of wedding cake through the bride's ring nine times and then sleeping with this under their pillow to dream of their future spouses. The tradition still holds, minus the actual threading. A bridesmaid who carries a piece of wedding cake in her pocket until the honeymoon is over will soon marry. After the first wedding in a family, part of the cake should be kept in the house until all the unmarried daughters are wed or they are destined to be spinsters.

ROYAL CAKES

Queen Victoria's cake was decorated with traditional cupids and a figure of Britannia. When Princess Marina of Greece married Prince George, Duke of Kent, in 1934, seven solid gold charms were baked into the lower tier. The cake itself was 9 ft (2.7 m) tall, weighed 800 lbs (363 kg) and was made with ingredients from the British Empire, plus Greek currants sent to the bride by Greek maidens.

The Queen had *twelve* official cakes presented to her by different baking companies — Huntley & Palmer made a four-tier cake; Peek Frean capped that with a six-tier affair made from ingredients from the Commonwealth countries and with a sugar figure of St George on a rearing horse on top; but McVitie & Price made the cake that was chosen for the reception — 9 ft (2.7 m) high and 500 lb (227 kg), it had four tiers supported by silver pillars and decorated with the armorial bearings of the bride and groom, with sugar plaques depicting Buckingham Palace, Windsor Castle and Balmoral, figures illustrating the sporting activities and interests of the pair, and dozens of crests, shields and badges.

Sarah and Andrew had two (one for real, one understudy) 5 ft 6 in (1.7 m), 17-stone (108 kg) cakes with five square tiers, painted thus: Tier 1 — Westminster Abbey, Buckingham Palace, Admiralty Arch and Dummer House; Tier 2 — crests of the naval ships in which Prince Andrew has served; Tier 3 — Sarah's coat of arms, her favourite painting, *Sunflowers* by Van Gogh, and a Pegasus (no one knows *why* a Pegasus); Tier 4 — Andrew's armorial bearings; Tier 5 — an entwined A and S in gold.

Caterers

(See also pages 147-149.)

All the caterers listed can bake — or organize — the cake.

N.B: almost all charges below are subject to VAT.

London

THE ADMIRABLE CRICHTON
71 Palfrey Place, London SW8
(01) 735 1740

John Robertson-Roxburgh and Rolline Williamson cook up mouth-wateringly delicious menus and come highly recommended by past clients. Hot and cold canapés start at £4.50 a head (a choice of eight canapés each plus cheese and anchovy straws and roasted nuts). Their long list of original eats includes apricots and almonds wrapped in bacon, sushi with duck and fresh ginger, croustade with chicken livers and grapes flambéd in Calvados, an orange muffin crammed with rowan jelly and finely sliced smoked ham, and goujons of beef sautéd in brandy with sour cream dip. A buffet for 200 with chicken and black grapes, pecans and Roquefort, rice with prawns and an exotic fruit salad beautifully presented in a flower-studded ice bowl would be £8.30 per head. A sit-down meal including Scottish salmon and sole, roast veal and chocolate marquise with raspberries would be £15.45. Their wine list ranges from a house white at £30.95 a case to Bollinger Special Cuvée at £153.

BY WORD OF MOUTH
47 Eglantine Road, London SW18
(01) 874 2417

Highly recommended by other wedding services. Michael Lloyd-Owen and his wife are party planners as well as caterers — an advantage if you want the whole day pro-fessionally organized, as you don't get middle-man charges for food and drink. They'll print menus, supply china and cutlery, erect a marquee, provide a live band, disco and fireworks and arrange a helicopter to fly you away. Interesting venues and first-class uniformed waitresses, barmen and toastmasters. A fork buffet may include starters of a terrine of salmon layered with spinach and monkfish mousse, parma ham filled with asparagus mousse or an avocado ring mould filled with olives, tomatoes and watercress; main courses of seafood quiche, beef salad Nicoise or veal with spinach, cream cheese and crispy bacon (all cold), hot or cold paella, or a variety of hot chicken dishes, beef Carbonnade or à la Bourguignonne or a seafood casserole. Dozens of salads, and puddings such as caramelized apples, grapes and oranges with brandy snaps, liqueur cake with Bavarian orange cream or fruit crème brûlée. No prices, as they prefer to do individual quotes for clients. They catered for Jane Gilmour's lavish wedding at Syon House near Kew.

CAROLINE'S KITCHEN
52 Pembroke Road, London W8
(01) 603 9788

Small catering business specializing in finger foods drawn from international cuisines, such as crispy potato skins with sour-cream dip, jumbo prawns with garlic mayonnaise, tiny spring rolls, Tandoori chicken with dip, sashimi, nachos or crudités with guacamole, a variety of kebabs. Suggested menus from £2.50 to £6 a head. Also cold buffet lunches with dishes from £1.50 a head (pâtés and salads) to £7.50 (salmon, lobster, partridge, etc.). Caroline believes in natural cuisine (super-fresh ingredients, a minimum of fats) and fine presentation. Staff and equipment can be organized if required. Free delivery in central London.

CLARE'S KITCHEN
41 Chalcot Road, London NW1
(01) 586 8433

Clare Latimer, who runs this small per-sonalized business, catered for the weddings of Michael Sellers (son of Peter) and Donald Sinden's sons. Hot or cold cocktail foods go from £3.50 to £4.50 a head, including crab sticks, stuffed vine leaves, ham and pepper Brie and barbecued meatballs. Buffets from £10.50 a head include dishes like pancakes stuffed with ham and asparagus mousse, chicken carabela with fresh grapes or mango; or for £12.50, things like filo parcels with crab and leek, Boursin and spinach or Camembert and cranberry, warm goat's cheese salad, lobster and scallops or ugli duckling (duck with ugli fruit). Excellent cheeses (including handmade English country cheeses) and an extensive wine list. They can supply staff, marquees, tables and chairs, etc.

FLAMBÉ
5 Broderick Road, London SW17
(01) 767 0865

Gillie Rowland-Clark has many loyal clients. She can organize marquees, butlers, wait-resses, invitations, flowers and so on, on top of her own catering service, which has ex-tended to receptions in the Tower of London and St James's Palace.

GASTRONOMIQUE
25 Red Lion Street, London WC1
(01) 242 9997; 405 2224

John Barraclough can supply staff, china, silverware, linen, flowers, a dance floor, disco and a venue to put it all in — from a livery hall or an elegant art gallery to a sailing barge. No charge for finding you a venue. All food is prepared by their team of cooks using fresh ingredients of the best quality. Finger buffets start at £4.50 a head and canapés from £3.00 a head. They have a suggested menu for weddings at £7.50 a head which allows 14 canapés (mini quiches, tartlets, chicken kebabs, scampi in bacon, steak tartare croûtes) plus half a round of wholemeal

sandwiches per person and tea or coffee. The standard delivery charge for central London is £10. Champagnes range from Comte de Robart at £8.15 a bottle and Charles Heidsieck at £11.50 to Bollinger Special Cuvée at £14.50. No corkage fee, but they may charge to chill or move cases of wine.

HUNGRY HAMPERS
Unit 241, Wandsworth Business Centre,
89-96 Garratt Lane, London SW18
(01) 870 7041

Jilly Swyers can plan your party, provide professional staff, a venue, a marquee and all the usual fillings. She will make a personal visit — in or out of London — to discuss your requirements. On top of catering, theme parties and dances are a speciality and for one nautical family, she made crackers sealed with a sailor's knot, containing presents for the bridesmaids. Her cocktail menu includes beef satay, chicken Parmesan, scallops and fried wantons and a suggested lunch includes a whole dressed salmon, egg cream mousse, salads, chocolate roulade, Brie and fruit.

LEITH'S GOOD FOOD
1 Sebastian Street, London EC1
(01) 251 0216

It is Prue Leith's company that feeds the mouths on the Venice–Simplon-Orient Express. For weddings, contact Polly Tyrer, who can arrange the whole party package or just the catering and cake. Good on themes, from Victorian extravaganzas to French peasant parties with a wedding breakfast *en plein air*. They can supply unusual venues and equipment and theatrical decorations. Their delicious variation on champagne is the Bellini, a blend of fresh peach nectar or passion fruit juice with champagne (or spark-ling wine). They can also do freshly squeezed

orange juice. Dishes of canapés — prawn bouchés, mini kebabs, salmon and tarragon bites, chicken satay, etc. — are spruced up with napkin gondolas. Cocktail menus about £4.50 to £6 a head. Lunches and dinners stretch from the traditional cold collation to delicacies such as turbot and salmon plaits or pears with Roquefort and leek mousse, followed by boeuf en croûte or duck with apricots and pistachio, and endless dreamy puds. Lunches from £8 to around £14 plus a head.

J. LYONS CATERING
Manor House, Manor Farm Road, Alperton, Middlesex (01) 998 8880

J. Lyons does the catering for the Insurance Hall in the City, The Belvedere in Holland Park and Syon Park near Kew. Their subsidiary, Town & County Catering, organize and cater for almost all outdoor events — Wimbledon, the Derby, Royal Windsor Horse Show, etc., as well as society weddings, usually in marquees. They cater for the receptions in the beautiful Orangery in Holland Park. Anything from simple cocktail eats to six-course dinner menus.

MOVABLE FEASTS
83-85 Holloway Road, London N7
(01) 607 1178; 607 1555

Run by Nick Huntington and Tony Clare. For large receptions, one of their senior staff will visit to discuss menus and estimate costs. They can advise on wedding cakes, cars, photographers, flowers, discos, marquees and venues. If the reception is to be held in a marquee, they ask for a service tent; otherwise they need use of a kitchen. Finger buffet prices for 70-plus guests start at £4 for 12

items of food a head or £4.80 for 17 items (which they suggest is appropriate if guests have travelled far). Tea and iced coffee are included in all menus. For lunchtime receptions (100 guests minimum), they offer a more substantial finger buffet (£7 a head for 17 items) which includes king prawns, cubes of sirloin steak with béarnaise dip and smoked trout sandwiches. Wines (on sale or return) from £2.60 for a Blanc de Blancs; Perrier Jouet champagne £11.60; Bouvet Ladubay *méthode champenoise*, £6. Glasses, ice, cooling tubs and bar supplied free of charge with wine.

THE PIE MAN FOOD COMPANY
16 Cale Street, London SW3
(01) 225 0587 (shop); 23 Pensbury Street, London SW8 (01) 627 5232 (kitchen)

Friendly young company that can provide all the trimmings, from ice to flowers to a venue, as well as home-prepared food. A good selection of canapés (Scotch pancake blinis, Tandoori chicken kebabs, prawn tarts, caviar and smoked salmon chequerboard) costs about £3 a head. A cold buffet with spinach and smoked haddock mousse or chilled cucumber and shrimp soup followed by exotic meat salads and chocolate roulade costs £8 a head; for £11, you graduate to crab conquests (Scotch smoked salmon wrapped around crab and orange mousse), Beijing beef salad, chicken, avocado and melon salad, crème brûlée with raspberries and heavenly strawberry and mango pavlova.

SEARCY TANSLEY & COMPANY
124 Bolingbroke Grove, London SW11
(01) 585 0505

These old hands have been established 150 years, catering for about 300 weddings a year, 2,000 of which have been tended by director Freddie Meynell. He and fellow directors will

visit you to discuss catering (they like to originate a special menu with you), marquee hire, venus, and any other services you would like help with — for which there is no charge. Their degree of involvement is up to you. They specialize in private house affairs, be it your own or theirs (30 Pavilion Road, their swanky Georgian house near Sloane Street) or a hired stately such as Ham House or Osterley Park — they have dozens of private contacts around London, the Home Counties and Hampshire. Their staff are trained butlers and maids. Freddie organized a romantic dance in a glass-walled tent in the floodlit rose garden at Ham House, and arranged for one couple to be rowed away in a skiff down a stream lined with hand-held flaming procession torches. They do receptions for 100 up to enormous sit-down feasts — for 1,500 plus. N.B.: Searcy's charge about 15 per cent less from mid-January to early April.

SPATS
47 Kendal Street, London W2
(01) 262 0870; any time (0836) 201216

James Forbes does lots of film location catering, but enjoys doing weddings — not least his own recent Highland wedding (see page 108), where guests tucked into an out-door lunch of local poached salmon, oodles of salads, and raspberries and cream. The informal sit-down lunch is his favourite formula, as it skirts the problem of guests standing with their heels sinking deeper into the grass while balancing a glass of champagne and a plate full of eats and trying to look attentive to the yakkings of some un-known relation. He tailors menus specially to your needs, but, for example, canapés include mussels with marinière dip, savoury profiteroles with smoked trout mousse, pepper

salami and ricotta cheese sticks, salmon trout caviar blinis, and Stilton and marmalade parcels. He can provide jolly young staff, all equipment, marquees, lighting, and his own Discochef's Jazz Discothèque.

TOWN & COUNTY CATERING
See J. Lyons Catering, page 144.

Country and Scotland
COUNTRY COOKS
Home Farm House, Kennington, Ashford, Kent (0233) 21917

Diana McKenzie finds most of her wedding receptions require irresistible pop-in-the-mouth savoury and teatime eats. She often makes the wedding cake herself and has it iced. Either you or she can provide the drink, and she will supply butlers, ice, glasses, etc. Each menu tailored and priced individually. She visits the bride's mother and discusses the whole occasion, recommending toast-masters, marquee hire, photographers — the lot. There is, she feels, an art to discovering just how the bride's mother sees the wedding, whether she wants 'caviar or farm food'. Diana sees it as an important part of her role to nurse her through the occasion, and especially to support her on the day. 'The most sophisticated women are often very nervous. I tell them how stunning they look — which they always do — because nobody else takes the time to say it.'

KIMPTON KITCHEN
Vann Road, Fernhurst, Haslemere, Surrey (0428) 52043

David and Elizabeth Gillespie have been catering for weddings for nearly 20 years. All food is fresh, home-cooked, well presented and plentiful; any left-overs are re-plated and

left with you. Finger buffets for afternoon weddings from £5.45 (devils on horseback, cheese pastry boats filled with prawns, celery and Stilton boats, tiny sandwiches, etc.). The heartier £6.55 menu includes French bread and pâté, chicken drumsticks and fingers of pizza and quiche. Wedding cakes cost £4 per lb. They can hire a cake table, silver cake stand and knife (free for use with their own cakes); glasses, ice and bar equipment; and a team of helpful, experienced staff. Their own off-licence can provide a wide range of champagne and sparkling wines at competitive prices or you can supply your own at no corkage fee. The Gillespies will handle marquee hire, obtaining estimates and going along to the site at no extra expense. They will also recommend a florist, photographer and can provide a Rolls Royce or Daimler.

DEDE MARKS
Wighill Lane Farm, Healaugh, Tadcaster, N. Yorkshire (0937) 832569

Dede Marks does many local weddings, but can venture south. She likes to work with the bride's mother to ascertain the desired food, but a canapé menu (from £3.50) might include bacon wrapped round chicken livers, smoked salmon squares, savoury choux puffs, bite-size sandwiches, baby chocolate éclairs, fruit kebabs and home-made biscuits. A sit-down meal, depending on the number of staff and whether food is hot or cold, starts at around £10. All food is sent out to receptions on baskets, decorated with flowers and handed round so that none is left curling up in a corner. She can recommend cake-bakers and is known for her efficient, happy staff.

Cakes

London

ANNE FAYRER CAKES AND FLOWERS
66 Lower Sloane Street, London SW1
(01) 730 6277

All manner of wedding cakes, from traditional ones in the round, iced to your colourway, to mad-shaped and hand-painted cakes. Underneath lies a traditional fruit cake recipe 'with all the fruits and lots of booze'. They have disguised cakes as champagne bottles, clapper boards, buildings (although they stress that they're not actually architects), a tiered cabbage cake and one with two rabbits springing from a top hat. Allow at least four to six weeks — but the longer the better — for richer, for maturer. They have sent cakes to South Africa and Australia, but locals are expected to pick up. Also bridal flower arrangements in central London. Three-tier cake on a 10 in (25 cm) base, from £105; this would feed 150 people, allowing for the top tier to be kept for junior's christening.

HARRODS
Knightsbridge, London SW1 (01) 730 1234

Where Paula Yates ordered her round, step-tiered cake. Standard cakes range from a single, 8 in (20 cm) square that feeds 40 to 50 (£45), to a four-tier, 15 in (38 cm) cake to feed 400 to 450 (£365). A round cake for 30–40 guests costs £30, and a five-tier for 420–460, £410. A four-tier, 12 in (30 cm) hexagonal cake for 180–200 hungry mouths costs £185. They offer five different icing effects at £8.25 per tier.

PARTY PLANNING SERVICES

Party planners will organize any or every aspect of your wedding, reception and/or engagement party. Taping their experience, contacts and time to your budget, they can make the whole event run smoothly. They are a godsend to those trying to organize a wedding from a long distance or at short notice or who just don't have the time themselves. Planners have trade contacts that you could never get access to yourself and they can get wholesale prices on champagne and suchlike. The money saved on such bargain buys can often cover the planner's fees. They can advise you where to economize and where not to, offer ideas, and take the headache out of organization.

But beware — despite what planners may say, costs can mount. Most (but not *all*) charge for consultations, secretarial work and travel, and prices may increase for work undertaken outside office hours. An hour with the *grande dame* of party planning, Lady Elizabeth Anson, will set you back £50 in the office, £65 out; and if you require her services overseas, that's £760 a day.

Make sure you are aware of all costs you may be liable for. At worst, you are paying for a middle man with no skills other than experience and efficiency. One decorator points out that it is much easier for him to deal direct with the client and not a party planner because only then can he get a clear idea of the client's requirements. So, if you do really need a planner, make sure you're on the same wavelength. In general, they suit those with the cash but no time for, clue about or proximity to, the proceedings. They're not for those who want a strong hand in the planning themselves but don't know where to start — in that case, you'd be better off asking your caterer's advice.

Do note that there is a difference between the middle-man planner (usually called 'Party' something) and those who are attached to, for example, catering, discothèque or marquee businesses; here, there is closer contact with the creative team and they are less likely to charge consultation fees.

Party planners

All these planners can arrange everything to do with your wedding, or simply help co-ordinate parts of it. (See also pages 142-146.)

London

CHANCE ENTERTAINMENT
313 Brompton Road, London SW3
(01) 584 3206

Andrew Chance can arrange any style or scale of music; first-rate videos and photographs; lighting by Starlight (see page 161); floristry by their own small team or, for grand events, by John Plested (see page 128). They have organized receptions for Egyptian weddings that entail canopies and thrones and a dramatic spotlit zephyr (procession), and did the whole shebang for a Los Angeles couple who came over to London to marry. (See also page 162.)

JOFFIN'S PARTY PLANNING
1 Heliport Estate, Lombard Road, London SW11 (01) 350 0033

Originally in the disco-band biz, they now have two warehouses bursting with equipment that enables them to cut right down on subcontracting. They have frame tents, their own caterers, a florist and all manner of musical equipment and lighting. They will also organize the design and printing of your stationery, can provide a toastmaster, PA system, video, a sophisticated tape of the ceremony and a photographer. They travel anywhere and do not charge a consultancy fee. (See also pages 155 and 163.)

JULIANA'S
1023 Garratt Lane, London SW17
(01) 672 3691

William Bartholomew's well-known travelling discothèque from the Sixties has blossomed into a full party-planning business. They have their own marquees, dance floors, a team of designers, caterers and florists and, of course, discos and bands. They're particularly hot on interior or exterior lighting and special effects, and can advise on security, etc. (See also pages 156 and 163.)

PARTY LINE
53 Wimpole Street, London W1
(01) 935 2377

Over the past ten years, Lady Colwyn has built up an impressive list of contacts and an invaluable list of venues. She feels her service is especially of value to those who live abroad — one of her London weddings had to be organized by a father living in Dubai. She contracts work out in order to get the most suitable person for the job — flowers, floodlights, catering, marquees, invitations, cars, etc. Her speciality is music: her husband has his own dance band, the Three B Band, and a 15-piece orchestra, Lord Colwyn's Orchestra. Lady Colwyn has hundreds of musical contacts and can organize anything from a soloist (harp, flute, vocals . . .), choir or chamber music, to a jazz or steel band. Contact her as far in advance as possible, although she can step in at the last minute if necessary. Her consultancy fee is based on time — the more complicated the planning, the more expensive. However, she is careful to work to a client's budget.

PARTY ORGANISERS
8a Sterne Street, London W12
(01) 743 3810

Anthony Myers is particularly recommended by fellow party services for his high standards. Most of their work is for private houses. In the business since 1969, they cover the whole range of services and contract everything out. Every five years they do a survey of all catering and tent companies to ensure they are up to date with the very best. For each job, they offer clients at least two or three quotations from different companies, chosen for suitability and to meet the budget. Anthony Myers advises you give plenty of notice, which makes it easier to get economic quotes. They charge a consultancy fee but no travel or other hidden expenses.

PARTY PLANNERS
56 Ladbroke Grove, London W11
(01) 229 9666

The best-known of all, run by Lady Elizabeth Anson, who organizes all the royal bashes. They can do absolutely everything from accompanying you on wedding-list expeditions to printing and writing out invitations, taking replies and compiling final lists. An impeccable and lengthy list of sub-contractees and hire companies — florists, theatrical equipment, wine merchants, cabaret — which is ever-expanding ('I've just held auditions for a marvellous choir that will sing unaccompanied in church', enthuses Lady Elizabeth). They can cope with rushed weddings, and organized one in a week. Fees are charged for consultation (on a sliding scale according to experience) and secretarial work, but they tailor their service to your budget and reckon they'll save you money in the long run.

PARTY PROFESSIONALS
6 Linden Gardens, London W2
(01) 221 3438

Valli Watson and Annabel Guinness are invaluable at taking care of all the dull jobs like confirming all the various services in writing, sending out invitations, organizing placement and writing cards (which they say drives bride and mother mad). Their experience means they get the best possible service from hotel banqueting departments, and they are *au fait* with the drawbacks and advantages of most London hotels. Consultation (£25 plus VAT an hour) and secretarial fees are charged, but again, they shop around for low prices that the client could never obtain.

Bouffant tent lining, twinkly lighting, floral design and catering, all planned by Juliana's.
(Photograph courtesy of Juliana's)

VENUES

Finding the right venue for the reception is largely a matter of logistics. It should be as near the church as possible. If you live in the country and have a fair-sized garden, you will probably want to make use of it; then you will need a marquee (though some couples risk a wedding *en plein air*) and to organize the catering. Otherwise, you may choose a local hired hall or house, in which case catering could also be your responsibility. Hotels, clubs and restaurants take care of the whole reception — venue, decor, food, drink — which is less hassle, and makes it easier to keep tabs on your budget, but may lack individuality. In the end, the actual cost is swings and roundabouts — for example, you may not pay for venue hire with a hotel, but you pay double the price for champagne.

(See also pages 130-149 and 155-161.)

Hotels

London

A typical hotel wedding package, based on a two- to three-hour cocktail party, includes hire of reception room(s), flowers, toastmaster, changing rooms for the couple, half a bottle of champagne a head and canapés. Prices range from about £20 to £30 a head. Wedding cakes are normally charged for separately. Musicians, bands and discos can usually be arranged. Contact the Banqueting Manager for details.

THE BERKELEY
Wilton Place, Knightsbridge, London SW1
(01) 235 6000

Slick and modern, rated in the top five London hotels. The glittering mirrored ballroom holds 450 for cocktails, and anything from 70 to 180 seated. Smaller reception rooms, too.

CLARIDGE'S
Brook Street, London W1 (01) 629 8860

Sumptuous but discreet Thirties' hotel (see colour plates 1-4, 8 and colour photograph opposite page 128) where the royals have their Party Planned extravaganzas. The Ballroom Suite holds 200 seated, 350 for cocktails, and the French Salon, in shades of pink with elegant wall mouldings, accommodates 70 seated, 240 standing. Or you can combine these and other rooms for 800 guests.

DORCHESTER
Park Lane, London W1 (01) 629 8888

Another suave art deco palace which can accommodate up to 1,200. Canapé menus from £9.50 to £15.50, plus drink (house champagne £26). No room hire.

GROSVENOR HOUSE
86-90 Park Lane, London W1
(01) 499 6363

Old hands at banqueting. Finger buffet from £15 a head, plus drink, plus hire of the turquoise and gold ballroom (£1,000).

HYATT CARLTON TOWER
2 Cadogan Place, London SW1
(01) 235 5411

For up to 180 guests, the Tower Suite offers fantastic views over the city (more guests, less view — in the Ballroom). Wedding package, £23 to £25 a head.

HYDE PARK HOTEL
Knightsbridge, London SW1 (01) 235 2000

Impressive reception rooms overlooking the Park. The usual package (though their canapés sound more exotic listed in French), £22.50 or £26.50 a head, for 50 to 700 guests.

INN ON THE PARK
Hamilton Place, Park Lane, London W1 (01) 499 0888

A modern hotel renowned for their high standard of catering; very switched on to weddings. Their £30.50-a-head deal includes two-thirds a bottle of champagne plus white wine, a wedding cake and a nuptial suite with champagne breakfast. For 30 to 400 guests.

THE RITZ
Piccadilly, London W1 (01) 493 8181

Gorgeous, Louis XVI-style opulence, an overdose of golden swags, carving, marble and chandeliers. In summer, you can use the Terrace, where flowers tumble from stone vases and the Italian Garden overlooking Green Park, where you can erect a marquee to boost guest numbers from 300 to 400. Finger buffets from £10 to £18, plus room hire from £100, plus champagne from £22.50 a bottle.

SAVOY
The Strand, London WC2 (01) 836 4343

Based in the heart of theatreland, overlooking the Thames. The River Room costs £500, plus canapés from £13 a head, plus drink. The prettiest reception room is the French château-like Lancaster, with its Wedgwood blue-and-white mouldings; this is more suited to dinner-dance receptions, with a menu of around £25, but no room-hire charge.

Other venues

London

Apart from hotels, options in London encompass private clubs, livery halls, historic houses and restaurants. Gentlemen's clubs such as the Turf, Boodle's, Brooks, Garrick, Cavalry and Guards, etc., provide superb reception spaces with excellent catering — but they don't want the world and his wife-to-be clamouring for their canapés. However, if you *are* keen, their only stipulation is that you are sponsored by a member.

THE BELVEDERE
Holland House, Holland Park, London W8 (01) 602 1238

An elegant, airy restaurant attached to the Orangery in Holland Park (see also page 153). Lavish lunches or dinners à la carte, a finger buffet (about £10 a head) or fork buffet (about £18); plus room hire, staff charges.

HURLINGHAM CLUB
Ranelagh Gardens, London SW6 (01) 736 8411

The townies' country club — an Edwardian stately with sweeping lawns, croquet, tennis, swimming and other genteel sports facilities. Wonderful for summer weddings, though you must be sponsored by a member (who vouches for your proper behaviour). A reception for up to 100 in the Drawing Room costs £175 for room hire, plus canapés from £5 a head or buffet from £8 a head, plus drink. More guests can be accommodated in the Quadrangle, which opens on to the gardens; room hire, £250 to £350.

INSURANCE HALL
20 Aldermanbury, London EC2 (01) 606 1561

Oak-panelled banqueting hall with stained glass windows, with catering by J. Lyons (see page 144). Room for 320 standing or 225 seated: £250 from 1 pm to 5.30 pm; £400 from 5.30 pm to 11 pm.

LEIGHTON HOUSE
12 Holland Park Road, London W14 (01) 602 3316

A magnificently decorative Victorian house, entered by the Arab Hall with its blue and

The Arab Hall at Leighton House: the guests pass through it en route for a garden reception.
(Leighton House Museum Royal Borough of Kensington and Chelsea)

gold Islamic tiles and mosaics. Available for evening receptions, from 6.30 pm to 11 pm, for 150 people. Catering by Leith's (see page 143). Hire of the house — and garden in

summer — £450. Contact the curator, Stephen Jones.

THE OLD RANGOON
201 Castelnau, Barnes, London SW13
(01) 741 9655

A colonial-style restaurant and cocktail bar .with a palm-fringed terrace and an acre of landscaped garden dotted with ducks, rabbits and guinea pigs. Receptions can be held in the restaurant and/or their own marquee, which accommodates 80 sit-down or 100 to 120 for cocktails. The restaurant holds around 120 sitting and 150 to 200 standing. A special music and dancing licence can be obtained. Flexible feasting, from finger buffets to grand carveries.

THE ORANGERY
Holland Park, London W8: c/o Town & County Catering (see page 145)

Classy and glassy, the conservatory-style orangery and summer ballroom have large arched windows opening on to leafy gardens, which can be tented over.

THE ROOF GARDENS
99 Kensington High Street, London W8 (01) 937 7994

The well-known roof garden, constructed in the Thirties above the old Derry & Toms department store (now Barkers) is still flourishing. Around the rather flash restaurant/nightclub is a cleverly countrified English Woodland Garden, a Tudor Rose Garden and a Spanish Garden, plus a maze of walkways, lawns, streams and trees. Take over the whole place or just a part of it for smaller numbers. Their chef organizes all catering, from around £12 a head for a buffet and £15 sit-down. No venue charge, just a minimum expenditure of £1,500.

STANLEY HOUSE
The Hamilton Suite: c/o King's Campus Vacation Bureau, King's College London, 552 King's Road, London SW10 (01) 351 6011

A magnificent Georgian building with two grand reception rooms, overlooking wide lawns which could hold a marquee; £425 for the day. King's can arrange all catering.

STATIONERS' HALL
Ave Maria Lane, London EC4 (01) 248 2934

A seventeenth-century hall with dark oak

panelling and carving and elaborate stained glass windows. As well as the Hall, there are the smaller Stock Room and Ante-Room. The Hall and Stock provide space for 400; £300 (lunchtime), £550 (all day). Contact Barbara Eden. Caterers must be chosen from their approved selection.

30 PAVILION ROAD
London SW1: c/o Searcy Tansley & Company (see page 144)

Searcy's own elegant Georgian townhouse. The upstairs library and ballroom lend themselves admirably to receptions for about 150; £350 to hire, plus food and drink (which must be provided by Searcy's when using their premises).

Country and Scotland

(For hotels, see pages 183-186. Most hotels listed there can cater for the reception.)

BEAULIEU
c/o J. Lyons Catering, John Montagu Building, Beaulieu, Brockenhurst, Hampshire (0590) 612102/612165

Banqueting for up to 300 in the grounds of Lord Montagu's Palace House and the thirteenth-century abbey. Or you could take the abbey over for a medieval banquet, held weekly in the evening. You get hunks of meat, mead, wine, entertained by a jester, minstrels and henchmen — and a disco afterwards. (You need to book ahead for 70 to 100 people at £14.25 a head.)

THE HUNTING LODGE
Adlington Hall, Macclesfield, Cheshire (0625) 827595

A converted Georgian mews set in lovely rambling gardens, facing the black and white wing of Adlington Hall. Good familiar English lunches and dinners (melon/prawn cocktail, roasts, apple pie/cheesecake, etc.) for 80-plus guests cost £12.25 a head. Cold buffets from about £10, and cocktail eats from about £4. All prices include room hire. A discothèque is available for £60.

KNEBWORTH HOUSE AND BARNS
Knebworth Park, Knebworth,
Hertfordshire (0438) 813825

In the grounds of Knebworth are two souped-up sixteenth-century timber-frame barns, accommodating 200 and 250 seated and 300 and 350 standing. No hire charge as long as you make full use of their caterers — canapés from about £8 a head, buffets from about £10, which includes napkins, candles and flowers. They can arrange a disco, band, light show, etc. The banqueting hall of Knebworth House itself can be used for dinner or cocktail parties.

PHYLLIS COURT CLUB
Marlow Road, Henley-on-Thames, Oxford-shire (0491) 574366

An early nineteenth-century mansion on the banks of the Thames, opposite the Royal

Phyllis Court Club-on-Thames: a perfect summer setting.
(Photograph courtesy of Phyllis Court Club)

Regatta enclosures. Both the Thames Room (holds 80, from £75 a day) and Ballroom (holds 250, from £150 a day) open on to the lawns that lead down to the river. One couple left their reception here by river launch, while a brass band blared away in another launch. You could also leave Phyllis Court by helicopter. Catering ranges from a simple cocktail buffet at £4.75 to a feast of salmon, beef, ham, chicken and salads, for £19.50.

PRESTONFIELD HOUSE
Priestfield Road, Edinburgh
(031) 668 3346

The main Jacobean hotel can accommodate 300 standing, in various dining rooms, for £400 a day. One room costs £100. Outsize receptions (up to 500 guests seated or 800 standing) can be held in their Round Stables (£400), the open centre section of which is tented over. Dozens of sit-down menu ideas, from £12 to £25; tea and finger buffets from £8 to £12. They can arrange for pipers and Scottish dancers and the grounds will run to two helicopters and 300 cars.

MARQUEES

There are two types of marquee — the traditional canvas tent with one or two central poles and guy ropes and the aluminium frame tent, a free-standing structure with no ropes or poles. This second type is perfect for weddings — no poles means everyone can see the action, no ropes means tipsy guests won't trip up and you can have French windows leading into the garden; you can extend the marquee directly from the house with no need for a canopied walkway. The best frame tents are designed and built in Germany to withstand Alpine conditions, and so they are quite safe and undraughty in high winds and wintry weather.

The lining is a matter of choice, and costs about half as much again as the marquee. It could fall in voluptuous ruches, in wide stripes (yellow/white or pink/white are *de rigueur*) or be pleated or plain. For a theme party, you could have painted murals instead of lining. With frame tents, you can remove the walls if it's hot. Flooring (at extra charge) can be of coconut matting laid directly on grass, or boarded with either matting or carpeting on top. Carpeting is expensive as you can only use it once. For dancing, the best surface is interlocking parquet. The marquee firm will require at least one site meeting to discuss layout for seating, dancing and sitting out (if applicable), to ensure that

they use the space to the best advantage; they can supply chairs and tables. Make sure there is somewhere for guests to put their coats and belongings. If extra electricity is needed, the marquee firm can install generators and they will arrange lighting and heating.

Rent-a-tent

(See also pages 150-154.)

London

CHATTERS
10-12 Glenville Mews, London SW18
(01) 228 5583

Will set up camp anywhere with their frame tents, all fixtures and fittings and lighting after the Starlight method. (See also page 162.)

JOFFIN'S MARQUEES
1 Heliport Estate, Lombard Road, London SW11 (01) 350 0033

Their own frame tents, or they can find you a specialist marquee from an outside com-

155

pany. Dance floors in oak parquet or black and white, coconut matting, carpeting and staging. (See also pages 147 and 163.)

JULIANA'S
1023 Garratt Lane, London SW17
(01) 672 3691

Traditional poled and modern frame tents. A wide range of colourful linings, French windows, floral trellised arches and a night sky — a black ceiling studded with white lights. Lighting includes gilt wall brackets, chandeliers, spotlights or individual pinspots, all with dimmers. Dance floors have interlocking sections of polished oak parquet. Also staging for speeches, bands and discos. Exterior floodlighting for the house, special effects for the garden, firework displays and even laser shows that you can plan yourself. (See pages 148 and 163.)

LEWIS MARQUEES
20 Enterprise Way, Osiers Road, London SW18 (01) 350 2207

Marquees that can stand up to uneven ground, bridge ponds and clear walls. They have pitched up at the Hurlingham Club, a roof in the Docklands and outside Buckingham Palace.

M & G MARQUEE HIRE
1053-5 High Road, Whetstone, London N20 (01) 446 4115

Traditional and frame tents plus lean-to house extensions. Linings are lavishly ruched from the ceiling down to the ground in creamy, silky material — as if you've got caught up in the bride's underskirts. M & G tented over one terrace and swimming pool and floated water lilies on the pool. Lighting from spots to crystal chandeliers; doors and windows; theme tents such as Caribbean calypso or an English garden with fountain, urns, live doves and a folly.

T.G. & T.S. PEPPER
Unit 5, Gateway Trading Estate, Hythe Road, London NW10 (01) 960 6078

Top-notch frame tents recommended nation-

Anna Joyce (née Thompson) hired a jazzily striped circus tent (left) *for her informal wedding celebrations.*
(Clare Faull)

Lucinda Rivett-Carnac's Hampshire house and garden (right) *were transformed into a theatrical setting for her wedding to Valentine Guinness. The event was orchestrated by Searcy's; the Clearspan tent (a frame tent with transparent walls) is from Carters of Basingstoke.*
(Philip Durell, Aardvark Photography)

Wall-to-wall tenting: the garden wall and a flourishing herbaceous border provide spectacular floral decor for Joanna Philipson and Hugo Lascelles' marquee.
(Philip Durell, Aardvark)

wide, superlative lighting by Starlight (see page 161) and all interior equipment, including a stock of 8,000 chairs.

Country and Scotland

CAMBRIDGE CATERING EQUIPMENT
6 North Road, Whittlesford, Cambridge (0223) 833100

Not only traditional tents, but all the fittings — coconut matting, Astra Turf, gilt or beech chairs, silver, linen, glasses, china, cutlery and bar equipment. They stock over 6,000 place settings.

CLYDE CANVAS
50 Lindsay Road, Leith, Edinburgh (031) 554 1331

All styles of marquees — they can even construct one to order — plus all the inner trimmings.

DEVON & SOMERSET MARQUEES
Orchard View, Stoodleigh, Tiverton, Devon (03985) 210

Jazzy, hexagonal blue-and-white striped frame marquees that can link together. A tent for 270 standing costs £368.

T.G. & T.S. PEPPER
Crosshill, Snaith, North Humberside (0405) 860249

(See London entry, above.)

WHITE HORSE MARQUEES
The Manor House, Hill Deverill, Warminster, Wiltshire (0985) 40705

Trad white marquees with vibrant stripy linings. Specialists in the wedding field.

DECOR AND LIGHTING

Your wedding bash could be the biggest show you'll ever take part in. Let the stage be worthy of the stars. It's an opportunity to let your imagination run riot, and it doesn't *have* to break the bank. Parties are all about creating mood, appealing to all the senses. Candles or fairy lights, scented herbs and flowers, essences dropped onto light bulbs, evocative soundtracks and music, swathes of lush fabrics, flaming torches, water (be it river, fishpond or swimming pool) — all these give atmosphere. It doesn't apply just to evening parties. Daytime receptions can be just as atmospheric. A rustic Thomas Hardy scene, a medieval jousting party, a boating-on-the-river theme. Raid the countryside for resources — sheaves of wheat and corn, masses of ivy to twist round tent poles; drape muslin; hang bunting; fly flags from a stripy tent; paint backdrops, use mad props; float water lilies or petals on pools. Colour themes are fine, but avoid matching *everything*. (See also page 123.)

On colour co-ordination

It's nice — up to a point — to be colour co-ordinated and a subtle matching of creams and ivories looks classy and thought-out. One all-yellow wedding, however, went way beyond the pale: the bride wore yellow net under her dress, the bridesmaids wore yellow, the groom and ushers wore yellow cravats and roses, the bouquet, head-dresses and corsages were yellow, the tent was lined in yellow stripes, the cake was yellow, the floral decorations were yellow — in fact everything was so yellow that the guests turned green.

Decorators

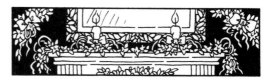

(See also pages 125-129, N.B.: in particular John Plested, page 128.)

PAUL DYSON
58 Cloudesley Road, London N1
(01) 837 5671

Display manager at Harvey Nichols, responsible for their marvellous windows, he also creates theme parties, organizing decor, lighting and costume. Talented and chock-full of ideas, he is a dab hand at co-ordinating your disjointed thoughts and wishes and turning them into reality. He kitted out one Christmas wedding ball in lapis lazuli blue and shocking red, in contrast to the preceding reception 'for dreary aunts'. At Ringo Starr's reception in a Mayfair club, the couple received guests at the foot of the stairs while Paul Dyson cascaded silver star sequins and rose petals from the top. He plans a totally candlelit wedding next.

MICHAEL HOWELLS
42 Bloemfontein Road, London W12
(01) 749 7414 (See also page 126.)

Fantasyland weddings. Artist, set designer (he did the 1986 Bolshoi Ballet tour) and floral artist, he aims to create a memorable morsel of magic for a day or night. For Ari McNair-Wilson and Nick Ashley's wedding, he wrapped up whole houses and barns with sashes and bows, so that as everyone came over the hill, it looked as though the valley

was full of presents. Apple trees were dotted with pink bows and there was a round tent in Laura Ashley fabric for the band. At Sophie Marten and John Alexander's wedding, Michael realized her Wyatt country house was too grand for conventional flower arrangements as decoration; instead he had two 18-ft (5.4 m) unicorns rampant constructed. At Prue Murdoch and Crispin Odey's reception in the Park Lane Hotel, he hired fibreglass statues, covered them in ivy and foliage and created a classical courtyard. His style is theatrical, operatic, but he can do simple things — he tented the ceiling of one village hall in blue and made white paper

Clearspan tenting (above) *leads from the house to the main marquee at Lucinda and Valentine Guinness' reception.*
(Philip Durell, Aardvark Photography)

Dramatic floodlighting (below and below right) *from Starlight makes all the garden a stage.*
(Philip Durell, Aardvark Photography)

mouldings and candelabra. At a dinner party, he scattered rooms with spices and herbs, so that each footstep would crush the pot pourri and release the scent. He redecorated a room as Marie Antoinette's dairy, floating rose petals on milk-filled pails, sprinkling more petals over the floor and hanging muslin on the walls. At a summer party, he played a continuous soundtrack of cicadas and tropical birds. He can arrange any props, backdrops and murals you care to dream up and props include people — liveried footmen, dressed-down dancers — anything to complete the theme.

STARLIGHT
Unit 5, Gateway Trading Estate, Hythe Road, London NW10 (01) 960 6078; (0223 811046)

Michael Lakin is the star of party lighting — recommended by one and all, he is the examplar of floodlighting, interior lighting and special effects. One florist marvels that he can light anything to make it look like something else. He can transform a garden into a magical Disneyland scene by splashing coloured light against foliage. He has shone tiny spotlights onto individual tables in a marquee, picking out only the tree centre-piece in a pool of light. One marquee was pitched on a roof garden, so he lined it with midnight blue muslin, dotted Christmas-tree lighting all over the ceiling, and then put more muslin over it so that it seemed just like a starry night. He can also illuminate the church in a subtle way, highlighting flowers and architectural features.

PARTY MUSIC

If you are holding a large party, it is worth hiring a band. Choose one that comes personally recommended, plays together regularly and is aimed at the right age-group — or is versatile. Most dance bands play a mixture of golden oldies, current pop music, etc. to suit all ages. You may want to run through their repertoire and let them know if there are any special songs you'd like played. A good band will play the right tune according to the mood of the party and not adhere to a standard routine. They should play at the right volume for the venue and the guests, so that you don't have to shout to make yourself heard. Check that they'll play for as long as you require and non-stop if necessary. Confirm the exact timing with them and make sure they'll have their equipment set up and instruments tuned in good time for the party.

If you want a band *and* discothèque, it is best to book these from the same firm so that they can work happily together. The requirements for a disco are the same as for a band: apart from professionalism and efficiency, they should be willing to play what you or the party mood requires, at the right volume.

It is traditional for the bride and groom to lead the dancing. Paula Yates professes never to have danced with Bob Geldof — even in ten years of living together — before their nuptial night. Then, they strutted their stuff to 'Hey, Hey, Paula' and 'I want to be Bobby's Girl', though the Rolling Stones finally foxed them. In Scotland, it was traditionally the bride's privilege to choose the music for a 'sham spring' which she danced with the groom, bridesmaids and best man. And surely the most energetic reception of all time was the one held in eighteenth-century New England, when the guests danced 92 jigs, 50 contra dances, 43 minuets and 17 hornpipes.

Bands and discos

London

All the following will travel nationwide.

ALAN BAILEY AND THE NEW CONNECTION
C/o Party Planners (see page 147).

A band with stamina who will play virtually anything — golden oldies, Sixties, chart hits, etc. They dress in white suits. Book as early in advance as possible.

CHANCE ENTERTAINMENT
313 Brompton Road, London SW3
(01) 584 3206

Andrew Chance can organize any music, from dance bands (Chance — of which Andrew is the drummer, Oliver Twist, Penthouse, Moonshine, Inflation) and discothèques (Chance, Raffles, Bentleys) to big bands (Kenny Ball, Acker Bilk), chamber orchestras, solo musicians and choirs for the church. (See page 147.)

CHATTERS
10-12 Glenville Mews, London SW18
(01) 228 5583

A band of travelling discos run by Tim Radford, who has now branched into marquees (see page 155) and party planning.

DARK BLUES

Dark Blues Management, 30 Stamford Brook Road, London W6 (01) 743 3292

Four bands: The Dark Blues (formed in 1962, they've played at countless royal events, and are still strummin' away), The Wallace Collection (who have played for Liza Minnelli and the Duke of Marlborough at Blenheim Palace), Event and Runcible Spoon — as well as The Dark Blues Disco. They can also supply steel bands, jazz bands, gypsy trios, string quartets and other speciality musicians. Their consultancy service will help you plan details such as where to put the bar, how big the marquee should be, how much space to allow for dancing, etc. Each band has a large repertoire ranging from current pop and disco music, through Latin American and ballroom standards, to rock'n'roll, jazz and Scottish reels.

GIBSONS

16 Pensbury Street, Pensbury Industrial Estate, London SW8 (01) 622 9798

Travelling discothèques run by Angus Gibson. They can do theme parties — Twenties, Thirties, Sixties, etc. — and travel not only countrywide but all over Europe. Suitable mainly for grand affairs — it was Gibsons that played at the Duke and Duchess of York's wedding thrash.

JOFFIN'S PARTY PLANNING

1 Heliport Estate, Lombard Road, London SW11 (01) 350 0033

Jonathan (Joffin) Seaward is lead singer of

Spot and the Dogs dance band and has seven discos with full lighting effects, plus, to hand, anything from a string quartet to a steel band. Any size, anywhere. (See pages 147 and 155.)

JULIANA'S

1023 Garratt Lane, London SW17 (01) 672 3691

The first name in travelling discos. William Bartholomew has dozens of them, to cater for all age groups and tastes; all carry the full gamut of musical styles. They are careful about sound levels and moderate the volume whenever necessary. They can fit extension speakers for sitting-out areas and have public address systems for speeches and announcements. They will advise on and supply special lighting, which runs to a striking laser show. (See pages 148 and 156.)

PASADENA ROOF ORCHESTRA

c/o David Curtis, Priors, Tye Green, Elsenham, Bishops Stortford, Hertfordshire (0279) 813240

For grand occasions. This renowned 11-piece orchestra (two trumpets, three saxophones, a trombone, piano, banjo/ guitar, drums, bass and a singer) play melodic, harmonic Twenties' and Thirties' dance music — Cole Porter classics, the Charleston, 'Don't bring Lulu', etc. They went all the way to Dallas for one night's entertainment.

Country

FAT CAT DISCO

The Malthouse, Teffont Magna, Salisbury,
Wiltshire (072276) 282

Run by Rupert Little and John Nicholson.
Good for events down south, as rates are
lower than the big London discos, and travel
expenses can be cut down. A wide range of
music, from Fats Waller and Louis Armstrong
to current hits. Top sound equipment, a
microphone available for client use, lighting
equipment and effects. Also interior tent
lighting, outdoor floodlighting and car park
illumination. They can organize dance floors
and firework displays with at least six weeks'
notice. One partner is always present at
parties.

*Highland hooley: James and Kerry Forbes a-rockin'
and a-reelin' at their evening party.*
(Alan Donald)

SECTION V
STAG AND HEN NIGHTS

(Sue Carpenter).

Don't have your last fling the night before the wedding. Zombie-like is not the best way to feel or look on your wedding day. Most couples play safe and actually have their parties the weekend before. The stock hen night brings out latent dirty talk and behaviour in women, the stag night is an excuse to get hammered and rowdy. Women tend to take care of themselves, men don't. So make sure the best man or another reliable friend is sworn to looking after your husband-to-be, as it will be everyone else's intention to get him uncontrollably drunk and to play practical jokes. On no account should anyone drive — taxis are the order of the night.

Disaster stories are legion. Hilarious in retrospect, they cause little mirth to the couple at the time. As one bride wailed of her husband's stag night (the night before the wedding), 'They got him plastered. Literally. They covered his leg in plaster. Then they put him on the train to Edinburgh.' The best man retrieved him just in time. Another groom was stripped, his arm put in plaster and then chained to Chelsea Bridge. *That* is what you call suffering from exposure. Luckily a policeman found him before he got hypothermia. Not so funny are the stories of grooms who get alcoholic poisoning and require stomach pumps; or those who are so senseless that they have accidents.

Some stag 'nights' are spread over a weekend or even a week. One groom took a barge down the Thames with ten chums, who joined and departed at various stages. Another took a crowd of mates to Corfu for a week, and it was declared by all as one of the best holidays they'd ever had, with non-stop schoolboy banter. As long as you are not required at home for some vital piece of organization, it is a therapeutic and relaxing move to take off somewhere with your best friends for a few days. Palm off most of the arrangements on your chief bridesmaid/best man.

If it's to be a one-night affair, find a sympathetic restaurant or club with a private room, if possible. One group of men went to a crowded Indian restaurant and ended up

165

chucking chicken korma round the room. When some landed in a dollop on the pristine cuff of an elderly gentleman, the group were let off lightly — the man simply smiled and said: 'So nice to see the young enjoying themselves.' Other diners might not be so enchanted.

It is par for the course for the chief bridesmaid/best man to produce sex shop props and to have ordered a human telegram. Check that the restaurant is agreeable to a gram. The Ritz and Savoy are hard ones to crack, but it has been done. Strippagram companies report such frequent problems with rowdy stag-nighters (Hooray Henrys are the least respectful, they say) that all their girls now have minders. Most companies won't send girls to private houses.

Male grams are used to the girls getting out of hand. One Vicargram, paid to strip down to a g-string, had the string snipped instantly and then had to shield himself with a menu while trying to sing 'You are my sunshine'.

Bridal shower

In America, the bride is given a 'shower'. At this variation on the hen party (usually lunch or a bridge party), friends produce token presents on a theme. It could be a kitchen shower (pots, pans, cooking things), a bar shower (glasses, coasters, cocktail shakers), or a closet shower (shoe trees and brushes, coat-hangers). A popular bride receives several showers. The groom may receive a 'honey do' shower in anticipation of his future household duties ('honey, do this'; 'honey, do that'), with gifts of aprons, dustpans, brushes and other useful equipment.

One bride-to-be had a round-the-clock shower at a civilized London restaurant, organized by an American friend. Each guest was allocated a different time and they then had to bring a present associated with that time. The girl who got 5 pm brought a cup and saucer. The one who got 4 am produced a copy of *Playgirl* and a bag of coffee. One person got confused and turned up at her given time — which, happily, was 2 pm.

He was then led by the bride into a contorted Kung Fu-style dance which required both arms to be held in the air. He says it happens all the time.

To have the event videod (see page 56-59) is increasingly popular. Just make sure you aren't filmed doing something you might later regret and don't have the wedding filmed on the same tape . . . .

Telegrams

ANTONIOGRAMS
(01) 558 5999

Good clean entertainment. Eccentric Antonio plays his piano accordian in OTT romantic-style, singing a personalized song (having been briefed on the victim's character) to the tune of 'My bonnie lies over the ocean'. He continues with special comic serenades, ending up with 'Farewell my love' and tears in his eyes. Then he presents the bride-to-be with a red rose. You may be able to persuade

Having your cake and eating it: hen-night surprise for Sally Rowbotham.
(Antoinette Eugster)

Pride comes before a Faull: schoolgirl strippagram turns the tables on the groom-to-be.
(Nick Dixon)

him to flash his furry underpants with the line 'all men are little lambs underneath'. £25.

THE LUSCIOUS LIP COMPANY
(01) 351 9400

Vicars and Casanovas for hen nights, Spank-ing Schoolgirls or Rolypolygrams for stag nights. About £18 for an above-board Kissa-gram or Tarzanagram; £23 takes you down to the g-string, and £35 gets you the full strip.

TELEGRAMS UNLIMITED
(01) 980 0939

For a hen night they offer leathermen, police-men, Superman, frogs and penguins. Gerald the Giraffe arrives and sings 'Don't step on my blue suede hooves' and then strips to a g-string. Gerald notes that 'girls on the receiving end often do a runner'. When a Gorillagram (in real life Mr Great Britain) arrived at one hen night, the bride ran into the kitchen and got out a carving knife. 'What about a Tarzan, then?' he whimpered in a small Welsh voice.

For stag nights, they do a stripping school-girl, nurse, French maid, nun or police-woman. The WPC (remember Di and Fergie's little jape?) is the favourite. She strips down to suspenders and bra; in general, Telegrams Unlimited find full strips cause too much trouble. Most work is in London, but they have worked in Paris and take bookings from all over the world. About £25.

 # THE DAY

While the wedding day is a tactician's dream, a piece of precision engineering that has to be planned down to the last minute, it is more likely to result in insomnia for all those involved. When the big day dawns, having done so much detailed organization, the best policy is to relax and trust that all the component parts will slot together in the correct order at the right time.

All major worries such as last-minute flower arranging, assembly of the cake and laying out food should be palmed off on helpmates on the big day. For the immediate families, there should be nothing more flustering than getting ready and getting there. You, the bride, have only to think about your beauty routine (see page 111), hair appointment if applicable, safe delivery of your flowers and getting dressed. Lay out or hang up your underwear, dress, shoes, make-up, jewellery, head-dress and veil the night before, so that you don't forget anything. Your honeymoon suitcase should be packed and your going-away outfit (don't forget hat, shoes, bag) ready to be taken to the reception if it is not at home. Make sure travel documents are in a safe place. If your photographer/video-man is filming you at home, be ready at the appointed time.

On the morning, put your engagement ring on your right hand. When the wedding ring has been placed on your finger during the service, you can transfer your engagement ring to the same finger.

Meanwhile, the best man will probably have been staying or lunching with the groom. (Warn your betrothed in advance that the marriage is off if they down more than two drinks. There have been horror stories of drunken grooms who could barely slur their vows out in church.) The two should aim to arrive at church half-an-hour to 20 minutes before the service. The ushers should arrive half-an-hour before.

Back at the bridal ranch, the bridesmaids and pages turn up (though the chief bridesmaid has probably been with you all morning), their car arrives, and off they go. Mother may accompany them or go separately, perhaps escorted by other members of the family. That leaves you and Father, who will be clock-watching like mad.

'The most frequent thing to be forgotten,' says Lady Elizabeth Anson, 'is the bouquet. It is usually sitting somewhere in a box, keeping cool, Mother's already left and Father's in a panic. You hope there's a pretty prayer book you can shove into the bride's hands.' Even the veil gets forgotten. Lady E. advises that

Duties: the bride's mother

She should have handed over all organizational responsibilities for the day. If not, may need to make last-minute touches to flowers, cake, food, etc. Keeps bride and household on schedule — up on time, visiting hairdresser if applicable, eating a light breakfast or lunch, starting to change on time and so on.

Leaves house before bride and father, perhaps with the attendants or son(s) and/or other daughter(s). Takes make-up for bride with her. At church, she is escorted by an usher to her place in the front left pew.

Is present at signing of register, is escorted by groom's father down aisle. Stands in receiving line (if applicable) at reception and thereafter acts as hostess, mixing and introducing guests, etc.

Afterwards, takes care of bride's wedding dress and accessories, the cake, wedding presents, etc. If reception is at home, directs the clearing-up operation.

Mothering mum

It is important to pamper both the bride's and groom's mother on the day. Their child's marriage is a major occasion in *both* their lives. Some thoughtful caterers, dressmakers, photographers and the like make a point of saying how lovely the bride's mother looks and what a fabulous spread. The groom's mother, meanwhile, may feel somewhat superfluous. She has no role as hostess and will have played a smaller part in the preparation and so will receive none of the praise and attention well earned by the bride's mother.

you are ready by the time Mother departs, so that she can perform the final inspection.

Off you go, with plenty of time to spare. Many's the bride who arrives 15 minutes early and then has to circle round the block ten times like an aeroplane stacking to land at Heathrow. In a town with congested traffic, there is little you can do to avoid this — better to arrive in good time than too late, even if you do keep passing your guests with a queenly wave.

The car draws up with a few minutes in hand. The blur begins. The click, whirr of camera and video; demure, veiled smiles at late guests; less demure adjustments to your attire; lining up attendants (usually little maids all in a row behind the bride, the chief bridesmaid bringing up the rear); Father with gritted teeth, pacing. You walk up the path, the first bars of your familiar processional music strike and you launch up the aisle on Father's right arm, slowly, steadily to the chancel steps where you join the groom and best man.

You turn and give the bouquet to the chief bridesmaid. The marriage service ensues (see page 36) and after the vows, Father, best man and attendants (optional) fall out and take their allotted pew. There may be a sermon

(please, dear minister, not procreation or divorce, again), winding up with a quick word about stacking extra chairs at the back and donating generously to the fund for the church roof. Then you and the groom proceed to the altar for the prayers and blessing.

The minister, the couple, their parents, attendants and best man then disappear into the vestry to sign the register. Now you lift the veil back off your face and, if Mother has

Duties: the chief bridesmaid

The chief bridesmaid is helper, supporter, morale-booster and confidante to the bride.

Organizes the hen night in conjunction with the bride, arranging the venue and any props or surprises such as a Rambogram.

Often stays the night before the wedding at the bride's house. In the morning, helps the bride dress and generally gives support and encouragement.

Precedes bride to church. Is in charge of the other attendants, checks their clothes, head-dresses and bouquets are in order.

When bride arrives at church, she arranges her veil and train.

Takes the bride's bouquet when they reach the chancel steps and hands it back to her when they sign the register, so that the bride can carry it down the aisle.

Helps to round and organize younger attendants for the wedding photographs. At the reception she is always on hand to tend to the bride and, like the best man, she is on standby for family duties, looking after little bridesmaids and pages, etc.

May help the bride change out of her wedding dress; may then take charge of it, but usually the bride's mother does this.

Duties: other attendants

No responsibilities other than to be present and correct and do as they are asked by the chief bridesmaid. Older ones may be called upon to help in general hostly duties and introduce themselves to guests. Youngsters are simply required not to tread on the bride's train or to scream/yawn/scratch throughout the service.

If the vestry walls had ears...
(Desmond O'Neill Features)

remembered your make-up and hairbrush, touch up your maquillage. Then it's time to march back down the aisle (not too fast — the congregation are dying for a proper look at you): the bride on the groom's left arm, followed by a crocodile of small attendants, the chief bridesmaid and best man, the bride's mother and groom's father and the groom's mother and bride's father.

You emerge into the sunlight for snaps and congrats, then bundle into the car or carriage bound for the reception. The best man, bridesmaids and pages bundle into the next car and both sets of parents hasten to the reception to take up their positions in the photographs and/or receiving line before guests arrive.

Duties: the ushers

Get to the church about half an hour before the service. There may be three or more ushers — one in charge, one who knows the bride's family and one who knows the groom's family.

Hand out service sheets and show guests to their seats — bride's side on the left, groom's on the right.

One usher — perhaps the head usher — should be delegated the duty of escorting the bride's mother to her seat. The front pews must be kept free for the immediate families; there may be a seating plan to follow. It is nice if someone is assigned to ushering the groom's parents, grandparents, etc.

Helps best man in his general duties — gathering guests for photographs, arranging transport, etc.

Transport logistics

This is one of the knottiest brain-teasers around. Consider this.

Arrival at church
Car A: bride and father
Car B: bridesmaids and pages (and possibly bride's mother)
Car C (optional): more bridesmaids and · pages
    Best man/groom's car: groom and best man

Departure for reception
Car A: bride and groom
Car B: bridesmaids, pages and best man
Car C (optional): more bridesmaids and pages
Best man/groom's car: no driver
No car: bride's parents

That one seems easy, though the answer is probably *not* that the bride's parents drive the best man's car. Add sisters and brothers and non-driving grannies and uncles on both sides, and you have a sophisticated puzzle. Think through your particular case in advance, make sure everyone knows his duties, who's collecting/giving lifts to whom, and that *everyone has the necessary car keys.*

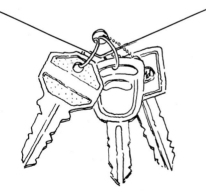

The reception

The recommended length of a standard afternoon reception is two to three hours: wedding at 2.30 pm, say, reception at 3.30 pm, departure at 6 pm. As Freddie Meynell of Searcy's points out, 'The atmosphere goes

Duties: the bride's father

Between the departure of mother for the church and his departure with his daughter, he must be a calming influence, supporting and not upsetting the bride in any way.

Escorts her to church and down the aisle. At the chancel steps, when the minister asks who gives the bride away, he offers the bride's right hand to the minister.

Stands until the vows have been taken and then joins the bride's mother in the front pew. He signs the register and escorts the groom's mother down the aisle.

At reception, stands in receiving line (if applicable) and, as host, mixes among guests and introduces them.

May give the first speech.

slowly down if the bride and groom don't go — it loses its charm. And when they've gone, it's time for guests to go.' Diana McKenzie of Country Cooks advises: 'Although the day will go fast for the bride, it is often a long day for the guests — the best receptions are short, sharp and to the point. I hate it when they go on into the evening; everyone is so jaded. A wedding reception is the only occasion where there is no natural hostess who knows all the guests and can introduce them. You may have two quite different groups of people. It's a very funny occasion if you analyse it. In fact, in the nicest possible way, a wedding is quite boring for a lot of people.' Be warned.

The receiving line

The grander the wedding, the less receiving. Perhaps this is because with 1,000 guests, you'd still be shaking hands two hours later. Whatever the style of your wedding, queuing is a killer. The latest lines in receiving are: (a) to cut the line down to bride and groom only; (b) for there to be two rooms — the first for guests to mingle and start partying, the second for the receiving line, cake and main reception; (c) for the bride and groom to stand near the back of the reception hall or marquee, so that guests can go up to the couple in their own time; (d) on a fine day, for the line to be at the entrance of the marquee or house so that people can mingle outside

Duties: the best man

The best man's job is one of the most demanding — confidant, peace-keeper, liaison officer, minder, guardian angel.

Organizes the stag night with the groom, prevents the mob (i.e. the groom's best friends) from giving the groom alcoholic poisoning and ushers him safely home.

Confers with groom and his family over service sheets, buttonholes, the groom's going-away outfit, honeymoon suitcase and travel documents, the going-away car. He may have to take responsibility for making sure some or all of these things are in the right place at the right time.

Helps the groom get ready and gets him to the church or Register Office on time.

Keeps the wedding ring safe until it is called for in the service.

Makes sure all the fees are paid to the minister or registrar, organist, bell-ringers and any other musicians.

He is generally on call for rounding up family to be in photographs, organizing lifts to the reception and parking. At the reception, he may be required to help in keeping-the-family-happy duties and speeding guests along the receiving line.

If there is no Master of Ceremonies, he organizes the timing of the speeches and cake cutting and announces their onset to the guests.

Gives the third and final speech, thanking the groom for his toast to the bridesmaids on their behalf. Reads out any Telemessages.

Makes sure the couple go and change on time and tells the guests when they are about to leave.

Makes sure everyone is gathered round outside to bid the couple farewell. If the couple are worried about a barrage of crazy foam and having their car wrecked, he and the ushers should try and prevent it.

After they're gone, he should be on hand to help out in general. He may have to take charge of the groom's wedding clothes if the groom's parents have not made provision to do so.

first. If you absolutely can't avoid a queue, make sure everyone in it is served with champagne.

Speeches

You should without exception go through the formality of having speeches, however informal or short the actual speeches may be. The wedding needs a focus — the three speeches, toasts and cake-cutting — and there are people who will be offended if they are not thanked. Speeches are advisedly kept brief, although there is a general feeling of being short-changed if there aren't a few anecdotes and jokes, particularly from someone known to be a good orator. Guests didn't know quite how to react at the society wedding where the bride's uncle said: 'Ladies and gentlemen, the bride and groom', the bridegroom: 'Thanks everybody', and the best man: 'Let's toast the bridesmaids'.

The first speech, proposing the health of the bride and groom, falls to the bride's father, uncle or an old friend of the family. This one is about the bride and is best kept brief, straight and affectionate; no jibes and only witty if he is a good speaker. If one or both of the bride's parents are dead or not present it is appreciated and touching to mention him/her and how proud he/she would have been.

The second speech, delivered by the groom, proposes a toast to the bridesmaids and pages. The toast is preceded by a chain of thank-you's, particularly to the new parents-in-law. One groom purportedly forgot the bride's mother in his bread-and-butter list, for which she has never quite forgiven him. The tone of this speech is straightforward and sincere, with the odd light touch.

The final speech, the best man's reply 'on behalf of the bridesmaids', is traditionally a vehicle for rattling a few of the groom's closeted skeletons. If the best man is a confident speaker, it can be very funny. If not, it can be embarrassing and in bad taste. He should avoid a complete character assassination and not dwell on past girlfriends, or go on for too long. Props can be fun — one or two — but not a whole *Blue Peter*-style teach-in, or a bag of tricks like the one produced by one Hooray best man: after a stream of sex aids, air freshener, etc., he pulled out a blown-up photograph of the groom in bed with another woman. A quick road to divorce. Another best man was enthusing about the effervescent bride who seemed to 'bubble up everywhere', when the groom chipped in 'like a bad drain'. That didn't go down too well with the new in-laws. It was customary for the best man to read out telegrams, but since Telemessages just don't have the same ring, this formality is often dispensed with. Otherwise, you could read out amusing messages (not private ones) or simply list the well-wishers.

That's news to me! Felix Schade's best man brings the house down when he presents Sally with a progression of props during his speech.
(Richard Greenly Photography)

Duties: the groom

Gives church fees to the best man so that he can pay them after the ceremony.

Gives going-away clothes and honeymoon suitcase to best man for him to take to the reception venue.

Gives second speech, in response to the toast to the bride and bridegroom.

Delivers a stream of thank-you's to the bride's parents, friends who have helped with the catering and flowers, and so on. Proposes a toast to the bridesmaids.

Has going-away transport organized for smooth getaway.

Going away

It's up to the best man to round you up at a pre-arranged time to go and change. You will be ravenous, so it's a good idea to arrange for a tray of food and champagne to be in your changing room. One couple's second pit-stop

Cake-cutting

Together the bride and groom hold the knife (upside-down for luck and a wish) and smile for the photos as they slice. Easier said than done — these cakes are like rock. You could do as the Queen did — a section was cut in advance, tied with a ribbon and iced over. When she and Prince Philip came to cut the cake, they were guided by the ribbon and only had to sever the icing. In any case, the show-cake is then whisked away and another, ready-cut replica brought in for the guests.

To live and slice by the sword.
(Moira Leggat)

after departing (the first was to clean the windscreen) was to buy crisps and peanuts for the journey to their hotel.

The best man should bring down your suitcases to the car in advance, before the crowd has gathered. Then it's time to make your second, less dignified, entrance of the day. Prepare to be mobbed.

Confetti, spaghetti, streamers, shaving foam, crazy foam — crazy guests. How do you contain them? A shower of confetti is all very well until it rains or gets into contact with the champers; then the cheap dye will run and could stain your outfit. Shaving and crazy foam are thoroughly unpleasant if you get a mouthful or an eyeful and they too can stain. Hurling rice (an ancient fertility ritual) is no better. Note Lady Elizabeth Anson's memo to guests: curbing hooligan tendencies is not a case of spoiling your fun, it's a case of not spoiling the whole day for the bride and

groom by taking things too far. The bride has bought a special outfit that is only going to be seen for a few minutes; why ruin it? Of course, some couples look forward to a frenzied departure. So, know your bride and groom. If there's any chance either of them will have a sense-of-humour failure, don't prompt it.

From bad to worse . . .

Sabotaging the car

Caterers and planners say they've seen many a happy wedding spoilt at this stage. The windscreen of one beautiful old Daimler was covered in horse manure, things get stuffed up exhaust pipes, the engine is tampered with, lipstick writing ends up scratching paintwork when the lipstick runs out and the metal casing takes over. One car was layered

Lady Elizabeth Anson on . . . going away

‘A lot of churches and hotels don't like confetti because it takes so long to sweep up. It's agony if people throw rice — like hail pellets. Our alternative is to provide big baskets of petals, and everybody takes a handful.

It's very important to time the changing of the bride and groom right — there is nothing worse than the couple going off to change and everybody drifting away so there is nobody left to throw a petal. ’

Hatless and happy: as the Duke and Duchess of York leave Buckingham Palace they are declared the fairest couple in the landau.
(Anwar Hussein)

Clare Faull (née Reilly) fights her way through a barrage of crazy foam (left). The car, meanwhile, suffers at the hands of playful ushers before the final getaway. (Sue Carpenter)

Rice lore

The practice of throwing rice and confetti originated in Greece, when sweetmeats were showered over the couple to bestow fertility and prosperity. On Sulawesi Island, Indonesia, there is a belief that unless the groom's soul is bribed with a shower of rice it will fly away after the wedding and never return. At Malay weddings the bride and groom feed each other continuously during the ceremony with uncooked rice.

in shaving foam inside and out, so that the couple could not avoid sitting on a cushion of froth and neither could they see to drive. The groom was so incensed that he felt like ploughing straight through the crowd.

Accidents will happen. One drunken usher took the vintage Roller for a drive, the chauffeur got awfully upset and chased after it and the usher turned back and somehow ran into the chauffeur. On another occasion, piles of cans were tied to the back of the car and a guest's foot got caught in one. As the chauffeur drove off, the crowd shouted and screamed, but the chauffeur and couple naturally thought it was all part of the fun and drove off, scraping the guest down the drive.

If you go away by boat, helicopter, balloon, etc., you avoid the horror, because — you hope — no one would dare sabotage them. If you have a hired car, a watchful chauffeur should be able to deter vandals. Otherwise, keep your car under lock and key until the last minute and let it be known that if he finds the car foaming at the windows, the groom will foam at the mouth. Or depart in a ready-

Prime beefs

Whether you're holding it or attending it, note the following points, which come up time and time again when the word 'wedding' is mentioned.

Guests: don't bring babies and young children to church or, if you must, sit at the back of the church and take them out if they start to create a disturbance. Give them a soft toy to play with rather than a toy car, say, which echoes round the church when inevitably tossed to the ground.

Hosts: a crèche is the perfect solution. St John's Ambulance will officiate for a small donation.

Groom, best man, friend of bride: keep speeches brief.

Hosts: don't have a long reception line; if a queue is unavoidable, do serve drink to everyone in it.

Guests: don't throw rice or squirt foam; if it's wet, don't throw confetti.

Hosts: supply rose petals to everyone instead.

Guests: don't sabotage the car with foam/manure/tin cans. **Groom:** Keep car hidden under lock and key.

mutilated old banger and have the real getaway car hidden somewhere nearby.

After they've gone

If the reception is at home, the best way of shifting guests after the bride and groom have gone away is for the bride's parents to stand on their doorstep and not go back inside.

If the reception is not at home, someone must be responsible for taking the presents, the top of the cake, the bride and bridegroom's wedding clothes and other items home once the couple have left. Make sure the clearer-uppers know who owns what equipment — for example, if cake knives belong to the family or the caterer.

Evening party

If you're having a shindig later that evening, the advice for shifting guests still applies. Mother and father will be gasping for a breather. For you, the usual routine is to 'go away' to great fanfares as normal, relax and change at a nearby hotel and then return a little later after the appointed party hour. You are not expected to be present in advance to act as hosts — you are guests of honour. So make a dramatic star appearance after most of the other guests have arrived. After the dance, you go away for the second time (more tears, hugs, waves), back to your hotel.

Some couples can't keep away and make another appearance at lunchtime the next day — particularly if friends are staying in the area for the weekend. A lazy outdoor lunch or picnic may be planned — anything to make inroads into those Tupperwares full of rice salad and coleslaw–or perhaps a country pub lunch, plus a little gentle opening of presents. Then, you can go away for the third time, getting full mileage out of your wedding weekend, and finally head for the airport.

(Sue Carpenter).

THE HONEYMOON

You will be *exhausted* after the wedding, all newly-weds concur, so aim on at least a week of pure relaxation. Most couples spend their first night in a hotel not too far from the reception or, alternatively, a short drive from the airport. If warned in advance, most hotels will lay on the honeymoon suite or one of their best rooms, lacing it with flowers and champagne. Splash out on a superb hotel (see listings below), even if it's only for one night, and indulge in the stuff films are made of. After a drawn-out candlelit dinner, take a steamy scented bath —

The term honeymoon derives from the old Northern European custom of drinking honeyed wine or mead as an aphrodisiac during the first month of marriage. An old Greek-Cypriot custom involves rolling a baby boy up and down the bridal bed before consummation to ensure the couple will be blessed with healthy male children. Peasants of Languedoc, France, would burst into the bridal chamber and offer the bride and groom soup from a chamber pot. The soup was meant to invigorate the couple and ensure their marriage would be quickly blessed with children. The Yezidi sect of North Iraq lock the couple in a room and after consummation the groom knocks three times on the door; a priest opens it and fires a gun to signal the start of festivities.

together–wrap up in enormous plushy white bath robes, drink a toast to yourselves and dive into your luxurious linen-sheeted, king-size bed. A late breakfast in bed next morning — the works — and then it's off, be it to the airport, ferryport or Southport.

Your destination depends largely on how well you know each other. If you're still in the first flush of romance, two weeks on an island, whether it's the Bahamas or the Isle of Wight, would go down a treat. But if you've known each other since school and/or co-habited for the past two years, you're not going to want to gaze into each other's eyes for a solid fortnight. Many couples find the solution in two-centre holidays, one untaxing week away from it all and one week of townie sophistication, sight-seeing or adventure living.

But, whether short- or long-haul, staying-put or outward-bound, try and make it as hassle-free as possible. India and Nepal may sound fabulously romantic — stretched out on the beach in Goa, trekking in the Himalayan foothills, boating across to the Lake Palace Hotel at Udaipur, haggling for trinkets in Jaipur — but forever being on the road can make you irritable and tired, requires more detailed organization and gives more room for things not going according to plan. Tropical conditions (stifling weather, dust-ridden trains, diseased mosquitos, gut-rotting food, leering natives) don't invite relaxed living. And many couples find they actually get on better if there are no distractions and diversions to remind them of the real world.

Honeymoon à douze

Some couples who already know each other inside-out abandon the idea of a togetherness

Still life with coconuts: Marina and Alexander Reese bask in the Jamaican sun after a cosmopolitan breakfast with friends who have flown in from Europe and the States to share the honeymoon. (Hugh Lillingston)

holiday and ask friends along. Unconventional it may be, but it can be a jolly good party: Alexander and Marina Reese hired an old plantation house for ten in Jamaica. People who marry abroad tend to prolong the party for days on end. Or you may want to stay with friends abroad. Just be sure you really want to be with others and that one partner isn't secretly wishing for time alone. Remember, you will have had little time on your own in the months of preparation and certainly you will have made dozens of compromises to fit in with Mother, the in-laws, etc. This could be time for a spot of selfishness.

Honeymoon surprise

It is traditional for the man to book the whole thing and keep mum. That's fine, but don't they know women get paranoid about what to pack? And his idea of a holiday paradise may not be yours. He may drop hints: 'It's quaint, lots of canals, romantic . . .' and you're convinced it's Venice until you arrive in Bruges. Not that Bruges isn't *lovely*, but it's like salivating for strawberries and cream and having sauerkraut slipped into your mouth. One man had mapped out an elaborate trail by Orient-Express to Paris for two days, on to Rome for two days, then off to New York for three days, then . . . . It was to be the trip of a lifetime, yet when his wife-to-be got wind of it, she persuaded him to cancel, and they ended up going to . . . Kenya. So be careful your surprise isn't a shock.

Once you've decided on the style of holiday, you can see how far your budget will take you and whether you want to blow it on distance or luxury.

Short-haul destinations

You may never have stayed put in one hotel for more than a night or two and certainly not a four- or five-star affair. A week at a charming, pampering hotel may be novel enough. Plonk the hotel somewhere by the sea or in clear-aired countryside, spice it up with a nearby town and don't stir. It could be in Britain or France, Spain or Italy — somewhere not too far, but with character, good food and sunny days. Or you could hotel-hop at a gentle pace through Britain or France (get the international *Relais et Châteaux* booklet). Some European hotels to yearn for are given below.

Paris
THE RITZ
15 place Vendôme, Paris 75001
Opulent; faultless service.

LANCASTER
7 rue de Berri, Paris 75008
Personal, pretty and discreet.

LA RÉSIDENCE DU BOIS
16 rue Chalgrin, Paris 75116

A proper Parisian house in Third Empire style.

South of France

HOTEL DU CAP-EDEN ROC
boulevard Kennedy, Cap d'Antibes

For film-star romance and glamour.

HOTEL MAJESTIC
boulevard Croisette, Cannes

A beach-side resort hotel.

HOTEL NÉGRESCO
37 promenade des Anglais, Nice

Edwardian grandeur, superb cuisine.

HOTEL DE PARIS
place du Casino, Monte Carlo

Top glamour in the centre of town.

Italy

CIPRIANI
Giudecca 10, Venice

On a tiny island opposite San Marco, with a glorious swimming pool.

GRITTI PALACE
Canal Grande, Venice

Magical, sumptuous, perfect.

HOTEL LE SIRENUSE
via C. Colombo 30, Positano

Terraced cliff-hanger overlooking the Amalfi coast.

VILLA D'ESTE
via Regina 40, Cernobbio, Lake Como

Historical palazzo by the lake.

VILLA SAN MICHELE
Via Doccia, Fiesole, Florence

Plushily converted Franciscan monastery in the hills above Florence.

Long-haul destinations

This could mean Rio or Zambia or Burma or the Great Barrier Reef, but it's more likely to mean Kenya or Thailand or Sri Lanka or the Seychelles. Certainly newly-weds feel a pull to the East (balmy seas, long beaches, spectacular sunsets plus culture shock), while Kenya (ditto plus safari) is the rich man's honeymoon cliché. Just don't overload your schedule — or suitcases — and remember the basics: jabs (you may have to go several weeks before departure; some have to be administered in two nail-biting instalments. If you go through your GP it is cheaper than a clinic), passport, visas, insurance, foreign currency, traveller's cheques and driving licence if you want to hire a car. There are a million other useful things not to be forgotten, but it's best to consult the definitive guide to your destination. Check out hotels below.

Kenya

MOUNT KENYA SAFARI CLUB
P.O. Box 35, Nanyuki

Top-notch hotel in 100 acres of gardens; organizes air and land safaris.

TREETOPS
House Arcade, P.O. box 47557, Nairobi (Book through Block Hotel Central Reservations Office, New Stanley)

For an overnight stay among the wildlife, in the footsteps of the royal family.

Seychelles

BIRD ISLAND LODGE
P.O. Box 404, Seychelles

Remote and tranquil, cottages in tropical gardens.

India and Kashmir

FORT AGUADA BEACH RESORT
Sinquerim, Bardez, Goa

Hotel-villa resort in beautiful gardens.

KASHMIR HIMALAYAN EXPEDITIONS
Boulevard Shopping Centre, Dal Gate, Srinagar

For a houseboat on one of the lakes.

LAKE PALACE HOTEL
Pichola Lake, Udaipur

A gleaming white palace in the centre of a lake.

RAMBAGH PALACE HOTEL
Jaipur

Creamy yellow palace in gorgeous gardens.

Thailand

ORIENTAL
48 Oriental Avenue, Bangkok

Stay in one of the writers' suites in the old colonial Author's Wing. The height of luxury.

Phuket, Krabi and the nearby islands are the best beach havens. Accommodation varies from primitive hut to resort hotel.

Caribbean

CORAL REEF CLUB
St James, Barbados

Resort hotel with villas in garden setting, watersports galore.

COTTON HOUSE
Mustique

A former cotton warehouse on the chic-est island.

GOLDEN LEMON
Dieppe Bay, St Kitts

Colonial hotel with walled garden.

HALF MOON CLUB
P.O. Box 80, Montego Bay, Jamaica

Top service and a mile of private beach.

LITTLE DIX BAY
P.O. Box 70, Virgin Gorda, British Virgin Islands

Luxurious thatched cottages in extensive gardens and its own marina.

PETIT ST VINCENT RESORT
Petit St Vincent

True hideaway paradise on a privately owned island.

RELAIS DE L'EMPEREUR
Petit Goave, Haiti

Luxurious, big-is-beautiful hotel.

Tour operators and travel agents

ABERCROMBIE & KENT
Sloane Square House, Holbein Place, London SW1 (01) 730 9600

Worldwide luxury tours; particularly good on Kenya, Egypt and the Seychelles.

CARIBBEAN CONNECTION
93 Newman Street, London W1
(01) 930 8271

Cushy hotels and villas in the Caribbean.

CV TRAVEL and DIFFERENT WORLD
43 Cadogan Street, London SW3
(01) 584 8803

Smart villas in the Greek islands, South of France and the Caribbean (hotels too).

KUONI TRAVEL
Kuoni House, Dorking, Surrey
(0306) 885044

Luxury tours all over the world.

TRAILFINDERS
42 Earl's Court Road, London W8
(01) 937 9631

They are excellent at putting together cheap multi-destination long-haul deals.

Hotels in Britain

(See also pages 150-151.)

London

CLARIDGE'S
Brook Street, London W1 (01) 629 8860

One bride describes 'champagne and flowers at every corner'. No bridal suites as such, but 50 very different suites in luxury-antiquish or art deco style, all with stupendous bathrooms. Service impeccable and in the morning, mammoth breakfasts are wheeled in with all the finery of silver and linen napery. Suites from £275.

THE RITZ
Piccadilly, London W1 (01) 493 8181

The original, out-of-control grandeur has been tamed into line and suites are merely comfortable; those ending in the numbers 22 overlook Green Park. Special honeymoon package incudes a suite, breakfast, flowers, chocolates and champagne for £300 a night. A weekend in an ordinary room is £360 for two nights.

SAVOY
The Strand, London WC2 (01) 836 4343

Two honeymoon suites with canopied beds overlooking the Thames. Suites £330 with all the trimmings; the same flowers-chocs-champagne treatment in a double room, £150.

Country

Most of these hotels are super-luxuriously converted country houses, maintaining their original style and atmosphere while adding mod. cons — all bedrooms have private bathrooms — and gastronomic cuisine. Don't expect any excitement — just peace and pampering service. Prices are for two unless otherwise specified. If you are honeymooning out of season, enquire about cheap winter breaks. Most of these hotels can lay on a wedding reception.

BODYSGALLEN HALL
Llandudno, Gwynedd, Wales (0492) 84466

Cushily restored seventeenth-century house in Snowdonia with oak panelling, stone mullioned windows and splendid fireplaces. Suitably romantic gardens include a rare original knot garden and a walled rose garden. Rooms can't be bettered — triple-sized beds, crisp white sheets, enormous baths. Double room from £65, four-poster room £95, including early-morning tea, newspaper and continental breakfast.

BUCKLAND MANOR
Buckland, Gloucestershire (0386) 852626

A Cotswold manor house with lovely gardens, offering croquet, tennis, putting and a heated pool. Two four-poster bedrooms, bathrooms fed from the Manor's own spring. Superb cuisine with vegetables from their garden; Mother Earth breakfasts. Four-poster suite £130, double rooms from £ 95, including tea, English breakfast.

CAVENDISH HOTEL
Baslow, Derbyshire (024688) 2311

Part of the Duke of Devonshire's estate, furnished by the present Duke and Duchess partly from Chatsworth House itself. Open fires, oak beams, fresh flowers, delicious home-made and local produce. The sort of place to return to one anniversary, as the fishing's exceptional and you can play golf. Double rooms from £57.50, excluding breakfast.

COMBE HOUSE HOTEL
Gittisham, Honiton, Devon (0404) 2756

An Elizabethan mansion in gorgeous grounds, perfect for walkers and fishermen (become a fishing widow the first day of your marriage). Plenty of carved panelling and woodiness, soft lights and flowers. King-size double beds. Landing facilities for helicopters. Double rooms from £61, including full English breakfast.

CONGHAM HALL
King's Lynn, Norfolk (0485) 600250

A Georgian manor house in 40 acres of parkland, paddocks, orchards, and country gardens. Jacuzzi, swimming pool and tennis court. Their own kitchen garden supplies most vegetables, fruit and herbs for the restaurant. Fine wines. Double room from £58, four-poster room from £70, including light breakfast.

GRAVETYE MANOR
East Grinstead, East Sussex (0342) 810567

Creeper-clad Elizabethan stone house. A small hotel for gastronomes. Home-baked bread and croissants, fresh produce from the garden, sophisticated cuisine. Good for Gatwick (25 minutes drive). From £58 for a double room (breakfast is extra).

THE GREENWAY
Shurdington, Cheltenham, Gloucestershire (0242) 862352

A sixteenth-century Cotswold manor with formal gardens and open log fires. Bedrooms individually furnished with fine antiques, views through stone-mullioned windows over the parkland. Candlelit dining in the panelled restaurant overlooking a lily pond. Double rooms from £61 a head, including a four-course dinner early-morning tea and English breakfast.

HAMBLETON HALL
Hambleton, Oakham, Leicestershire (0527) 56991

Recently revamped by Nina Campbell, this old hunting lodge is well placed for country sporting pursuits. Top-ranking for its food and intelligently selected wines. Double room from £82, including breakfast.

LORDS OF THE MANOR
Upper Slaughter, Bourton-on-the-Water, Cheltenham, Gloucestershire (0451) 20243

Golden Cotswold manor in a pretty-pretty village with stream, lake and meadows. Fifteen bedrooms, two with four-posters. Superlative cuisine with home-made soups and pâtés, vegetables and herbs from the walled garden, Cotswold trout and locally

Middlethorpe Hall in York. (Photograph courtesy of Middlethorpe Hall)

Opulent in aquamarine: the Sir Percy Blakeney Suite at the Royal Crescent Hotel in Bath. (Photograph courtesy of the Royal Crescent Hotel)

smoked salmon. Double rooms from £50, including continental breakfast.

LE MANOIR AUX QUAT' SAISONS
Great Milton, Oxfordshire (08446) 8881

The gastronomic experience of your life — Raymond Blanc is showered with praise by every living Foodie. A fifteenth-century manor with ten rooms, from £95. Set dinner is £37 — and rising.

MIDDLETHORPE HALL
Bishopthorpe Road, York, North Yorkshire (0904) 641241

An elegant William III country house overlooking York racecourse (become a racing widow from day one). Finely tended gardens and parkland include ha-has, a white garden, a walled garden and a small lake. Liveried staff. Double room from £70, four-poster room £100, including early-morning tea, continental breakfast and newspaper.

MILLER HOWE
Rayrigg Road, Windermere, Cumbria (09662) 2536

Which is more spectacular — the food or the views? In the heart of the Lake District, it's like a private country house with special touches like biscuits in the bedroom. Prices from £50 to £90 per person per night for a double room and include dinner, bed and breakfast and VAT, but there is a 12 per cent service charge on top of this.

PLUMBER MANOR
Sturminster Newton, Dorset (0258) 72507

Small Jacobean manor in Hardy country, with six bedrooms in the main building and six in the converted stone barn. Family-run, by the Prideaux-Brunes. From £45, including breakfast.

ROOKERY HALL
Worleston, Nantwich, Cheshire (0270) 626866

A *maison à la grand château*, bursting with antiques including a genuine William IV four-poster. Set in wooded parkland with croquet lawn, hard tennis court, walled kitchen garden and fishing. The ex-Dorchester chef receives accolades, as does the endless wine list. Double rooms from £62.50 a head, four-poster £90, including six-course dinner, early-morning tea and breakfast.

ROYAL CRESCENT HOTEL
Royal Crescent, Bath, Avon (0225) 319090

Splendid town hotel in the centre of the crescent. Elegant rooms, some in the Palladian villa, others in the Dower House, both within the grounds. The Jane Austin Suite (£210) has a Regency canopied bed, and all suites have a spa bath fed by the therapeutic hot springs. From £75; suites from £180; breakfast extra.

SHIPDHAM PLACE
Church Close, Shipdham, near Thetford, Norfolk (0362) 820303

Billed as a restaurant with rooms, this is run by Justin de Blank, he of the smart bakery-delis. Set five-course dinner is £18; the two double bedrooms are £42 and £55, including breakfast.

SPRINGS
Wallingford Road, North Stoke, Oxfordshire (0491) 36687

A mock-Tudor mansion in landscaped gar-

dens overlooking Springs Lake. Convenient for Heathrow (30 miles away). Tennis court, heated pool, croquet lawn, pitch and put, sauna, boating on the Thames nearby, riding, squash and golf. Double room from £82.50, including full breakfast. Special honeymoon deal with dinner, breakfast, and fruit, flowers and a half-bottle of bubbly in the room, £110.

STON EASTON PARK
Ston Easton, Bath, Avon
(076121) 631

A Palladian stately, sumptuously decorated yet cosy, set in gorgeous countryside. Double rooms from £87 to £165, including breakfast.

THORNBURY CASTLE
Thornbury, Bristol, Avon (0454) 412647

A proper stone castle with battlements, built in the early 1500s, with its own vineyards and gardens surrounded by high walls. Two baronial dining rooms with heraldic shields and open fires, award-winning cooking. Rooms retain character — oriel windows, arched doorways — but are plushily kitted out. Doubles from £82.50, four-posters £135,

Plushy and pink: the Duke's Bedchamber at Thornbury Castle near Bristol.
(Photograph courtesy of Thornbury Castle)

including continental breakfast, morning tea and newspaper.

Scotland

CROMLIX HOUSE
Kinbuck, Dunblane, Strathclyde
(0786) 822125

Quiet private house, prettily redecorated by Designers Guild. High standard of cuisine. A double room is £40.00 per person and includes dinner, a full Scottish breakfast and VAT.

GREYWALLS
Muirfield, Gullane, Lothian (0620) 842144

Beautifully homely house with compact rooms and a panelled drawing-room-cum-library with cosy sofas and crackling fire. Bang on the Muirfield golf course (become a golfing widow . . .); wild, windswept walks down to the sea. Prices vary.

INVERLOCHY CASTLE
Fort William, Highland (0397) 2177

Lochside castle where Queen Victoria stayed (you could sleep in her suite). Magnificent outside and in, with cuisine that ranks it number one in Scotland. Views of Ben Nevis. Doubles are a princely £132.25 for bed and breakfast, dinner is extra.

COLOUR PHOTOGRAPH CREDITS

Photographer   Mark Houldsworth
Stylist   Sue Carpenter
Flowers   Jane Packer Floral Art
Make-up   Lucie Llewellyn
Hair   Pascal at Neville Daniel
                     Mats

Details for front cover and plates 1 to 12

For addresses and details of shops and stockists, see individual entries under the name of each designer or shop in the Clothes chapter, page 64.

Front cover and plates 1 to 4, beginning opposite page 64: photographed at Claridge's, with their kind permission. Hair: Pascal at Neville Daniel.

Front cover: complexion: Balanced Make-up Base in Ol Ivory, Face Powder in − 1 Transparency, both by Clinique. Powder cheek colour in Chamois by Prescriptives. Eyes: Glossy Black Mascara by Clinique. Shadow by Shiseido. Lips: Moisture Lipstick in 103 Sandalwood by Revlon. Dress and jewellery, as plate 1. Model: Denise.

Plate 1: Edwardian-style dress in ivory duchesse satin and Chantilly lace with embroidered and beaded bodice, from Tatters. Ivory silk shoes with lacy heart-shaped tongue, by Elizabeth Stuart-Smith. Cream silk tulle veiling pinned into a bow, Dickens & Jones. Long fingerless stretch lace gloves, by Cornelia James. Pearl choker; diamanté, crystal and pearl drop earrings; diamanté and gilt ring, all Butler & Wilson. Model: Denise.

Plate 2: Thirties-style slippery silk satin dress with short train, from David Fielden. Satin

court shoes by Pancaldi, from Sasha Hetherington. Model: Denise.

Plate 3: Cressida: silk ottoman dress with stand-up collar and bow, leg o' mutton sleeves and train by Catherine Walker for the Chelsea Design Company. Pearl and diamanté stud earrings, Harvey Nichols. Cosima: silk georgette sailor dress trimmed with embroidered lace, with peach silk lining and bow, from Tatters. Pop sox, Harvey Nichols. Ballet pumps, Gamba. Peach ribbon on pumps, Peter Jones.

Plate 4: Fifties-style duchesse satin dress with Chantilly lace bodice, sleeves and overskirt, and layers of net underskirts, from Tatters. Ivory Biedermeier lace tights by Wolford, from Harvey Nichols. Ivory woven satin court shoes, Manolo Blahnik. String of pearls; pearl and diamanté drop earrings, Harvey Nichols. Short silk tulle veil, Ritva Westenius. Model: Cressida.

Plates 5 to 12, beginning opposite page 96: hair (all except plates 8 and 9): Mats. Additional styling (plates 6 and 7): Rose Coutts-Smith.

Plate 5: halter-neck dress in silk satin covered with cobweb lace leading into a train; silk lace fingerless gloves, both by Ellis Flyte. Pearl brooch with diamanté droplets. Butler & Wilson. Model: Lauren.

Plate 6: antique pale yellow silk camisole with lace trim, Eve's Lace, Stand X5/X6, Antiquarius, 135 King's Road, London SW3 (01) 351 0175. Net and silk petticoat, Ritva Westenius. Antique lace stole over petticoat, Adrienne, Stand Y2/Y3, Antiquarius, as above, (01) 351 5171. Yellow silk satin sash, Laura Ashley. Fingerless stretch lace gloves, by

Cornelia James. Ivory Biedermeier lace tights by Wolford, from Harvey Nichols. Satin ballet pumps, Gamba. Yellow ribbon on pumps, Peter Jones. Pearl necklace; pearl and diamanté stud earrings, Harvey Nichols. Pearl bracelet with diamanté clasp; diamanté ring, Butler & Wilson. Model: Lauren.

Plate 7: antique cotton camisole, Eve's Lace, as above. Silk dupion worn as skirt, Dickins & Jones. Crisp linen Edwardian-style jacket with Brussels lace lapels; matching linen hat, both from Adrienne, as above. White muslin draped over hat as veil, Peter Jones. Marcasite bow and pearl drop earrings; diamanté hand and pearl brooch; diamanté and gilt ring, all from Butler & Wilson. Stretch lace gloves, by Cornelia James. Model: Lauren.

Plate 8: Max: silk Peter Pan shirt; silk dupion knickerbockers, Chelsea Design Company. Yellow ribbon tied at neck, Peter Jones. Pop sox, Harvey Nichols. Ballet pumps, Gamba. Cosima: silk dupion dress, Chelsea Design Company. Pop sox, pumps and ribbon, as Max. Photographed at Claridge's, with their kind permission. Hair: Pascal at Neville Daniel.

Plate 9: Max: red velvet sailor suit with cream silk inset and bow; matching hat, Chelsea Design Company. Pop sox, Harvey Nichols, satin ballet pumps, Gamba. Cosima: Red velvet sailor dress, Chelsea Design Company. Pop sox

and pumps, as Max. Red silk roses on pumps and hair combs, Ritva Westenius.

Plate 10: Lauren: ivory silk satin and silk tulle Arabesque dress trimmed with silk roses and pearls; silk rose half-circlet on head, both from Ritva Westenius. Ivory Biedermeier lace tights by Wolford, from Harvey Nichols. Satin ballet pumps, Gamba. String of pearls, Harvey Nichols. Diamanté and pearl drop earrings, Butler & Wilson. Eve: red silk taffeta and net Arabesque dress with low laced back and bow; red silk taffeta rose hair comb, both Ritva Westenius. Red glass drop earrings, Butler & Wilson.

Plate 11: complexion: Country Moist Liquid Make-up in Beige Light 07, Face Powder in -1 Transparency, both by Clinique. Powder Blush in Rouge Imperial by Chanel. Eyes: Glossy Black Mascara by Clinique. Les Quatres Ombres shadow in Ocres by Chanel. Lips: Rouge Extrême lipstick in Brun Précieux by Chanel. Silk satin cowl-neck dress covered in cobweb lace, Ellis Flyte. Long beaded silk tulle veil, Ritva Westenius. Pearl choker with pearl and diamanté clasp; pearl, diamanté and crystal drop earrings, Butler & Wilson.

Plate 12: inset: mint cowl-neck dress as above, matching cobweb lace gloves, Ellis Flyte. Veil and jewellery as above. Model: Eve.

BIBLIOGRAPHY

Baker, Margaret, *Wedding Customs and Folklore* (David & Charles, 1977)

'Good Housekeeping' *Complete Book of Cakes and Pastries* (Ebury, 1981)

Lansdell, Avril, *Wedding Fashions 1860-1980* (Shire Publications, 1983)

Monsarrat, Ann, *And the Bride Wore...* (Hodder & Stoughton, 1975)

McWhirter, N.D., ed., *The Guinness Book of Records* (Guinness, 1983)

Reader's Digest, *Strange Stories, Amazing Facts* (Reader's Digest, 1975)

INDEX

Aardvark Photography 51
Abbey Studios 52
Abercrombie & Kent 182
Accessible Too 97
Adams, Mary, Flower Design
    Studio 125
Admirable Crichton, The 142
Alexandra, Princess 30, 31
Allen, Trevor 17
Alternative Service Book 25
Amies, Hardy 65, 70
Anello & Davide 92
Annabelinda 81
Anne, Princess 30, 65, 110
announcements 11
Anson, Lady Elizabeth 26, 51,
    70, 112, 132, 137, 147, 168,
    174, 175
Antiquarius 67
Antique Claude 17
Aquila Press 38
Ashley, Laura 84, 95, 118
attendants 22, 102, 169-71
auctions 18
Ausdan Stud 63

Bailey, Alan, and the New
    Connection 162
Baker, Maureen 65
Bally 92
banns 23-5
Barber, Amanda 70
Bartlett Street Antique Centre
    88
Bates van Hallan, Bill 52
Beauchamp Place Shop, The
    95
Beaulieu 153
Belgrave Press Bureau 51
Belleville Sassoon 77
Belvedere, The 151
Berkeley, The 150
best man 172, 174
Biddulph & Banham 77
Bird Island Lodge 181

birthstones 13-14
Black, Valerie 16
Blahnik, Manolo 93
Bodysgallen Hall 183
Book of Common Prayer 24-5
Borovick Fabrics 75
bouquets 115-21
Bourdillon, Tatti 70
Bradleys 91
bridal shower 166
bride's father 171
bridesmaids 102, 121, 169
bride's mother 19-21, 40, 110,
    168
Brooks, Pam 71
Buchan, Roberta 81
Buckland Manor 183
Buckle, Jane, Bridal Wear Hire
    86
Buckley, Catherine 78
Butler & Wilson 102
buttonholes 122
By Word of Mouth 142

cake 138-142, 174
Callaghan, David 14, 17
Cambridge Catering Equipment
    158
Campbell, Nina 42
Cap-Eden Roc, Hotel du 181
Caribbean 182
Caribbean Connection 182
Caroline's Kitchen 142
caterers 142-6
catering 130-46
Cavendish Hotel 183
CB Helicopters 63
ceremonial duties 168-74
Chalfont Cleaners and Dyers
    87
champagne 134-5
Champneys Health Resort 112
Champneys at Stobo Castle 112
Chance Entertainment 147,
    162

Chatters 155, 162
Chelsea Design Company 78,
    106
Chic of Hampstead 95
children's clothes shops 106
choirs 31-2
Choirs for Weddings 31
Christie's 18
Church of England 23-5
churches in London 27
Church of Scotland 25
Cierach, Lindka 7, 65, 68, 69,
    70, 71
Cipriani 181
Clare's Kitchen 143
Claridge's 150, 183
Cleaners and dyers 87
Clive, Richard 52
Cloonan, Anna 71
Clyde Canvas 158
Clyne, Chris 81
Cochrane, Sally 90
Collingwood 18
Concord (Cleaners) 87
Conran Shop, The 42
Conservatory, The 128
Constant Sale Shop 95
Combe House Hotel 184
Congham Hall 184
Coral Reef Club 182
Cotton House 182
Country Cooks 22, 171
Coverdale, Les 58
Cowdrey, Colin 138
Craig, Paul 97
Cromlix House 186
Curzon Lawrence Flowers 125
CV Travel and Different World
    182

Daily Telegraph 11
Daniel, Neville 113
Dark Blues 163
Davies, C.I. 76
decor 159-61

department and chain stores 84, 95-6
designers 67-9, 70-5
designer shops 77-84, 95-6
Designing Woman 96
Designing Woman for Brides 81
Devon & Somerset Marquees 158
Dickins & Jones 76
diet 110
Dorchester 150
dresses 64-87
    antique 79
    attendants' 102-6
    colour 65
    fashions 67
    going-away 94-6
    hire 86-7
    material 75-7
    problem figures 66
    restorers 90
    second-hand 86-7
    style 65
    white 67
Dressing Room, The 95
dressmakers 7, 65, 68, 70-5
    amateur 68
    professional 68
drink 133-5
Droopy & Browns 81
Dyson, Paul 159

Edelstein, Victor 64, 71
Elizabeth, Queen 30, 41, 68, 141
Elliott, Grace 75
Elliot, John and Annette 52
Ells & Farrier 76
Emanuel 68, 72
engagements 9-10
engravers 38
Etzdorf, Georgina von 77
Evans, Caroline 126
Eximinious 42
Eyre, Esther 16

fabrics 75-7
Fabula Flowers 126
Fat Cat Disco 164
Fayrer, Anne, Cakes and Flowers 146
Fennell, Theo 16
Fielden, David 67, 78
figure types 66

Fisher, Melanie 75
Flambé 143
Fletcher, Nichola 17
florists 7, 125
Flower Garden 128
flowers 114-29
    artificial 116
    bouquets 115-21
    choosing 114
    in church 122
    foliage 119-20
    head-dress 121-2
    preserving bouquets 119
    at reception 123
    silk 116
    symbolism 116
    time schedule 124
Flowers by Maxwell 128
Flyte, Ellis 67, 72, 91
Forbes, James 58, 130
Forest Mere 112
Forge, Gilly 97
forms of address 34
Fort Aguada Beach Resort 181
Foster, Carol 129
Fox, Frederick 98
France 180-1
Fratini, Gina 64, 74
Freed, Frederick 93
Frieda, John 113

Gage, Elizabeth 17
Gallery of Costume and Antique Textiles 79
Galliano, John 67
Gamba 93
Gandhi, Mahatma 41
Garrard & Co. 17
garters 91
Gastronomique 143
Geldof, Bob 31, 35, 41, 138
General Trading Company, The 40, 43, 116
Gibsons 163
Gieves & Hawkes 109
Glanville Sharpe 93
gloves 101
Gold and Silver Studio 17
Golden Lemon 182
Good Housekeeping 139
Goodman, Mary 94
Gordon, Angus 113
Gravetye Manor 184
Gray, Rosemary 129
Green, James 63

Greenly, Richard 52
Greenway, The 184
Gretna Green 25
Greywalls 186
Gritti Palace 181
grooms 107-9
    dress 107-9
    drunken 168
    duties 19-21, 173
    mother 169
Grosvenor House 150
Guardian 11

Hackett 109
hair 110-11
hair and beauty specialists 112-13
Hale, Sophie 74
Half Moon Club 182
Hambleton Hall 184
Hancocks 14, 17
Hari & Friends 113
Harrods 38, 43, 84, 95
Harrods Hair and Beauty Salon 113
Harvey Nichols 95, 102
hats 96-100
Hat Shop, The 98
health spas 112
Hempel, Anouska 96
Henry, Jules 17
Hetherington, Sasha 67, 79, 86
highland dress 108
Hill, Trevor 94
honeymoon 179-86
    abroad 180-2
    in Britain 183-6
    à douze 179-80
Hope's Shoes, Emma 94
hotels 180-6
Howells, Michael 126, 159
Hugh at 161 112, 113
Hungry Hampers 143
Hunting Lodge 153
Hurlingham Club 151
Hustler, Tom 48, 50, 52, 130
Hyatt Carlton Tower 150
Hyde Park Hotel 151
hymns 30

Independent, The 11
India 181
Inn on the Park 151
Insurance Hall 151
Inverlochy Castle 186

invitations 33-9
  'At home' 36
  engraved 33, 35, 38
  informals 35
  maps upon 36
  unpretentious 33
  wording 34
Ireland, David 94
Italy 180, 181

Jackson, Caroline 127
James, Charles 68
James, Cornelia 101
Jeeves of Belgravia 87
Jenners of Edinburgh 42
jewellers 13, 14, 16-18
jewellery 101-2
Joel & Son 76
Joffin's Marquees 155
Joffin's Party Planning 147,
  163
Jones, Peter 43
Juliana's 148, 156, 163

Kashmir Himalayan
  Expeditions 182
Kent, Duke and Duchess 31
Kenya 181
Killery, Marina 98
Kimpton Kitchen 145
Knebworth House and Barns
  154
Kuoni Travel 182

Lace of Salisbury 83
Lake Palace Hotel 182
Lancaster Hotel 180
language of flowers 116
Leggat, Moira 53
Leighton House 151
Leith's Good Food 143
Lester, Patricia 67
Lewis, John 40, 42, 43, 76, 85
Lewis of Manchester 42
Lewis Marquees 156
Liberty 40, 44, 76, 85, 95
lighting 159-61
lingerie 90-2
Lingers 92
Lipman & Sons 109
Little Dix Bay 182
Lonsdale Engraving 38
Lords of the Manor 184
Loudon Papers 38
Lownes, Victor and Marilyn 9

Lunn Antiques 88
Lyons, J., Catering 144

M & G Marquee Hire 156
Majestic, Hotel 181
make-up 111, 170
Maison Henry Bertrand 76
Mann, Rosalind 51
Manoir aux Quat Saisons, Le
  185
Mappin & Webb 18
Margaret, Princess 30
Marks, Dede 147
marquees 155-8
marriage
  certificates 23
  of divorced persons 27
  licences 23-4, 27
  proposals 9-10
  services 24-5
McKenzie, Diana 22, 171
Membery's Children's Clothes
  106
menus 37
Meynell, Freddie 135, 171
Michaeljohn 113
Middlethorpe Hall 185
Miller Howe 185
milliners 97-100
Milton, Camilla 65, 74
Monckton, Harriet 138
Monks' Dormitory 83
monograms 35
Monsoon 95
morning suits 107-9
Moss Bros 109
Mount Kenya Safari Club 181
Movable Feasts 144
Mr Gubbins 79
Muir, Alex 100
music
  ceremony 29-32
  reception 162-4
musicians 31-2

NAFAS (National Association of
  Flower Arrangement
  Societies) 123
Négresco, Hotel 181
Nethwoods 100
Nutter, Tommy 109

O'Connor, Sarah 126
Ogden, Richard 17
Old Rangoon, The 152

O'Neill, Desmond 54
Orangery 153
Order of Service 36
Oriental Hotel 182
O'Toole, Melanie 88

Packer, Jane 7, 118, 119, 128
pages 102-6
Pamela Furs and Things 98
Paris 180-1
Paris, Hôtel de 181
parties 36, 147-9
  evening 178
  hen 165-6
  music 162-4
  planners 147-9
  stag 165-6
Party Line 148
Party Organisers 148
Party Planners 148
Party Professionals 148
Pasadena Roof Orchestra 163
Pepper, T.G. & T.S. 156,
  158
Petit St Vincent Resort 182
Philippson, Anne L. 88
Phillips (auctioneers) 18
Phillips, Lucienne 96
photographers 45-8, 51-4
photographs 11, 45-55
  amateur 50
  black and white 46-7, 48
  in church 48
  colour 46-7, 48
  group shots 48
  portraits 51
  in the Register Office 48
Phyllis Court Club 154
Pie Man Food Company, The
  144
Plested, John, and David Jones
  128
Plumber Manor 185
Pongees 76
Portman Press Bureau 46, 52
Portobello Road Market 108
presents 40-4
Pressed for Time 119
Prestonfield House 154
printers and stationers 38-9
Proposal of Salisbury 84
Pugh & Carr 128
Pulbrook & Gould 128
psalms 30
Queen Mother 30

Rambagh Palace Hotel 182
Rayne 94
Reagan, Ronald 138
receptions 36, 130-7, 171-8
  duties of best man 172
  marquees 155-8
  music 162-4
  receiving line 171
  speeches 172-3
  venues 150-4
  see also catering
Regal Brass Consort, The 32
Reger, Janet 92
Register Office 26, 27
  photographs in 48
Relais de l'Empéreur 182
religious ceremonies 23-32
Résidence du Bois, La 181
Rigby & Peller 91
rings 10, 12-18
  antique 15
  suppliers 16-18
  sizing 16
  styles 15-18
Ritchie, Shireen 59
Ritz, The (London) 151, 166, 183
Ritz, The (Paris) 180
Roman Catholic Church 25
Romer, Helena-Jane 138
Rookery Hall 185
Ropner, Avvy 129
Roof Gardens, The 153
Royal Crescent Hotel 185
Royal School of Needlework 90
Russel & Bromely 92

Samuel, H. 14
Sanctuary, The 112
Savoy 151, 166, 183
Searcy Tansley & Company 135, 138, 144, 171
service of blessing 26
Seychelles 181
Schofields of Leeds 42
Scotch House, The 106, 109
Shipdham Place 185
shoes 92-4
Shrubland Hall Health Clinic 112
signing the register 31
Silk House, The 74, 77
Silvan 77
Sireneuse, Hotel Le 181

'Something old, something new... 64
Small, Susan 65
Smith, Graham 99
Smith, Jane, Straw Hats 99
Smiths of Bath 84
Smythson 39
Somerville, Philip 99
Sotheby's 18
South of France 181
Spain 180
Spats 130, 145
special licence 24
speeches 172-3
Spencer, Ivor 133
Springs 185
Spry, Constance 117, 128
Standbrook, Lyn 86
Stanley House 153
Starlight 161
Starzewski, Tomasz 74, 86
Stevens, Moyses 127
Stationers' Hall 153
Ston Easton Park 186
strippagram 167
Stuart-Smith, Elizabeth 94
Studd, Sara 74
superstituions 64-5

Taroni 75
Tatler, The 138
Tatters 67, 79
telegrams 166-7
Thailand 182
30 Pavilion Road 153
Thompson, Anna 138
Thornbury Castle 186
Times, The 11
Tizzie Dee 84
toastmasters 133
Tops Video 59
Trailfinders 183
transport 60-3
  balloon 62
  boat 62
  helicopter 61
  horse-drawn carriage 60, 61
  limousine 60
  logistics 170
  sabotage 176-8
  supplier 63
  vintage car 60
Treetops 181
trousseaux 90-2
Trumpet Voluntary 32

ushers 170

veils and head-dresses 88-90, 121-3
venues 150-4
vicargram 166
Victoria, Queen 116, 141
video-makers 59
videos 45, 56-9, 166
  amateur 57
  booking 56
  in church 57
  coverage 57
  in Register Office 57
Villa D'Este 181
Villa San Michele 181
Vintage Rolls Royce Hire 63
Vollans of Knaresborough 54
Vreeland, Diana 66

Wales, Prince of 9, 29, 31, 41
Wales, Princess of 9, 13, 25, 29, 30, 31, 41, 69, 106, 110
Walton Street Stationery Company 35, 39
wedding
  abroad 28
  advance planning 19-22
  announcement 11
  cake 138-41
  day 168-78
  lists 40-2
  present shops 42-4
  reception 130-46
Wedding Dress Exchange 86
Weddings in Paradise 28
Westenuis, Ritva 81
White Horse Marquees 158
White House of New Bond Street, The 92
Whistles 96
Woodward, Kirsten 99

Yates, Paula 29, 31, 35, 41, 65, 138
York, Duchess of 7, 9, 10, 13, 18, 25, 29, 30, 31, 41, 65, 68, 75, 96, 106, 110, 118, 121, 138, 141
York, Duke of 9, 10, 13, 29, 30, 31, 41, 107, 119, 121, 141

Zales 14